KINSLEY, D. A. **Favor the Bold.** vol. II: **Custer, the Indian Fighter.** Holt, Rinehart and Winston, 1968. 241p il bibl 67-13482. 6.95

A fast-paced account of George Armstrong Custer's post-Civil War career as told by a part-Indian author. Eminently readable, but of questionable scholarly value since there are no footnote citations for the numerous quotations used in the book. In addition, words supposedly spoken by the participants in some of Custer's spectacular activities could not possibly have been recorded in any source but the author's imagination. Suitable for background reading at the high school level.

Collected and Edited by
H. G. Merriam

# WAY OUT WEST

## *Recollections and Tales*

NORMAN
UNIVERSITY OF OKLAHOMA PRESS

❦ BY H. G. MERRIAM ❧

*Northwest Verse* (Caldwell, Idaho, 1931)

*Edward Moxon, Publisher of Poets* (New York, 1939)

*Readings for an Air Age* (in collaboration with Baxter Hathaway and John Moore) (New York, 1943)

*Recollections of Charley Russell,* by Frank Bird Linderman (editor) (Norman, 1963)

*Montana Adventure: Recollections of Frank B. Linderman* (Lincoln, 1968)

*Way Out West: Recollections and Tales* (collector and editor) (Norman, 1969)

LIBRARY OF CONGRESS CATALOG CARD NUMBER: 68–31372

# Prefatory Note

THE WRITINGS IN THIS BOOK have been selected from *Frontier* and *Frontier and Midland,* edited and published at the University of Montana as a regional magazine from May, 1920, through June, 1939. In the autumn, 1927, issue a section devoted to historical materials was begun with this headnote: "Each issue will carry some authentic account, diary, or journal, preferably of early days in this region of the country." The first account to appear was "A Wisconsin Youth in Montana: 1880," by John R. Barrows. The editor, aware that it was reminiscence, had doubts about publishing it as history. One year later, in the November, 1928, issue, a section entitled "Open Range" was inaugurated with this headnote: "Each issue will carry accounts of men's personal outdoor experiences. Only accounts of actual experiences are solicited." From that date the "Historical Section" carried only documents contemporary with events they recorded, and any reminiscential account which was contributed went into "Open Range." The materials in this book are from the latter section. From the "Historical Section," selections have been made, edited, and published as *Frontier Omnibus.*[1]

The writings are presented here in the belief that they are informatively entertaining and valuable as secondary sources of history. The able historian, especially the social historian, lends a learning ear to what people of the time he is investigating have to say of that time, even when recalled in later years.

[1] Edited by John W. Hakola; foreword by H. G. Merriam (Missoula, Montana State University Press, and Helena, Historical Society of Montana, 1962).

Moreover, reminiscences have an interest over and beyond recorded events since in them one senses the personality and character of the tale teller. The teller is boastful or modest, sober or humorous, cheerful or morose. He is observant or unobservant, scrupulous about details or careless with them. He is in tune with his time or out of tune, conducts his life routinely or with zest. He ducks difficulties or stands up to them, shuns dangers or faces them, takes life in stride or rebels. In short, in reminiscence the human element is present.

Through reading reminiscences, the social historian interprets events. The general reader gathers pictures of people, places, and events and comes to some realization of other times and other ways of living than those he experiences. He may even look into another kind of society. Of course, no one can completely re-create a former period of time and its life, simply because he cannot fully shake off his contemporary conditions and influences; but he can, by garnering facts and pictures of an earlier period and playing his imagination upon them, enjoyably create an approximate replica. That is what, along with entertainment, the accounts in this book can give an alert reader.

The men of the early West sometimes came close to being heroes, if they were not actually such. They were often "giants in the earth." Yet the greater value for the reader of these recollections lies not in judging values in the activities of the recorders but in realizing the everydayness in their attitudes and activities, however difficult or dangerous they were. The courage of the two Indian lads who expiated what was recognized by them as a crime, the day-to-day exposure to danger by the army scout, the persistence of the driver of bands of horses through dust and drought, the skill of the cowboy handling cattle—these and other pictures arouse admiration. In the early life in any country unusual hardships have to be overcome; if they can be met without fuss or ado, so much the better. The writers of the recollections in this book did not live in soft times, yet they seemed to relish life.

Some of the writers of these reminiscences had little or no

formal education; they lived apart from books. Their school was everyday experience. Their full time, energy, and ingenuity were required for meeting the circumstances and conditions of their lives. Their accounts appear here as they were sent to the magazine. However, I have at times altered or supplied punctuation; I have changed a few titles and have made a few deletions.

I hope that readers may have a good time romping through this book, that especially those with an eye and an ear cocked toward history may realize that men and women like themselves met life as it came to them.

H. G. MERRIAM

*Missoula, Montana*
*February 10, 1969*

# Contents

CONTENTS

# ALMOST MYTHICAL

# Other Gods, Montana![1]

HOMER M. PARSONS

Never did Olympians dwell
  In your woods of spruce and fir;
Moloch yawn, or great Thor hurl
  His thunder;
Never did the sirens call,
  Never did the harpies sway
In your boughs, or banshees wail
  Thereunder.

*No, but with the melting snow, Bunyan has appeared,*
*Breaking off a pine tree to brush his shaggy beard!*

Bitter Root and Yellowstone
  Never saw a bassarid;
Never dreamed of glades wherein
  The fairies
Danced and capered on the green;
  Never once the goat-foot god
Blew his merry pipes upon
  Your prairies.

*No, but when the soft chinook April's green unlocks,*
*Here comes Bunyan with his big blue ox!*

[1] *Frontier*, Vol. X, No. 1, p. 2.

# Captured by the Utes

## ALDEN B. STEVENS

THE INDIAN HAS OFTEN BEEN THOUGHT OF as unemotional; however, his emotion is shown in the journals of Lewis and Clark, is enlarged upon by Vardis Fisher in *Tale of Valor* (Garden City, New York, Doubleday, 1958), is found in the writings of James Willard Schultz and Frank Bird Linderman—in fact, is in the writings of any person who really knows the Indian—North, South, East, or West.

Alden B. Stevens, a New Yorker, spent several years in the Southwest engaged in anthropological and ethnological studies. His tale appeared in *Frontier and Midland*, Vol. XV, No. 3, p. 227, as "How Joe Crawford's Great Grandmother Was Captured by the Utes."[1]

*Note by Alden B. Stevens*: This is a free translation of a story told in the Navaho language by Joe Crawford, a young Indian who lives [1935] near Fort Defiance. He told the story as if it had occurred in the remote past to some unknown or mythical woman. Later, he said the story was that of his own great grandmother. Joe's grandfather, old Billy Crawford, is said to be half Ute, though he himself doesn't admit it. Joe could not say how or where the name of "Crawford" got into the family. Old Billy never went to school, so perhaps some trader attached it to him or to Joe's mother's husband.

THE TRAVELER WAS VERY TIRED and cold. He had come a long way since morning, and he had eaten nothing on the trail. His feet were sore and his legs ached. Snow had been falling since sunset, and added greatly to the difficulty of walking along a trail he did not know. There was a moon, but very little of its light filtered

---

[1] Unless otherwise noted, all headnotes in this book are by the editor.

through the falling snow, and the traveler realized that he must soon find a place to spend the night or he would freeze.

He thought he saw a light in the distance, and turned his steps in its direction. As he approached he saw that the light was made by a fire inside a hogan, and he knew that he was safe for the night. It seemed to him that he had walked many times the distance before he reached it, but this only increased his satisfaction when he came to the hogan and looked in at the door.

A young girl and an old woman were inside, but no man. So the stranger hesitated; but the old woman beckoned him to enter, for she saw that he was a Navaho and that he was tired and cold. She pointed out to him a place on the floor where he could sleep, and when he had removed his coat and shoes (for it was quite warm in the hogan) the young girl brought him food. He ate all he wanted, and as he ate he noticed that the old woman was watching him closely, though she said nothing until he had finished.

As soon as the stranger had finished his meal the old woman began asking him about himself—where he was from, where he was going, how many sheep he had, how many children he had, and other questions such as these. She asked him so many things that the girl remonstrated with her, saying the man was tired, and needed to sleep. But the old woman paid no attention and continued to ask the traveler about the world outside. He told her of many things she knew nothing about—of great puffing things which were not animals but which lived and ran along metal trails, far to the south, sometimes faster than a good horse. He told her of cities filled with pink-faced men who did not understand the Navaho or Hopi languages or even Spanish. She had heard of these men and asked if they understood Ute, and he said they did not, but spoke a new language.

All this interested the old woman, for she lived far away, north of the Hopi country, near the great cliff houses, and she had heard little of the habits of the strange white people to the south. She begged the traveler to tell her more, for, she said, "Few strangers come this way." Even the words she used seemed to

4

him different; they were Navaho, but they were somehow not the same as his. The girl again said their guest should be allowed to sleep, but the old woman answered, "No, no, I want to get what I can from him, then I shall tell him my story." So when the traveler had told her everything he knew, the old woman began.

"Long ago," she said, "when I was young, I herded sheep for my family. I was nearly ready to marry, but I was not quite sure I liked the man well enough. He was a little strange. He talked to himself most of the time, but some days he would not talk at all. A few days before the wedding was to have taken place, I was herding my sheep in a valley some distance from my family's hogan. I should not have gone so far away, because the Utes were about, making raids on the Navahos and stealing their sheep and their girls. I kept a sharp lookout, but everything seemed very quiet and peaceful. Later in the afternoon, however, I saw a large number of men riding toward me, running their horses very fast. At first I was not sure whether they were Navahoes or Utes, but soon I saw that they were Utes, and I jumped on my horse and started toward our hogan. I was very frightened. But the men came fast and they caught me and tied my arms behind my back. Then one of them tied a rope around my horse's neck and led me behind him.

"We started north. The Utes drove some of my sheep before them, and at sunset we camped at the prairie dog hill. They ate some of my sheep, but they did not hurt me. Early in the morning we went on northward, going into a deep canyon with steep sides, and traveling along the sandy bottom for many miles, until the canyon opened out into a plain. From there we traveled very fast northward, and that night the Utes ate more of my sheep, but I would not eat any. I did not know what would happen to me. The Utes killed as many of my sheep as they could carry on their horses, and the next day we went on through the place where the ground is blue, and then we came to the great river of the north. When we had crossed the water the band divided, half going one way and half the other. Soon the group I was with

5

began to split also. Finally, there were only three men left together, and they stopped and talked. I could not understand their language, but I knew they were talking about me. The man who had been leading my horse struck one of the others, who fell, and I knew that the first man was to have me.

"After a little while we reached his old camp. He told me to get supper, and I started to gather some firewood, but all the time I was planning how I could get away from him and go back to my own people. I built a fire and carved some meat from the sheep he had brought tied to his saddle—my own sheep. I cooked it for him and he ate it, but I would not eat anything.

"For many days he did not let me out of his sight at all. Then he began to trust me a little more, for he saw that I was quiet and was not trying to run away. But I was only pretending to be content, and I was still thinking about my people and my own country. I wanted to go back to them. I did not let him see this; I made him think I wanted to stay.

"One day the Ute was sitting on a rock ledge sharpening a stick. He worked for a time on this and finally had a very sharp point on one end of it. All the time he was working on the stick I was watching him through the corner of my eye, for I thought I saw my chance coming, and I did not want to fail to escape when I could.

"When he had finished the point and smoothed it by rubbing on a stone he put the point of the stick into his ear to clean out the wax. I picked up a heavy rock and started toward him without making any noise. But he turned and saw me; so I pretended to be carrying the stone to the fireplace. Soon he started to clean the wax from his other ear, and my heart beat very fast as I thought of my home. I did not like to do it, because I had come to like the man who had stolen me, but still I wanted to see my own people again. So I came close to him, carrying the large stone in my hand. He did not hear me this time, and he did not turn.

"Suddenly I ran at him with the stone in my hand, and I struck the end of the stick with the flat side of the stone as hard as I

6

could, and the point was driven through his ear into his head the length of a thumb. He fell over on his side without a sound, for he had died instantly. For a minute I was sorry, because he had been kind enough to me; kinder than most Utes would have been. But then I thought of my own people and my own country, and I was glad because I was going home.

"I saddled my horse and started south. I followed the trail on which we had come as nearly as I could remember it, but several times I got lost. I was in the country of the Utes, and I had to watch for men all the way, because if anyone saw me, I should not have been allowed to go on. I rode as fast as I could, and I even rode at night, for there was a moon; but my horse grew tired and I had to stop.

"I went on the next day and the next day after that. I had very little food and I did not dare to stop or try to get any, so for the last two days of my trip homeward I ate nothing at all. But I forgot how hungry I was when I began to see familiar places, because I knew that I was almost home.

"When I came into the valley in which our hogan was I saw my uncle taking a little dirt from the ground, and when I approached he looked up but did not seem to know me at first. Then he saw that it was really his niece, and he dropped the dirt he had picked up. I saw that it had come from a footprint I had made a long time before, in the soft mud. The mud had hardened, and my uncle was taking a bit of it to use in a death ceremony for me, because everybody thought I was dead.

"But instead of the death ceremony my family had a great feast to celebrate my return, and everyone was very happy. A little while after this I married the man I spoke of when I began my story. Now, what do you think of my story?"

But the traveler had fallen asleep, and did not hear her question. The old woman was angered, and kicked at him, but he only moaned, and went on sleeping.

7

--◦◅{ THEY TOOK LIFE AS IT CAME }▻◦--

# The Ballad of Danny Kirk[1]

## ADA FARRIS

Danny Kirk was a Western Man.
A ridin', swearin', gamblin' han';
He was plum locoed over Hanner Work,
And he wanted to change her name to Kirk.
   *With a ki and a yippi and a yi oh!*

But the gal she couldn't make up her min',
'Cause an Injun over on Porcupine
Wanted to marry Hanner too—
Now what in tunket was a gal to do!
   *With a ki and a yippi and a sigh oh!*

The Injun had some govermunt lan',
A house, and some mules, too—quite a span.
His name, Tail-Feathers-Goin'-Over-The-Bank,
Was shortened into jist plain Hank.
   *With a ki yi yi, oh fie oh!*

Said Danny to this gal, Hanner,
"All I got is a horse and a ole bandanner.
Will you marry me, or be Hank's squaw?"
But all that Hanner said was—"Naw!"
   *With a ki yippi yi and a sigh oh!*

Well, spring it went and summer come,
But things, they didn' begin to hum,
Till roundup time hove into sight—
And Danny Kirk drew Dynamite!
   *With a yip, yip, ride 'im Cowboy oh!*

This Dynamite was the darndes' hoss;
No han' could ride 'im, not even the boss;
He'd corkscrew and sunfish both together;
A cowhan' just nacherly had to pull leather!
   *With a ki yippi yi and a yi oh!*

[1] *Frontier and Midland*, Vol. XIX, No. 3, p. 201.

The folks rode in from the Bar X Nine;
Hank come with the Injuns from Porcupine;
An' all o' them bet their very las' buck,
That Danny Kirk would be out o' luck
  *With Dynamite, ki yi oh!*

Hanner was there with her hair in a braid,
But she was skeered—she was sure afraid;
She knew that her cowhan', Danny, must
Be bucked right off and bite the dust!
  *With a ki yippi yi and a sigh oh!*

But it goes to show—you never can tell;
Danny Kirk, he rode—he never fell;
The bronc bucked Dan right into space
An' nobody ever found a trace!
  *Oh ki yippi yi and oh yi oh!*

They watched him fly above the trees;
Ole Timers said a prairie breeze—
The kind some folks call a tornado—
Took and carried Dan clear to the town of Laredo!
  *Or to ki yippi yi, O-hi-o!*

And Hanner she sighed and Hanner cried,
And sad to relate, she up and died—
Well, nearly—but then she made up to her Hank,
And was Mrs. Tail-Feathers-Goin'-Over-The-Bank.
  *With a ki yi wink-o'-the-eye Oh!*

# A Courageous Duel

E. A. Brininstool (1870–1957) sent this remarkable account to
*Frontier* in 1934, and it was published in the spring, 1935, issue as "An
Unequal Duel." He was a poet (*Trail Dust of a Maverick*), a colum-
nist for a Los Angeles newspaper, and a prolific writer of western
history. Perhaps his most widely read book is *A Trooper with Custer*
(Columbus, Ohio, The Hunter-Trader-Trapper Company, 1925).

"Then you don't think, Lieutenant, that young Boyle accidentally shot himself?"

"No, Major, I don't. It looks to me like Indian work. No white
man would have taken the pains to conceal his body in the place
we found it, either."

"But what could the Indians have against Boyle? He has always treated them well. Besides, he wasn't scalped or mutilated."

"I know, Major. He was shot in the back of the head—it
wouldn't have been possible for Boyle to have done it himself.
My scouts found the spot where he'd been murdered—presum-
ably from ambush—and his body dragged down into that deep
ravine where we located it; besides, there were moccasin tracks
about. No white renegade did that job. I think it was the work
of some of those young Cheyenne bucks who thought it would be
smart to count coup on a white man; and as Boyle was alone,
they figured they could get away with it undetected. I think I'm
on the right trail, and I don't believe it will be long before we run
down the murderers." Lieutenant Robertson nodded significantly
to Major Carroll.

It was a puzzling case. Boyle, a young rancher whose home-stead claim was about three miles from the camp of the First United States Cavalry, under command of Major Carroll, along Lame Deer Creek, Montana, had been missing for several days. He had gone on a hunting trip, but failed to return. His absence had been reported to Major Carroll, who had ordered out a search detachment. His body had been located in a deep and remote ravine, by Lieutenant Robertson's Indian scouts. It was at first surmised that Boyle had fallen, his gun accidentally dis-charged, and that his death was therefore due to his own carelessness.

But the keen-eyed scouts in Robertson's command had pointed out certain tell-tale signs—moccasin tracks, along the ridge at the head of the ravine; blood on the leaves, evidences of a struggle, or of a body having been dragged along the ridge and then flung into the ravine. Several empty shells had also been found in a clump of brush about fifty feet from the blood-spattered leaves.

"No white man—Injun," grunted Lone Wolf, one of Robert-son's trailers.

For several days no fresh clue was obtained. Then one after-noon two members of the Indian Police rode up to the Agent's office.

"Head Swift and Young Mule gone five, six days," they reported.

Here at last was a clue! Head Swift and Young Mule were Cheyenne youths about eighteen years of age. Both were well known on the reservation—and none too favorably. Indolent, restless, they spent their time principally in roaming the hills, and were looked upon as a disturbing element among the young Indians on the reserve.

Their sudden disappearance was at once reported to Major Carroll. These two young braves belonged to the Northern Cheyennes, a part of old Dull Knife's band, which had made a masterful retreat after the Fort Robinson outbreak twelve or thirteen years previously. These Indians had since remained in comparative quiet until about 1886, when they became restive,

14

and gave signs of discontent, rendering necessary the establishing of an annual camp of Regular Army troops in their vicinity.

It was early in September, 1890, that young Boyle's body had been found. It was several days later that the Indian Police reported Head Swift and Young Mule to have taken to the hills.

The young bucks were suspected of hiding out for some good reason; a scouting party had been made up to run them down and bring them in for an interview.

"But, we've scoured the hills high and low, Major," reported Lieutenant Robertson, "and we can't find hide or hair of them. They're laying low."

"Keep after them and bring them in at all hazards," was Major Carroll's order.

Twenty-four hours later old Brave Wolf, a warrior of many battles, trotted in to the Agency and dismounted at the office. He asked to see the Agent at once.

"Head Swift and Young Mule no surrender," he indicated through the interpreter. "They kill man; no come in; want heap fight."

And then followed a most astounding and seemingly unbelievable confession. The two Cheyenne boys had sneaked in to the Indian camp under the cover of darkness and told their parents the whole story, admitting the murder of Boyle. They realized that their lives would be the forfeit if they surrendered. They would never give themselves up, but would die fighting.

"Fight all the troops," declared old Brave Wolf. "Tell so'jer chief bring heap men."

To Major Carroll hastened the Agent with the amazing proposal.

"What!" exclaimed Major Carroll in undisguised astonishment, "those two boys challenge me to a duel with all my command, is that what you mean?"

Brave Wolf nodded emphatically. "All," he said, "Injun boys heap brave; no surrender; fight all, or say they raid agency; kill heap white people."

It seemed preposterous—positively ridiculous that these two

rash Indian youths should thus defiantly challenge three troops of seasoned cavalrymen to a duel to the death!

"Why, that's a joke," exclaimed Major Carroll. "It would be useless for me to order out my command on any such fool's errand. They'd never show up. Where are these boys now? I'll send out a dozen men to bring them in."

One of the older of the white scouts with Carroll's command, shook his head. "Dunno 'bout that, Major," he mused. "These 'ere young Injuns git plenty of fanatical notions in their fool heads sometimes, and if they told Brave Wolf that they're ready to fight the troops to death, I reck'n you won't be disapp'inted, as fur as they are concerned."

Old Brave Wolf gravely nodded assent. "They come," he soberly reiterated. "No stay 'way if so'jers come now; they fight; heap brave."

"Well," declared the astonished cavalry leader, "I guess if that's really the case and they mean business, we can accommodate 'em. Orderly, have 'Boots and Saddles' sounded at once. Lieutenant Robertson, you will have a sufficient guard deployed about the Agency at once, in case of trouble, while we are accommodating these young Indian fools."

Following this command there was a scurrying of troopers, a saddling of horses and a jingling of accoutrements, as the men, laughingly and with much banter, made ready to depart.

During the previous few days' excitement, the entire Cheyenne village had been gathered by the Agent and placed in camp about the Agency, the better to watch their actions and prevent any possible disturbance. Excitement had been tense, and it now looked as though the climax were at hand.

"Prepare to mount; mount!" came the order, when the troopers had assembled.

And then, led by old Brave Wolf, the troops under Major Carroll, with Lieutenant Robertson and Lieutenant Pitcher, started on their strange mission.

Among the command it was looked upon as a joke, as Major Carroll had said. That two Indian youths, mere boys, would have the nerve to attack three troops of cavalry in open combat, was unbelievable; it was the consensus of opinion that the trip would be nothing but a fool's errand.

"Two agin two hundred?" snorted Trooper Callahan to Trooper McCarthy. Both veterans shook their heads in unbelief.

A half mile from the Agency, at a sign from old Brave Wolf Major Carroll gave the command "Halt!" This was the spot, said Brave Wolf, which the young bucks had chosen for their battleground. Here was to be enacted the strangest drama ever enacted upon the stage of frontier life. The road at this point ran through a narrow valley, flanked by rock-crowned hills, covered with a forest of low pine, forming an amphitheater. No more spectacular spot could have been chosen.

Here the troops were posted, some mounted, others dismounted. Excitement was at fever heat. Upon the hills surrounding the valley had gathered the entire population of the Cheyenne village, the bucks taking position close in upon the hills, and the squaws and children where they would not be endangered by rifle fire yet could watch their tribesmen die like true Cheyenne warriors.

It was an ideal autumn afternoon. Nature was at her loveliest, in colors of gold and brown. The haze of Indian summer was in the air. Peace and quiet were in the scene.

Across the valley was heard the death chant of the squaws. The stage was set, and it only lacked the two actors to step forth and play their respective parts.

"Where can they be?" was the eager query which ran through the command, as keen eyes searched various vantage points.

Major Carroll and Lieutenant Robertson were scanning the distant clumps of timber through their glasses. "I don't believe they'll ever show up," declared the former, closing his glasses with an impatient snap.

"Well, Major, there they are!" suddenly exclaimed Robertson, pointing toward two figures on horseback which had glided phantom-like from the darkened background of pines. "It looks like they mean business after all."

17

Glasses were again leveled, and it was seen that the two young Cheyennes were fully armed and decorated in war costume. To the ears of the astonished troops were borne the echoes of the Cheyenne death song, solemnly taken up and echoed by the distant squaws.

The plumed war bonnets of the youthful fanatics nodded in the breeze, while nickeled ornament on wrist and arm, the gaily decorated regalia, and the glint of rifle barrel, flashed in the sunlight.

Exclamations of excitement ran through the command. The troopers watched the young braves urge their ponies toward the top of one of the highest and steepest ridges, down which there was an open space to make a charge. All their actions could easily be watched and noted by their tribesmen, every detail observed.

Reaching the very pinnacle of the ridge, the young Cheyennes suddenly wheeled their ponies, and for an instant sat gazing down the lane of death. Then the war whoop echoed from the ridge, and then ——

"Here they come!"

And come they did, with fanatical fury! Down the slope, with Winchesters loaded, magazines filled, and cartridge belts sagging with lead. It was a sight the like of which had never been upon the American frontier!

"Hold your fire!" came the orders from troop commanders. "Not yet, men!" Excited troopers thrust carbines forward and triggers clicked as hammers were raised.

Down the steep hillside headed the two Cheyennes directly for a line of troopers that had just been led up the southern crest of the valley by Lieutenant Pitcher. Ponies straining every nerve, moccasined feet drumming at heaving flanks, rifles streaming leaden death, and over all the Cheyenne death chant!

Dismounted, the troopers waited the command to fire, the horse-holders in the rear. When the order came, a hundred carbines belched forth a roaring blast; others in reserve crashed out. The pony of the foremost brave stumbled, regained its feet, again pitched forward, hurtling its rider through the air.

18

Apparently unharmed, his companion continued to ride straight into the jaws of death, right at Pitcher's command, firing rapidly. But apparently his aim was high. Fifty carbines and revolvers roared in return, and yet, in some miraculous manner the daring warrior escaped death until he had actually penetrated the line of troopers, when both horse and rider crumpled under the leaden hail.

"Look out for the other Indian!" came the warning cry.

The dismounted Cheyenne, flung to the ground when his pony went down, had meantime regained his feet, and turned down the valley in the direction of the Agency. Volley after volley saluted him, and he returned the fire as rapidly as he could work the lever of his Winchester. Bullets rained around him, kicking up the dust and ricocheting off into space like angry bees. Finally, seemingly badly wounded, he limped painfully into a dry wash to make a stand to the death. In his wake streamed excited troopers, firing volley after volley.

"We crawled through the brush toward him," said Lieutenant Robertson, in his report, "not aware that he had been killed, and suddenly stumbled upon his body. I was startled, awe-struck, by the weird beauty of the picture he made, as he lay in his vivid color of costume and painted face, his red blood crimsoning the yellow of the autumn leaves upon which he fell."

# Scouting in Montana in the 1870's

## J. W. REDINGTON

J. W. REDINGTON, a Montana volunteer, was a United States scout and courier in the Nez Percé and Bannock Indian wars and assistant adjutant general of Oregon, 1879–83.

In *The New Northwest* (Deer Lodge, Montana), August 24, 1877, appeared this note: "J. W. Redington, formerly of Portland, Oregon, more recently correspondent of the *Salt Lake Tribune*, has had a lively experience—perhaps a fatal one. He accompanied the relief party going to Gibbon, pushed on when Gibbon's courier was met, reached the battlefield, started on Howard's trail, got lost and swamped, traded off his horse for an abandoned Indian pony, reached a deserted cabin which he described, found some flour scattered around which he ate, left a letter for the editor of this paper in the cabin dated August 16th—lost and not knowing where he should go next. The letter was mailed to us from Bannack August 23rd."

Redington wrote the following account some years before it was printed in *Frontier*, Vol. XIII, No. 1, p. 55. It was in the files of the Montana Historical Society, and David Hilger, then the society's director, gave permission for publication of it. In 1932, Redington wrote the editor from the National Military Home in California that he had also had experience with the Modoc Indians in Oregon. Redington's humor, sharp at times, is of the old-fashioned kind found often in the writings of men who have lived in two periods of time—two eras, they call them.

THE TIME TO GET THRILLS, real frontier thrills, was in the Territorial days of Montana, along through the 1870's. Of course, the Indians saw it first, but in the many times ninety-nine years they had had the vast domain they had never raised a grain crop to help carry out the country's supply of flapjacks, had never built a skyscraper or taken out a ton of gold to swell the wealth of the world, bought an auto or a share of oil stock. So of course it was decreed that the white race should come along and take it away from the red race and set it to work producing.

My awakening to the real size of Montana was when I covered eight hundred miles getting to the front during the Nez Percé Indian War in 1877, and I made it in ten days by swapping saddle horses three times.

And my first scouting thrills were received when I met Billie Woodward, advanced scout of the Montana volunteers, near Silver Bow, in 1877, while the brilliant stars were scintillating, and together we scouted ahead of the command through Deer Lodge Valley and its vast surroundings the rest of the night.

The battalion was under command of Major W. A. Clark, with General C. S. Warren, adjutant, and was composed of men who had dropped the tools of their industries and patriotically volunteered to take the field in defense of the country against the foes of civilization.[1] They were a fine body of men, and the present generation has much to thank them for. Major Clark had made a ride on his wiry war horse from Deer Lodge to Butte to recruit a company there.

When I left the Montana Volunteers on Big Hole River, Sergeant Wilson told me he thought I could strike the trail of the regular army in about fifteen miles, but they turned out to be the longest miles I ever measured. I was supposed to be alone, and it was a vast and lonely country to be alone in, but every hour or so a hostile Indian scout would show up on some sightly butte, and we would warily watch each other just out of range.

[1] From Missoula, Governor Potts had telegraphed Clark to go to Butte and enlist volunteers. By taking the shortest trails, he rode horseback the forty miles from Deer Lodge in three hours. He had no trouble raising three companies of volunteers, and within a few hours the battalion, of which he was appointed major, headed for Missoula. After traveling all night, the troops reached Deer Lodge only to learn that the Indians had turned up the Bitter Root Valley. (W. D. Mangam, *The Clarks, an American Phenomenon* [New York, Silver Bow Press, 1944], 57.)

The Big Hole battlefield was a sight to see, and was the scene of one of the fiercest little battles in all frontier history. The burning horse flesh, still smoldering in the Indian campfires where the animals had fallen when shot, gave out such an awful odor that it is easy to imagine that I can scent it yet.

The pretty pines along the mountainside were sadly singing their requiems for the twenty-one regulars and six volunteers whose lives had just been snuffed out in their prime; thirty-one had been wounded in the early-morning battle, and eighty dead Indians told the tale of the winning of the West and its great cost in human toll.

There was no stuttering about picking up trails along there, for the main big trail of the hostiles, Chief Joseph and his band of Nez Percés, led right off to the south—horse tracks and mule tracks, and the tracks of two hundred troopers and doughboys following them up.

It was a magnificent mountain country along there on the backbone of the Bitter Roots with the soaring summits that mark the dividing line between Montana and Idaho, with lush grass on the mountain meadows up to your horse's knees, and the best water in the world. It was all I had to fill up on for a few days, and it was certainly nourishing and satisfying.

The still-smoky droppings in the trails, made by Indian ponies who had not been housebroke, showed that the hostiles had their scouts out watching for any approaching army.

My sticking to the trail and admiration of the country were rudely broken in upon by a bunch of about seven Indians dashing at me across a meadow. As an act of courtesy I also dashed off, into a wooded swamp, and their bullets hit high on the trees close by. They might have been soft-nosed bullets, but they sounded like hot tamales or scalded snowballs the way they spattered out when they struck and mussed up the woodland.

By changing my course and coming to another edge of the swamp I could look out and see the Indians sitting on their horses and firing a few shots into the swamp at the point where I entered it. It was rather tough traveling through the swamp, but after a horse had sunk halfway to his knees he found firm bottom, so I took a southerly course, aiming to again strike the trail further on.

Being a swamp angel in a miry morass was a strange and sloppy stunt, but if the swamp cover had not been there the hostiles would soon have made some other kind of an angel of me and sent me climbing the golden stair, which might have its compensations. The two hours' delay was a lucky strike for me, and kept me from rushing up on the hostile camp without a letter of introduction.

It was very kind of the beavers who had dammed a creek and flooded that piece of timber, for it certainly gave me the cover that saved my scalp. They must have known I was coming.

Late in the day I got out of the swamp and again struck the trail and followed it on through the night. Next morning my horse petered out just as I reached the last camping ground of the hostiles. I abandoned my horse and captured another among a small bunch that had escaped from the Indians. I saddled and mounted him, but he balked and would not budge an inch. I caught another, and he was perfectly willing to co-operate and carry me on.

At the next Indian camp I came to, the still-warm ashes showed that the Indians were not far ahead. I was pretty hungry, and was lucky enough to find a piece of Indian bread about as big as your hand that had been overlooked in the ashes. It was made of straight flour and water, but just then it was a sweeter morsel than any angel cake that ever happened.

The saddest sight at this camp was an old, helpless Indian lying on a few old buffalo robes, with only a bottle of water alongside. He looked as though the snows of a hundred winters had fallen on his head, but still there was not a trace of baldness. He volunteered a wan smile at the sight of a human being, and made a feeble motion with one arm, pointing to his forehead, making a mumble with his poor toothless mouth. My compulsory schooling had not embraced his language, but I could under-stand that he was inviting me to shoot him in the forehead and end his misery. Instead of accommodating him I fed him half

23

of the piece of bread I had found, which he ate ravenously. He seemed quite disappointed when I made a motion of flapping my wings to indicate that I must skiddoo and be on my way.

This old Indian had doubtless carried sons and daughters through mumps and measles, cramps, colic, pains in the stomach, and all the ailments that kids are heir to, and brought them up to the scalping and voting age, and now they had abandoned him in the lone mountains because he could no longer ride a horse and was an incumbrance.

Such inhumanity gave me a new angle on Fenimore Cooper's Leatherstocking noble red men, and made me think of them as friends of the forest.

My new horse had evidently not had much of a rest from hard riding by some other Indian, but I pushed him along while the pushing was good, and neither of us retarded our gait by filling up on food, for there was none to fill up on.

I thought that the small advance force of the regular army was on the trail ahead of me, but found out afterwards that it had turned off so as to take a short cut via Rattlesnake Creek and Bannack City, and that during the night I had missed the turning-off point.

History may prove that I never crossed the Alps with Napoleon as I thought I had, but it can never deny that I was the first white person who went through the Bloody Dick gulch country after hostile Nez Percés.[2] Some pioneer afterwards told me that the only blood ever spilled there was from the mouth of an old English miner who was eternally talking about "blasting 'is bloody heyes," and bloody this and bloody that, so that the title of Bloody Dick stuck to him and his gulch.

But how I ever got through that region swarming with hostiles in those wild days, without an armored car, and live to sit at a hammerless typewriter and tell about it is one of those great mysteries of fools riding in where angels fear to fly. The logical thing would have been for me to be taken at that stage of the

[2] The gulch leads into Lemhi Canyon.

game. So I must have been born under a thirteenth lucky star or a twenty-third skiddoo moon.

Lucky for me my horse began to peter, for if he hadn't I would have rode right on into the hostile camp, a few miles ahead. I had been reading in "Our Dumb Animals" that a merciful man is merciful to his horse, so in the interest of humanity I picketed him on good grass below the Farnsworth mine, at the head of Horse Prairie, and staked myself out on the bushy benchland above, intending to resume the stern chase at the first streak of daylight, with no delay about cooking breakfast, as there was nothing to cook, and no dishes to wash.

But hard riding had brought the sounder kind of sleep, so there were several streaks of daylight chasing each other around when I woke up the next morning. And down on the bottom a bunch of Indians were dashing away to the south, driving a bunch of horses, among which was mine. They even took the picket pin.

This was the war party of the hostiles which had raided the Horse Prairie country and murdered several men, including William Farnsworth, whose body, covered with a quilt, lay on the meadow where the hostiles had shot him. A few more days and he was to have been on his way to the New York home where a bride awaited him.

As I hiked down Horse Prairie the first ranch I struck was John Clark's, and that pioneer was waiting and watching for any more hostiles that might be coming along, although he had no more horses for them to steal. When I saw the size of his rifle I was glad that he had not mistaken me for a hostile, for one of his bullets was enough to muss up an elephant.

The next ranch I came to looked like a total wreck, as the hostiles had played tag with almost everything they could smash, although they did not burn the buildings. They must have known that I was coming and would need it, for they overlooked a keg of old-fashioned soggy brown sugar, and the way I filled up on it made up for lost time and missing meals.

The heel blisters I raised as big as four-year-old watermelons were the result of the long hike I had to make before I consolidated with the army, but very soon Colonel Rube Robbins made me a Christmas present of a horse captured from the hostiles, and I was no longer afoot.

Scouting into the Yellowstone Park we were welcomed by several members of the Cowan party as they straggled out after being shot up by the hostiles.[3] They had scattered, each for himself, and each thought that all the others were dead, and they were mighty glad to again see a white face.

Mr. Cowan had shown wonderful vitality by crawling along down the river for quite a way after being left for dead. He had been badly wounded in head and hip, and his ghastly paleness made a strong contrast with his ink-black hair. The fine carriage that his party had taken into the park was badly wrecked by the hostiles, and they had taken most of the brightly varnished spokes to make handles for their riding whips.

In the camp on the Yellowstone at the mud geysers General Howard had a bunch of Bannocks under guard for stealing government horses. They had been advance scouts under Captain S. G. Fisher,[4] and told mysterious stories about his outfit being wiped out by the hostiles, etc.

Captain Fisher had not been heard from for a week, so I volunteered to go out and try to find him. Captain R. H. Fletcher, in charge of scouts, called for two volunteers among the Bannocks to go with me, and they all wanted to go, so as to get out from under guard. They finally selected two lucky ones, and we started off. But before going several soldiers warned me that the Bannocks would shoot me before we had gone a mile from camp.

We forded the Yellowstone and rode up the river to the lake, and then took the trail of the hostiles up Pelican Creek, and were

[3] George Cowan and his wife, Frank Carpenter and his sister Ida, and four other men were sight-seeing in Yellowstone Park when attacked by a scouting party of five Indians from Looking Glass's band. Helen A. Howard gives a full account in *War Chief Joseph* (Caldwell, Idaho, Caxton Printers, Ltd., 1941), chap. XIX. Frank Carpenter wrote of the incident in his *The Wonders of Geyser Land* (Black Earth, Wis., Burnett & Son, 1878). Cowan was found lying badly wounded in the brush by Captain S. G. Fisher and J. W. Redington.

[4] Captain S. G. Fisher was General Howard's chief of scouts.

26

soon traveling through a steady rain and the deep darkness of night. The Bannocks were certainly good trailers or else we would never have gotten through the awful stretch of down timber that we encountered. Twice the Bannocks tried to get behind me, but Colonel C. E. S. Wood,[5] chief of staff, had warned me against such possible treachery, and as one of the Bannocks rode a white horse, which was visible in the dark, I insisted that they keep in front.

We kept plugging away all night, and just before daylight found Captain Fisher and his little outfit of seven scouts. The rest of his fifty Bannocks had gone back on him when he started to charge the hostile camp, but he stayed with the job with only seven.

Captain Fisher took me up to the top of a ridge, from which we could look across a deep canyon and see the Nez Percé camp on the next ridge, and it looked as though they were putting up log fortifications to give the soldiers another battle.

Captain Fisher made a rough sketch of the surrounding landmarks, and with this and a brief report of his movements, started back for the command, taking along one of the Bannocks. But he went under protest, not wanting to be again put under guard.

Returning through the down timber, my horse gave out, and we captured a mule, on which I made another ten miles, and then he gave out, and we captured another horse, and when we had reforded the Yellowstone and reached the old camp, the soldiers were gone and ashes were cold and darkness was again with us.

[5] Charles Erskine Scott Wood (1852–1944) was a Pennsylvanian educated at the United States Military Academy and later at Columbia University. As a lieutenant he was General Howard's aide-de-camp in the Nez Percé campaign; later he was engaged in the Bannock and Paiute campaigns. After his army career he practiced law in Portland, Oregon, until 1919. Because he was a humanitarian and was sympathetic with the struggle of radicals, he often defended them in court, although his legal clients were big business firms. Several of his writings—*The Poet in the Desert* (Portland, Oregon, privately printed, 1915; reprinted by Vanguard Press, Inc., 1929), *Heavenly Discourse* (New York, Vanguard Press, Inc., 1927), and *Too Much Government* (New York, Vanguard Press, Inc., 1931)—are outspoken against social injustice. He also wrote a book of Indian myths.

We followed the soldiers' trail down the river, crossing the treacherous crust of the sulphur basin between the Sulphur Buttes, with big bunches of sulphurous steam belching out of the darkness and puncturing the night air. It was a ticklish place to ride over in the night, and when your horse sank in several inches it seemed as though you would not have very far to fall before entering the infernal regions. All night we rode, passing within earshot of the roar of Yellowstone Falls, on over Mt. Washburn, overtaking the command the next afternoon. On the information furnished by a veteran soldier named Irving, who had been a prisoner of the hostiles and had escaped, the command was taking this short cut, which certainly saved it many a weary mile.

The soldiers fixed up the Baronet bridge, burned by a war party, and marched on up Soda Butte Creek and passed Cooke City, where several pioneer miners volunteered to serve against the Indians. Along here Captain Fisher and his little bunch of Bannocks rejoined the command and again rode out far in the advance, on the heels of the enemy. I went with them, and we rode through the lofty region of Clark's Fork of the Yellowstone, following down that stream after dropping through one of the steepest canyons on earth.

Up there the Seventh Cavalry joined the command, and with fresher horses made a forced march down Clark's Fork. The rain came down in torrents, and we had to ford the river many times where the bluffs would come down to the water's edge and make travel impossible without crossing over, which had to be repeated a few miles further on.

Scouting three to five miles ahead of the soldiers, we had a chance to see it first when there was anything to be seen. One thing we saw was where the hostiles had cleaned out a prospector's camp, and one of the dead men there had a miner's pick driven through his neck into the ground. We rescued one of this party from the brush, wounded further downstream, and he told us all about it.

We were a pretty hungry outfit when we found the carcass of a fine, fat, dressed antelope lying right in the trail, but it looked too suspicious of poison, so no one dared to think of eating the meat.

Buffalo Horn was one of our Bannock scouts, and he was a wonder to get more out of a horse than a white man could get out of half a dozen. He had an eye like an eagle, and nothing escaped it. He noted how the hostiles' horses could outtravel the cavalry horses, and mapped out in his head a war that would sweep over Idaho and Eastern Oregon and capture heaps of horses. He told me all about it as we rode along. The following March I made a pretty readable column-and-a-half story of it in the *San Francisco Sunday Chronicle*. A few months later Buffalo Horn started his war just as outlined, and with warriors from the Bannocks and Malheurs raided Idaho and Oregon, and had horses to burn. After the battle on the Bear Fork of Birch Creek that year of 1877 our scouting outfit captured a Snake hostile who told me that, in the battle with Harper's Volunteers near South Mountain, Buffalo Horn was badly wounded, and three days after was abandoned along the Owyhee River. Having become an encumbrance unable to travel, and of no further use to the other hostiles, he was cached in the brush and left for the wolves. Such was the philosophy of the noble red man.

The Nez Percés made a hurry-up march down Clark's Fork, but left nothing behind in the camps we came to just after they had gone. Every move from camp was a complete one, and not a single mirror, dresser, Morris chair, music box, or electric chandelier was overlooked or left behind.

Fifty well-mounted Mountain Crow Indians joined us along Clark's Fork when we were five miles ahead of the command, and they were proud of the Spanish brands on their prancing horses, which they said had been stolen away down in Mexico and brought back by their war parties. They said it was no trick to swipe horses from the Mexicans, but they often had a tough time getting them through the tribes between Mexico and Montana.

We forded the Yellowstone just above the mouth of Clark's

Fork, and it was such a swift stream that my horse was washed off, but Captain Fisher skillfully threw his lariat over the horn of my saddle, and his muscular mule pulled us out.

Although the main hostile trail led down the Yellowstone, we saw Indian scouts watching us from the bluffs to the north; they charged down, but our outfit sent them charging backward. When we had driven them over the bluffs we caught a sight of what was on the other side, and there was the whole hostile out-fit right under us, strung along the benches and bottoms of Canyon Creek.[6]

At sight of 2,500 head of hostile horses the Crows went wild, charged one corner of the rear of the herd, and cut out 300 horses, which they stampeded over the hill and rushed back to their reservation. Horses were all they were after, so they did not stop to help the whites in the impending battle.

It was quite a joke to see our little scouting outfit make a charge against another flank of the hostiles. The charge was promptly repulsed. When the cavalry finally appeared above us on the bluffs we all thought there would be a charge of the 600 right there that would wind up the Nez Percé War. That seemed the proper procedure. But there was no charge. General Sturgis[7] dismounted and deployed the troopers, and they followed up the Indians in skirmish line. The impression was that the commander was too cautious on account of losing a son by Custer's intrepidity the year before. So the battle of Canyon Creek lasted the rest of the day, the hostiles contesting every foot of the ground while gradually drawing off up a box canyon.

The scouts bushwhacked around all over the battlefield, get-ting in many cross fires on the enemy. One Indian behind a point of rocks held them back for ten minutes, and when the point was taken I counted forty empty shells on the ground where he had been crouching.

At one spot we rode up on a knoll and had just reached the top

[6] Canyon Creek flows into the Yellowstone about halfway between Laurel and Billings, Montana.

[7] General S. D. Sturgis of the Seventh Cavalry had charge of the defense of the plains. He joined Howard's command near Canyon Creek.

30

when a shower of bullets came right at us. They spattered all around us, before and behind, but not a man or horse was hit. Strange how such things happen.

Captain Fisher led the scouts up a coulee and into a connecting pocket, where we got in a fine flank fire on the enemy, but the bullets soon began buzzing so briskly there that we had to get out, and consider it a sort of miracle that we ever did get out.

Some one of those cruel hostiles took a pot shot at me, but aimed too low, so that the bullet went through my horse and lodged in my knee. One of my fellow Boy Scouts took his mouthful of tobacco and slapped it onto the wound, making it stay put with a strip of his shirt. It smarted some, but caused hurry-up healing, and the few days' stiffness did not hinder horse-riding.

After the battle was over and darkness had come on we had to cut steaks from the horses and mules shot during the day. The meat was tough and stringy, for the poor animals had been ridden and packed for months, with only what grass they could pick up at night. But it was all the food we had.

By charging the Indian scouts over the bluffs we had saved twelve miles, for the main hostile outfit had gone down the Yellowstone six miles and back up Canyon Creek six miles to where the battle occurred. They had captured a Concord stagecoach, and were hauling it up Canyon Creek, but dropped it when they saw us coming over the bluffs.

It took a great deal of the forceful energy of troopers and troop horses to overhaul those hostiles at Canyon Creek, but at the last it was all a forceful failure because of the lack of old-time dash and charge in the Seventh Cavalry, Custer's old regiment.

Some of us scouted back to the Yellowstone to see if anyone had been killed where we had seen a big smoke ascending.

We rescued from the willows a bold frontiersman named Ed Forrest, who had that year started a ranch and stage station on the river, and had been attacked by the hostiles. They had also attacked the McAdoo sawmill further down. The stage had just arrived at Forrest's when the attack was made, but the passengers all escaped to the thick willows on the river. Among them was a

31

lady named Fannie Clark, who insisted on cooking a square meal for us scouts, soon filling us up with fried ham and flapjacks. The hostiles had captured everything Forrest had in his new cabin, but as he had been jumped before, he wisely kept an extra outfit of food cached in the brush. The smoke we saw was from Forrest's two haystacks, which the Indians burned up.

Mr. Forrest was certainly a booster, and told us that right there was the best growing country in all Montana. He invited us to help ourselves to a small patch of string beans he was raising, and they were so good, and we were so hungry for the vegetables, that we ate up the whole business raw, stems and all. Some day when my prairie schooner comes in without minding the moaning of the bar, and I again have a home garden, I shall plant a whole acre of baked beans and invite Ed Forrest to come and help himself to them all.

Forrest had a hound dog and Miss Clark had a little black-and-tan and they kept barking at the Indians and defying them to come and get them in the brush, but instead of doing so they shot in the direction of the barking. So as the barking had to be stopped, Forrest had to sever the windpipe of the small dog; but when he started to do the same with his own bigger dog he only got the hide cut through when he broke away. But nursing the cut kept the dog too busy to bark any more. The other stage passengers had started up river afoot during the night, and finally reached a settlement. The kit of dentists' tools and false teeth left by one of them in the stage was scattered all along the ground by the Indians, who then drove the stage in great style down the river to the mouth of Canyon Creek, turning up that stream, with half a dozen hostile war horses tolling along behind the coach. This we saw from the bluffs over which we made the short cut.

The water of Canyon Creek was villainous stuff. When we gave it to wounded men the painful expression on their faces increased a thousandfold. At that time of year there was no running water there; it stood stagnant in pools.

There was rough country up Canyon Creek and beyond, and the cavalry horses wore out very fast. There was scout skirmishing and a running battle, but the hostiles outran the horses and skipped along on their way to Sitting Bull's camp.

The Musselshell where we struck it was certainly a lovely stream, with grassy meadows, shady trees, and good running water.[8] And there were millions of buffalo berries, which we broke off in great clusters as we rode under the trees that bore them. The acid taste was very welcome after a long fast on fruit, and not a codling moth was in sight.

And those berries are certainly the best puckerers on earth. They put on a pucker that never comes off. It is a long time between drinks of the Nez Percé War and World War, but this kind of pucker lasted all the way through. While being recently rebuilt by Major Hardin, skillful surgeon at an army hospital, he turned me over to the Letterman dentist for finishing. That gentleman had great trouble stretching my mouth enough to get in his diamond drills, and had to stand on the outside during the entire operation. He pronounced it the most complete puckering that ever came within his practice. And right there I put in a good boost for the Musselshell buffalo berries, for they made the pucker that kept puckering for forty-three years.

There was no appropriation for the army in 1877, so when the Nez Percé War was over and the scouts were discharged they received yellow vouchers showing that they had certain amounts coming to them, payment being subject to future appropriations by Congress. These vouchers only brought thirty cents on the dollar at frontier trading posts where scouts had to buy things they badly needed. They were all pretty ragged from hard service, and were nicely nicknamed Sternouts.

The surviving warriors of Chief Joseph's army will be surprised when they read here of how the darkness of night helped our scouts to ride up so close to their camp that we could count their fires, hear the yelping of their dogs, and the squabbling of squaws. We would go into camp in early evening many miles ahead of the army, make big fires with wood if there was any,

8 This river runs from near Harlowton, Montana, about seventy miles east, where it turns north, runs another seventy miles, and joins the Missouri.

33

otherwise with buffalo chips, cook supper if there was anything to cook, and stick around in the open until after dark. Then, leaving our fires burning, and our horses having partly filled up on good grass such as Montana was plentifully supplied with, we saddled up and rode a few miles and made another camp without fires.

Then about half our force would scatter out in ones and twos and scout the country most of the night. Sometimes we had forty-five scouts in the bunch, sometimes only ten, and it seems now the greatest luck in the world that our little outfit was not wiped out. We kept close track of the hostiles, and every night one of us as a lone courier would make his way by the stars back to the army to report on how the enemy was heading and any indications of his being reinforced by other hostiles.

It was wonderful how those scouts could tell you how to find your way by the Milky Way and Big and Little Dipper and the old standby the North Star. Most of them had never studied Latin or Greek, or much of anything else, but they certainly studied stars. And in regions swarming with hostile Indians most small parties did their traveling at night and hid as well as possible during daytime.

The genial George Huston figured out that the Nez Percé hostiles were heading for the Judith Basin,[9] and thought we could locate them there and arrange for a battle and wind-up. Knowing that the enemy would be looking backward for us to come up on his main trail, we waited until after dark, made a detour to get under cover of the timbered mountains, and rode all night. At the first streak of daylight we had reached a point on the mountain where we could look right into Judith Basin where we saw a stirring movement that seemed like the hostiles getting their big band of horses in motion for another day's march.

But as daylight increased we saw that what we saw was a little bunch of 3,000 buffalo grazing around, and the smoke from a few fires curled up into the ambient air. We zigzagged down from

[9] The Judith Basin, almost exactly in the center of Montana, was the favored buffalo hunting ground for the Nez Percés.

the mountains, and in one canyon Horn Miller showed us the charred ruins of a cabin where he and two others used to trap two years before. The Sioux besieged them there for three days, and then they escaped in the night, but one of the partners was killed, and the Indians burned up the cabin. No insurance.

We found the Judith Basin the best grass country on earth and our hungry horses soon filled up when we halted at the smoldering fires where the Indian camp had been the night before. It was easy to figure out that the Indians had cooked supper there and then gone on during the night. They had an abundance of buffalo meat, and on part of the big pile they had left lying around we cooked a big breakfast.

There were fully 3,000 buffalo grazing in the Judith Basin, and they were only just wild enough to move out of our way as we rode alongside of them. Among themselves the scouts agreed that some day white people would make a productive proposition out of that rich region.

In one part of the Judith we found the remains of a wrecked Indian camp, and wondered how it happened. From the way things were torn up around there, there had certainly been quite a little battle. George Huston figured out that the camp had been occupied by Dumb Bull's outfit of River Crow Indians, who were drying buffalo meat and were attacked by the Nez Percés. There were tons of dried and partly dried meat lying around, and a flock of Poe's ravens rose gracefully from where they had been holding inquests on the rigid remains of several Indians who no more minded people knocking on their chamber doors, nevermore. We found by moccasin tracks that several Indians had skipped out afoot, and when we passed Reed's Fort later in the day we found that the scout's conclusions were correct. Dumb Bull was there, and was feeling pretty sore about the way the hostiles had cleaned him out of all his horses. But still he declined the invitation to come along with the scouts and get some sweet revenge.

When we reported back to the army that the Nez Percés had not made a stand in Judith Basin, General Howard concluded

35

that a stern chase with worn-out cavalry horses and footsore infantry after well-mounted Indians could not be made a success. So he really planned the plan that resulted in the final capture of the hostiles. He sent an all-day-and-all-night courier to General N. A. Miles,[10] away down the Yellowstone, asking him to take every man he could muster and angle in ahead of the hostiles, cutting them off from Sitting Bull, while he would change his course, quit the direct pursuit, strike the Missouri at Carroll, and give the enemy the idea that they were no longer pursued, so that they would let up on their forced marches and give the two little armies a chance to bottle them up between them.

The plan worked out all right. Orders came out to our scouting outfit to continue on the direct trail of the hostiles, and play tag with them, and make them assure themselves that we had no supports, and that the army had turned back and gone home. They knew that when we were only a few miles ahead of the army the scouts were pretty saucy.

Our outfit carried out the program to perfection. We always had a few extra horses, which we hastily abandoned when the hostiles' rear guard turned on us and chased us out of the country after we had exchanged a few shots with them. After this had occurred several times the Nez Percés became assured that the army had turned back and that they had won a great victory by outtraveling the soldiers. So they quit pressing the accelerator, slowed down, and finally went into camp and began drying buffalo meat for the coming winter. And they must have thought that winter was going to last about ninety-nine years, judging by the amount of meat they had piled up at their last camp near the Bear Paw Mountains.

Everybody knows how General Miles's gallant little army headed off the hostiles and wound up their war, but most people do not know that it never would have been possible but for General Howard's plan and the way our scouts fooled the hostiles.

When we crossed the Missouri, Cow Island certainly looked

[10] General Miles was encamped at the mouth of the Tongue River. He defeated Joseph at the Battle of the Bear Paw Mountains.

sick.[11] Tons and tons of winter supplies had been landed there by steamboats, as it was the head of navigation in the fall. The larger part of these supplies belonged to the Canadian police, and were to be hauled by bull trains to Fort Walsh, across the border.[12]

After defeating the small guard at Cow Island, the Nez Percés had a picnic helping themselves to all the stores. They loaded every pack horse they had with the best groceries and canned goods, and for many miles up Cow Creek and Bull Creek we could trail them by the packages of fine-cut tobacco, beans, and coffee that trickled and dropped off their packs. But they refused to take the big stack of long barrack stoves that were going to steam-heat Fort Walsh, so they set fire to the big pile they could not take along, and the stoves were warped and twisted artistically.

While scouting through the Whoop-up country[13] north of the Missouri, we bumped into the old pioneer Liver-eating Johnson,[14] who jogged along with us for a while. He said he was just sort of pi-uting around, and he certainly had room to do so, for there was not another soul in sight, and it was a notoriously bad region, where everybody got whooped up, both red men and white.

One of our scouts told me that Johnson was safe anywhere, for the Indians were superstitious about him, and let him alone, and kept out of range of the big telescope rifle he carried. It was also said that he really did not eat the Indian's liver, but had merely drawn it across his mouth, so that the other Sioux could see and

[11] Cow Island, in the Missouri River near the Little Rocky Mountains. At this point Cow Creek flows in from the north. The Nez Percés traveled seventy miles to it from a point in the Judith Basin in about thirty hours.

[12] Fort Walsh, in Canada, one of several forts established by the Northwest Mounted Police. In the 1870's the I. G. Baker Company of Fort Benton, Montana, opened branches in Forts McLeod, Walsh, and Calgary to supply their needs.

[13] The Whoop-up Trail runs from Great Falls, Montana, to old Fort McLeod in British Columbia. The Whoop-up country lies in northern Montana just east of Glacier Park and runs up into Canada to Lethbridge and Calgary and beyond.

[14] Liver-eating Johnson hated Indians and was given the nickname, it is said, because of his threat to eat the liver of any Indian who came near his place.

37

think he had eaten it after shooting the Indian and jumping over the breastworks at Fort Pease and cutting out the liver.

In one section we wound among many small lakes, on the edge of one of which we found the stiffening body of a colored courier who had been carrying dispatches from one command to the other. He had been shot through the head, perhaps about two hours before, and his .50-caliber needle gun lay longside him, with an empty shell in the chamber. His buffalo moccasins lay close by, and his dispatches had been torn up into little bits and scattered around. A box of cigars had also been broken into short bits, but not too short to use for filling in the scouts' pipes. His horse was gone, and it was a great mystery why his murderers did not also take his gun and belt of ammunition.

It is difficult to recall the names of the reckless roughriders who made up our scouting outfit in Montana, but Captain S. G. Fisher was one of the best, and so was George Huston. Horn Miller was one of the best old souls that ever lived, and his partner Pike Moore was a close second. There was Potter and Nutting, and John T. Lilly, and Stoner, and Gird, and the always genial Hank Flannagan, and Captain Wilbur, a Civil War veteran, and there was a good-natured youth whose name I have forgotten, but I have not forgotten how he swiped my horse, even taking the picket pin, the dark night he was discharged. St. Peter will never let him in and show him where to find wood, water, and grass, or even buffalo chips that are dry enough to cook with.

Colonel Rube Robbins was chief of the Idaho scouts, and had with him Cal Morton, Jack Campbell, Colonel Frank Parker, and others, and they were relieved from further duty and started home from Judith Basin with the First Cavalry.

Charley Rainey and Baptiste were the main daredevils of Fisher's Scouts, and how they ever came out alive they or nobody else will ever know. They certainly tempted death on many fierce forays.

The life of a scout was surely an odd one, and he was in a class by himself. One reason why he preferred to go alone, especially on long courier trips, was that when two scouts separated to reconnoiter their horses nickered at each other and sent vibrations through the air to enemy's ears. When there was only one horse there was no nickering. Being out alone in the great solitudes gave a scout a chance to practice the closed mouth, and his horse learned the noiseless, rubber-tired tread.

Although the scouts rendered the most valuable kind of military duty in the field during actual war, and their job was to be in advance preventing the soldiers from running into murderous ambuscades, through some War Department red tape they have been given no standing as soldiers, and are classed as mere civilian employees of the Quartermaster Department. This puts them in the noncombatant class, as though they were clerks back at department headquarters a thousand miles from the front, while really they were notoriously combat units. They were subject to army regulations and the articles of war the same as soldiers, and if the formality of mustering them in was overlooked through no fault of theirs, they rendered just as good military service as though they had been mustered in a dozen times over.

Our scouts never took orders from quartermasters, for they volunteered their services to the general in command, and took orders only from him or his staff officer, Lieutenants C. E. S. Wood and R. H. Fletcher, in charge of scouts. The quartermaster had charge of the packers and men in the rear, but not of the scouts, and the only excuse for classifying the scouts as noncombatants is that, while there were no paymasters out with the army in the field, the quartermaster did the paying when there was any done. The paying with yellow vouchers at the close of the Nez Percé War was a joke on the scouts when they came to raising any cash on them.

And merely because the quartermasters kept track of the list of scouts and the pay they got and didn't get, the War Department turned the whole scouting outfit over to the Quartermaster

General's Department, thus robbing the scouts of their hard-earned standing as soldiers, although there is no act of Congress or law to justify such injustice.

In 1917 Congress granted a pension to all survivors of Indian wars, and Congressman Keating of Colorado, author of the bill, says that of course he intended it to include men who had served as scouts and couriers in Indian wars. But with rank injustice the Pension Department has refused to pay pensions to such scouts and couriers, and claims that they were civilian employees of the Quartermaster Department and not entitled to pensions.

Well, as most of the old scouts are dead, it will make no difference to them. As Herbert Bashford or some other poet wrote, their guns are rust, their bones are dust, their souls are with the Lord, we trust. But it is pretty tough to have official high-salaried swivel chair warmers smirch their war records and make noncombatants of them at this stage of the game.

Scouts traveled light, and providing for tomorrow was not near so important as making it easier for your horse. Along late in the afternoon the scouts would spot a little bunch of buffalo, and two would scout up a coulee and get as near the game as possible without being seen. Then they would come up the bank and make a dash for the buffalo and shoot half a dozen. Two long strips from each hump would be cut and tied on behind the saddles, and the rest would be left for the wolves watching around to come to the feast. These humps would furnish enough meat for the outfit for supper and for breakfast next morning. The practice had daily repetition. It was most excellent meat, and that cut from yearlings of young dry cow buffalo was tender enough to absorb through a straw if there had been any straws.

Some misguided humanitarian wrote up Chief Joseph's account of this war, in which he denounced the soldiers for shooting women during the Big Hole Battle, forgetting to mention that the lady Indians there fought as fiercely as did the gentlemen Indians, and that just as one officer yelled out, "Don't shoot the squaws, boys!" a squaw raised the flap of a wickiup and took a pot shot at him, sending a bullet through his hat. Joe also forgot to mention how his noble red men murdered poor Mrs. Manuel at her little home on White Bird, beat out on the cookstove the brains of her little baby, and cut off the tongue of her little girl, after leaving Jack Manuel for dead on the outside, and then burned up the house.[15] He also omitted to mention how his kindly Indians shot Mrs. Norton and Mrs. Chamberlain on Camas Prairie.[16]

On the Yellowstone the army ran out of tobacco and most everything else, and filled up on trout without salt. These fat fish were lazily lolling around in the river, and luckily it was no trick to catch them. Most of them were wormy, but in those hungry days everything went. After Colonel Parker and I had filled up on them and were scouting around an outpost he said to the officer commanding it, who was just then eating a stand-up lunch, "Say, Lieutenant, don't you know that those trout are full of worms?" The lieutenant finished swallowing a big mouthful and replied, "Well, if the worms can stand it, I can," and started in on another fish.

The soldiers seemed to miss their tobacco more than they did their hardtack. They cut out the pockets where they had been carrying tobacco, and chewed the rag, and burned out their pipes trying to get smokes from dead leaves and grass.

One trooper rolled out of his saddle blanket and into the river, and when he swam out he said he had dreamed that big plugs of army tobacco were hanging from the trees over his head, and

[15] Howard, *War Chief Joseph*, p. 129, wrote: "The postmaster of White Bird, John J. Manuel, and his little daughter, Maggie, although both badly wounded, managed to escape into the brush." On p. 138: "Patrick Brice, a husky miner from Florence, was returning homeward when he found the little girl, Maggie Manuel, hiding from the Indians in the bushes. . . . Brice constructed a rude chair from the burned remains of the child's home on White Bird Creek. He strapped it to his back and started to carry the girl to Mount Idaho by a devious route of fifty miles." He was stopped by a raiding party and after a parley was allowed to proceed. There is an interesting story about the parley (pp. 138–39). In a note on p. 330, Maggie, when she was living in Butte, Montana, in 1934, stated that she "saw Chief Joseph drive a knife into her mother's breast while she was nursing her baby in their cabin home" and here again is an interesting tale.

[16] *Ibid.* Mrs. Norton "was shot through both legs, but later, like Mrs. Chamberlain and her daughter, recovered."

as he was reaching up for them he rolled into the river. He said that as soon as he felt the chill of the mountain water he realized that it was all a pipe dream. A sad feature about it was when a courier would come to the command and have a dozen soldiers flock around him and beg him for a morsel of tobacco, and when he told them he had none they showed every symptom of wanting to tell him he was lying about it, although he was sticking to the frozen truth.

There was a very big rifle among the hostiles that had been taken from a murdered cattleman in Idaho. The Indian carrying it generally selected a safe spot at long distance, and almost always hit somebody when he fired, and the report sounded like hitting the air with a pile driver. This gun was looked for after the surrender, but was never found.

In General Howard's account of the Nez Percé War he wrote: "A thrill of joy ran through our weary and almost discouraged command when we were reinforced by a bunch of scouts under Captain S. G. Fisher. Night and day, with force and without, Fisher fearlessly hung upon the skirts of the enemy. The accuracy and fullness of his reports were a delight to those engaged in chasing hostile Indians across a vast wilderness."

In her thrilling book, "*Boots and Saddles*," Mrs. Custer wrote, "After the Seventh Cavalry reached Dakota frontier, General Custer accepted the volunteer services of a scout named Charlie Reynolds, who remained with him until they both fell in the Battle of the Little Big Horn. Year after year Scout Reynolds braved the awful winters of Dakota alone. I have known him to start out from Fort Lincoln when our officers, accustomed to hardships as they were, were forbidden to go.

"When I watched the scouts starting away on their lonely trips I invariably thanked heaven that I was born a woman, and consequently no deed of valor would ever be expected of me. But I felt, though, were I compelled to be brave, I would far rather go into battle with the inspiration of the trumpet call and the clash of arms, than go away alone and take my life in my hands, as did the scouts.

42

"When I think of how gloriously Scout Reynolds fell, fighting for his country, with all the valor and fidelity of one of her soldiers, my eyes fill with tears. For he lies there on that battle-field unwept, unhonored and unsung. Had he worn all the insignia of the high rank and the decorations of an adoring country, he could not have led a braver life or died a more heroic death. And yet he is chronicled as 'only a scout.' ". . .

Dick Shovelhead was an Indian or sort of a near-Indian, a mixture of Shoshoni and something else, but he had a smattering of civilization, and as he and I were making a sort of side-scout near the Yellowstone we came to another one of the camps that the hostiles had left a few hours before. Following up a sort of human sound we heard, we found a very old squaw, a real pale-pink peony, helpless on a bunch of brush, and she began telling us in broken English that there were bad Indians nearby, and that white people had better "Klatawa," skiddoo, get out. Then she told us that her Nez Percé people had abandoned her, and that we were welcome to shoot her, and began singing the Indian death song. She could sing about as well as I could, but her poor old cracked voice could carry the chant, wild and weird. Dick proposed to shake dice to see whether or not we would put her out of her misery, as requested, but I side-stepped and showed him that the ethics of civilization frowned on such murder.

The old squaw was wasted to parchment, and when the poor old umbra saw her chant was bringing her no nearer to the golden stair, she made a pathetic effort to sing "Nearer My God to Thee." This pretty nearly brought Dick to tears, and he said something about once having a poor old mother himself, which all the other scouts had doubted, he was such an awful, although artistic, swearer.

But he brushed away the tears and said "A-w-e-e, that old son-of-a-gun! If she had you helpless on the battlefield she would cut off and make you chew your own ears. Don't I know? Haven't I seen it done? Come on, let's go!"

Dick also said that this Jersey Lily's Indian name meant the "Graceful Gazelle," although she looked as much like a gazelle as I did.

43

From the Musselshell on north it was almost impossible to look anywhere without seeing bunches of buffalo, and along the bottoms of the upper Missouri there were lots of bear, deer, and elk. Near the mouth of Rock Creek we passed a herd of at least 3,000 antelope, so fearless that they would hardly move out of the scouts' way. But through the Yellowstone Park, where meat was most needed, the Indians had scattered the game ahead of us, after shooting what they themselves needed.

While we were scouting through the magnificent Montana mountains, up to and over 10,000 feet, we took off our hats to Senator Ashley of Ohio, who first applied the territorial name meaning mountainous, for nothing could be more appropriate and distinctive. There were mountains to burn.

The Nez Percé War was tough on horses and pack mules, and many had to be abandoned along the trail, completely played out. Those that were left in the high mountains, after resting up a couple of weeks, always worked their way down to some settlement, as the horse's instinct told him to follow down some stream and get to lower levels before deep snows came.

When the scouts had a skirmish with the hostiles they would sometimes capture enough horses to get a remount all around. A courier generally got out every inch of speed there was in a horse, taking chances on getting another after he had delivered his dispatches.

Very often we would find at an Indian camp a little bunch of tired horses that had been left by the hostiles when they moved, only a few hours before, and they would be all dead lame. The Indians had abandoned them because they could not keep up with their big herd, but had cut one foot on each so that the scouts or soldiers could get no work out of them.

By having war parties out ahead on both flanks, the Indians raided ranches and captured many horses, so that they could ride a near-fresh one every hour. But the troopers had to get along with the horses they started out with on the long chase, and many of them were horses too heavy for mountain work and all of them had to live on what grass they would pick up at night,

44

after being ridden all day. This is where the hostiles had a big advantage in a stern chase. They picked out the roughest regions they could, so as to wear out the cavalry horses that had to follow them.

The infantry soldiers in the Nez Percé War certainly went through trials that tried men's soles. The soles of the government shoes they wore were fastened on with brass screws, and when the soles warped and twisted, those screws would wiggle up into the feet and cause all kinds of agony. Many a miry meadow these soldiers had to march across, many a creek they had to wade. And when their shoes were thus thoroughly soaked they often marched across a keen edged lava bed for a few miles, so that their shoes soon became total wrecks, with no chance to get any more. So they had to make moccasins from the coarse burlap that came on army bacon. But this was not lasting, and sometimes there was blood from bleeding feet along the trail. They were allowed ten minutes rest every hour on the march, and certainly needed it. These men marched anywhere from 1,400 to 2,000 miles on that campaign, and if the crooked zigzags had been ironed out the figures might be double that. Such hard, patriotic work was not well rewarded in those days, as soldiers received only thirteen dollars a month, and had an assessment of two bits stopped every payday for the support of the Soldiers' Home at Washington. And there were no paydays for eight months in 1877. And if one of those hard-worked soldiers should go to the Washington Soldiers' Home he would be barred out unless he had served twenty years in the regular army. The Indian used to call these soldiers the "heap-o'-walks," and the title was certainly appropriate. But that twenty-year feature has now been abolished. . . .

When the last battle had been battled at the Bear Paw Mountains by Miles's men, the infantry marched back to the Missouri River, but could not march back home to the Pacific Coast because early snows had already filled up the mountain passes. So they took the steamer *Benton* and went down the river 2,500 miles to Omaha, thence by rail to San Francisco, and up north

45

by steamship to Portland. It took twenty-five days to go down the river, the soldiers camping on shore every night. The boat did not dare to run downstream at night on account of snags and changing channels. A few times every day the boat would run onto sand bars and be walked over them on stout stilts. In those days those upper Missouri boats were shot full of holes by the playful Sioux as they went on their way upriver or down.

PARTNERS IN THE EARLY WEST

# Stranger from the Ridges[1]

WILLIAM C. BUNDRANT, JR.

Everybody's lookin',
Children quit their playin',
Women quit their cookin',
Menfolks all a sayin'—

> "Who's that comin' down the street
> With trail dust on his feet
> And gold dust in his beard?"

Stranger's come to town,
Follered by his houn';

> "Where you hail from, stranger?"
> "Up thar in the ridges."

Beddin' on his shoulders wide,
Carbine swingin' at his side;

> "What brings you down here, stranger?"
> "Fetchin' grub and ca'tridges."

His eyes like sparkling jewels show
Through the foliage of his brow;

> "Where you headin', stranger?"
> "Back thar to the ridges."

Stranger's leavin' town,
Follered by his houn';

> "Who's that goin' down the street
> With trail dust on his feet
> And gold dust in his beard?"

[1] *Frontier*, Vol. XIII, No. 2, p. 114.

# Partners

## FRANK B. LINDERMAN

FRANK BIRD LINDERMAN (1869–1938), a contributing editor of *Frontier*, was trapper, hunter's guide, assayer, insurance man, friend of the Indian (adopted member of three tribes), and author. He wrote *Indian Why Stories* (New York, Charles Scribner's Sons, 1915); *Indian Old-Man Stories* (New York, Charles Scribner's Sons, 1920) and other tales and legends of Plains Indians; *American: The Life Story of a Great Indian, Plenty-Coups, Chief of the Crows* (New York, The John Day Co., 1930); and *Recollections of Charley Russell* (Norman, University of Oklahoma Press, 1963), his friend of thirty years.

In the early 1880's Linderman was a trapper in the Flathead country of northwestern Montana and had several partners, Black George being the most colorful of them. The picture of the lad with down on his chin and the heavily bearded man, a fugitive from justice, is amusing, as is that of the slim lad serving as the go-between for two older, hardened outdoor men.

Both mules and men had to be worked over, the country and the climate doing it for the men, as the first two of the tales that follow show. They were published in *Frontier and Midland*, Vol. XIV, Nos. 1 and 2, pp. 62 and 153; the third appeared in the same volume, No. 4, p. 325.

Among Linderman's unpublished manuscripts is a collection of tales entitled "The Doctor and I." The doctor was a Helena physician, Dr. Oscar M. Lanstrum, who for some years was the titular head of the Republican party in Montana. He told these tales to his friend Linderman from his experiences. "The Secret of Keep Cool," which first appeared in *Frontier and Midland*, Vol. XIV, No. 4, p. 328, is one of these accounts.

## *I. Black George*

I HAD RIDDEN into Demersville, Montana Territory, consisting then [the early 1880's] of a store owned by Jack Demers and the saloon of Johnnie Foy. The early spring day was stormy. Sleet, driven by a north wind, that iced the grass and stung my face, obliged me to ride with my head bent downward. Near the saloon my horse shied at a canvas-covered bedroll that was sheathed with ice. Leaning against the roll I saw a Winchester, its muzzle up and exposed to the storm.

"Somebody has gone on a spree and forgotten his rifle," I thought, getting down to attend to the gun that might become rusted. There was no ice in the barrel. Throwing a cartridge into its chamber, I fired it. Then after wiping the piece as well as I could on the tail of my buckskin shirt, I shoved the rifle into the bedroll among the blankets. My horse had turned his rump to the storm. When I turned him back to lead him to the store I saw Black George staring drunkenly at me from the saloon window. He came to the door.

"How!" he called, coming out into the storm to stand before me, his lower legs encased in tattered Red River leggin's that had once been very fine ones. He was just under six feet tall with long black hair and beard that were both streaked with gray. His buckskin shirt, almost black with wear, was open far down, exposing his hairy breast. His hat was pulled down over his eyes. I noticed that his knife scabbard held no knife. Later on I learned why.

"Old hand, ain't ye," he sneered, sticking his hands under his cartridge belt flat against his stomach. "Takin' care of my rifle for me! A damned pilgrim takin' care of Black George's rifle!"

But by now I had caught a twinkle in his half-befuddled eyes. "You'd do it for another man," I said.

"How do you know I would?" He smiled, and we were friends.

Black George was a good partner. Little by little I gathered bits of his story, even his real name. He was a gun fighter. On the other side of the range where he hunted buffalo, he had made a killing or two. In one of these affairs he had used his butcher-knife in deadly fashion. "I felt her go bump, bump, bump, over every rib the feller had," he told me. Afterward when on a spree Black George never packed his knife. "It ain't a white man's weapon nohow," he said when he told me the story.

It was said that Black George had fled from the other side—that the hangmen of 1884 had nearly "got" him "over in the basin." And this may be true. The story of the doings in Montana Territory during the year 1884 is a wild one.

Black George was a slave to whisky. I have known him, in the dead of winter, to snowshoe fifty miles to get drunk. And once after trapping all winter I heard him say to the trader who had bought his furs, "Gimme a sack of salt for a grub-stake, Bill. I'll take the rest out in drinkin' whisky."

In his cups he was a little disagreeable, apt to be quarrelsome; yet he was always white with me. When at last we split the blanket because he wished to go farther north, I asked him to write to me if he found fur plentiful in a country he expected to visit.

"Nope," he told me, "I ain't never wrote no letters, and I ain't goin' to begin with you."

He was a cool-headed man. I shall never forget one night when he was fighting a burly half-breed, rough and tumble. The fellow was down, and had somehow managed to get Black George's right-hand thumb between his teeth. Men were thick around the pair, so that when they went down I could not see them on the dirt floor of the little saloon. Black George made no sound. I did not know what was happening until it was over. Black George never packed a six-shooter, and I have said never wore a belt-knife while he was drinking. Now, being unable to force the breed's jaws apart, Black George managed to get out his jackknife. This he was trying to open with his teeth when somebody kicked his elbow, knocking the jackknife into the crowd. It was now that I learned what was going on. We soon made the big fellow let go the thumb, which was badly mangled. Nobody in the Northwest had then ever heard of infection. Even the worst wounds got little attention, and yet they nearly always healed quickly. Black George's thumb gave him trouble, however. It refused to heal and kept growing worse, until finally we appealed to the surgeon who was with a detachment of United States Regulars. To show appreciation for his services we gave him a fat cub bear.

I have said that Black George was cool-headed. He was, and yet I once saw him when he seemed to have suddenly lost his natural calmness. The cats, all of them, generally sulk in a trap. Their eyes, greened with fright, follow every move a trapper makes. Their ears are aback, their mouths open to a hissing growl, and their bodies crouched as though for a leap. Fearsome as they appear in a trap they are nearly always dispatched with a club. One extremely cold day George and I, who had met where our trap-lines crossed each other, came to a trap that held a large lynx, not far from our cabin. "Big feller," said George, striking the animal a sharp blow on the head. "Let's us pack him to the shack where we can skin him out in comfort."

Taking a buckskin thong from his pocket he speedily tied the near front paw to the off hind paw, and then lifted the animal up so that he might poke his own head through the loop made by the tied legs. The body of the lynx was thus under George's arm against his body, nearly halfway down his side. The head of the beast was in front, so that its tail end was toward me when I fell in behind my partner to go to the cabin. The jostling, upside down, revived the lynx. If its head had been where its tail was I might have noticed signs of returning life in time to have warned my partner. But as it wasn't, the first I knew George's hat went flying. I cannot describe what followed. Both George and the lynx moved too swiftly for any recorder. I know that the lynx bit, spat, clawed, and growled, and that Black George swore strange oaths, all in a whirl of flying snow, before they came apart. "Kill him! Kill the ——— ———! What you laughin' at? Want to see a feller gutted? Hell!"

I sobered instantly, and although limp from laughing killed the lynx. Then off I went again into gales of laughter while

George, muttering, made a hurried examination of his bloody arm and breast. His buckskin shirt had saved him much, perhaps his life.

The only medicine that Black George packed was turpentine. I used this freely on his wounds at his direction. "I'm sorry I laughed, George," I said, honestly enough, when the cabin began to smell like a paint shop.

"S'll right, Pardner. It must hev looked right funny fer a spell, I reckon."

"It did; it did," I said, remembering the start and the finish, particularly.

"Hell," grunted George, pulling his shirt away from his deeply scratched breast.

I turned away from him, holding my breath against a return of my mirth. George saw this, and somehow it tickled him. He began to laugh, himself; and what a blessing this was to me! We had it out now, each furnishing a new start occasionally by mentioning some incident of the "fight."

"Don't never fool with 'em none," said George at last, very soberly. "Kill 'em plumb dead before ye take 'em out of a trap. Their cussed toenails can raise more hell with a man than a sharp butcher-knife."

## II. Men and Mules

RED ABBOTT WAS A TRAPPER, Joe Montgomery a prospector. Both had drifted into the Flathead country without partners. Both were experienced; and they were as different as men could be. Red was tall and thin, his eyes pale blue and cold. His long hair and beard were red, and his temper touchy as a set trigger. He talked but little, never mentioned his past, and would let whole days go by without uttering a word. Joe was short, inclined to stoutness. His hair and beard were dark, his eyes gray and warm. He was not explosive, never garrulous, and he never swore. He was good in camp, doing his full share of work there, though his left arm was stiff at the elbow.

I met Red and Joe at Jack Demers' store on the Flathead River in the spring of 1888. They were outfitting there, and so was I. They had known each other less than half a day when I made their acquaintance. The Kutenais had been giving a little trouble, so that for company we three threw in together, setting out for the upper Swan River country on the twenty-eighth of April, Red and I to trap beaver, Joe to prospect the country for placer gold, share and share alike. To me Red and Joe were old men, and yet neither could have been more than forty.

We had eight pack animals, one of the a large Missouri mule named Biddy that belonged to Joe. Because I knew the upper country I was given the lead. Joe took the swing, and Red the trail immediately behind old Biddy; and Biddy was as mean as a magpie. Besides being too tall to pack with ease she would not follow the narrow Indian trails through the forests. She had to be herded, and whenever turned back from her wanderings she would always kick viciously with both heels, so that by the time we made our first camp "Biddy" was a swear-word with Red.

We stopped on the edge of a swale where there was green grass for our stock. Rain had been falling for more than two hours, the night promising to be wet and cold. Lodge poles were handy, so that while Joe busied himself with the packs Red and I pitched an Indian tepee that belonged to me. I noticed that one of Red's hands was bleeding freely. "Hurt your hand, Red?" I asked him.

"Biddy! She kicks, damn her," he muttered, driving a peg out of sight in the soft ground with a single blow.

"I wondered how this happened," I said a moment later, examining an ugly rent in my tepee.

"Biddy! That damned mule packed it all over hell today with me right after her," growled Red glancing over his shoulder at Joe, who was coming toward us with some packs to put inside the tepee.

The day had been difficult. We were yet unacquainted, the brush had been wet, the trail through the spruce timber had been full of bog holes, and finally rain had fallen. Red and I wore buckskin, and buckskin absorbs water readily, so that we were both wet to the skin. Besides this, herding Joe's unruly mule

54

through dripping bushes had worn Red's temper thin. Joe bared his stiff arm to hold it near the tepee fire, the sleeve of his collarless, red flannel shirt steaming while he briskly rubbed his useless elbow. If he had noticed Red's wounded hand he did not mention it. Red moved back from the fire, spreading his blankets, while I cooked the supper. None of us talked. I knew that nearly all good mountain men were cranks, and that my new partners were both first-class mountain men. (I was no longer a mere pilgrim myself.)

However, the bright fire, the supper, and the pelting rain that could not reach us mellowed the outfit a little. Joe wondered, audibly, if our stock would take the back trail during the night. Red didn't believe they would. "They got too damned much sense," he said, gruffly. "That is, *most* of 'em have."

I thought his emphasis a little tactless, though Joe didn't appear to notice it. Nevertheless, I wished that Biddy had never left Missouri. I felt certain that she would yet cause trouble between my partners. However, I would keep out of it. I'd have nothing to do with the mule, and after this I'd pack my tepee on one of my own horses.

The weather held us in our first camp for days, the green grass lending cussedness to Biddy meanwhile. When finally Joe and Red were packing her for a move she suddenly whirled and let both heels go at Red, breaking the stem of his prized meerschaum pipe short off in his mouth.

"Well, well!" said Joe, mildly, scowling a little at the big mule whose switching tail was challenging all comers.

I saw Red struggle with his temper and throttle it. "It's jest the life that's in her," he managed to say, spitting out the piece of pipestem. "Tell you what I'll do, Joe," he went on, his lips twitching with suppressed anger, "I'll trade you that there brown G-Dot geldin' for the mule right now."

Perhaps Joe guessed what was in Red's mind. Anyhow, I felt that if Joe accepted the trade Red would lead Biddy out of camp and kill her, perhaps by inches. But Joe would not part with the mule. For weeks Biddy continued to build up a strange enmity between my partners. Red became formal, painfully polite whenever he addressed a necessary question to Joe; and Joe adopted nearly the same tactics with Red; so that our camp conversations were neither long nor interesting. Each drive we made seemed to bring the situation nearer a break. Even the weather, which remained wet and cold, appeared to be conniving with old Biddy to bring on an open rupture between my two partners.

The tension in the tepee tortured me. I began to feel afraid. Nevertheless, Red and I, going our separate ways, caught beaver from every camp. Joe seldom left the tepee, never stuck a pick into the ground, and had not even panned any gravel. I knew that Red must have noticed Joe's lack of industry. I feared that he might accuse Joe of laziness and so open the long-dreaded ball. This I would try to prevent by asking Joe why he didn't prospect.

"You and Red don't set your beaver traps until you see sign, do you?" he asked.

"No," I told him, "not until we see beaver sign."

"Well, I don't prospect until I see gold sign; and so far this country is barren of gold," he said.

He was right, though I knew nothing of mining then. As peace-preserver I hastened to acquaint Red with Joe's reason for not prospecting. He made no comment whatever.

And so things went on until one day Joe left camp early carrying a pick, shovel, and gold pan. I felt a thrill at this. Joe had seen *sign*. Perhaps he might strike pay gravel. Then old Biddy would be forgotten, and we'd all be happy. Red, too, appeared to be glad that Joe was at last going to prospect. He actually hummed a lively tune when Joe's back disappeared in the timber. I left him in camp fleshing a beaver skin, and went down to the river to look for a set or two.

This was our first clear day. The bright sun gladdened me. Rich grass, tall weeds, and countless blossoms were everywhere, and rank. Our stock was rolling fat. The river was rising. June was at hand and beaver trapping nearing its end for the season. However, I set a trap or two, starting back for camp in the middle of the afternoon, wondering if Joe had struck gold.

56

When near the tepee I heard weeping, loud sobs that stopped me in my tracks and held me there. My fear returned. What could have happened in camp? Had Red and Joe —— what *had* happened?

"Thud, thud, thud!" The sound of heavy blows reached me, and then a string of awful swearing followed by sobs that made me shiver. Running a little way toward the camp I jumped upon a huge pine tree that had been overturned by wind. I could see the whole camp now. Biddy, angrily switching her tail, was tied to a fir tree. Red, shaking with sobs, was seated upon a log near the mule. I looked hastily about for Joe. He was nowhere in sight.

Biddy, suddenly, began to pull back on the rope that held her, sitting down like a dog in her frantic efforts to break it. The top of the fir tree trembled. Red, as though prodded with a goad-stick, leaped to his feet and began to belabor the mule with six feet of a broken lodgepole. "Whack, whack, whack!" The heavy club landed upon Biddy's shining ribs, head, and rump, accompanied by swearing, unheard-of oaths, until, exhausted, Red staggered back to his log to rock himself and sob.

His actions disgusted me, lowering him a long way in my estimation, though I wasn't very sorry for Biddy. She had made our lives miserable. But what if Joe should come in and catch Red beating his mule? I ran into camp. "What are you doing, Red?" I asked, looking again for Joe.

He actually smiled. "By God, I been a-workin' that Biddy mule over for Joe. He won't never do it himself," he said, letting old Biddy go free. "I'll bet you a beaver hide that that there mule will stay in trails from now on," he added, with a quick glance in the direction Joe had taken in the morning.

The strange thing about it all is that old Biddy *did* stay in trails afterward; and because of this Red and Biddy became friends. When one day late in June while we were crossing the range the old mule slipped and fell on a mountainside that was covered deeply with crusted snow, sliding more than a quarter of a mile, pack and all, it was Red who helped her out again, Red who ministered to her badly skinned shoulder and hip. If Joe ever

57

knew what had converted his mule he never spoke of it to Red or me. We split the blanket on the third of July. I was once with Red afterward, but never saw Joe again.

### III. The Secret of Keep Cool

THERE WAS AN AIR OF INSTABILITY about most mining camps, something in their pretentious frame buildings, with high, false fronts and no foundations, that was like hope established without faith. Marysville was different. Her big, English-owned gold mine, the Drum Lummon, had paid fabulously for years, and that it would go on paying forever became a camp tradition. The thunderous booming of its huge 110-stamp mill was music so continuous and contenting that if it ceased for a minute at night all Marysville sat up in bed to wonder and wait for its resumption. There was a satisfying air of permanency about Marysville. Her miners and millmen were not drifters. They were largely family men, and mostly Cornish, with children in the public school. Besides its big Drum Lummon, the camp was surrounded with other famous gold mines, so that Marysville felt established, rich, not only in her mines but in her traditions; and she generously cherished the little mysteries in her surrounding hills.

For instance, there was the secret of Keep Cool, a small gulch with a placer pay streak. Dick Lewis and Tom Benton had struck Keep Cool in the sixties, and had stuck to their gulch ever since, sluicing its gravel each season. They had come up from the gold diggings in California, prospecting all the way to this district; and in those days the Blackfeet were hostile here. "Keep cool, Tom," Dick admonished, when Tom cheered lustily at the sight of heavy colors of gold in his first pan of gravel. "You'll fetch the Injins down on us first you know." And so they named the gulch "Keep Cool." But civilization followed them. It grew up around them, and yet the partners, old men now, were mining in Keep Cool. Nobody knew if their diggings were rich or poor; and nobody cared, so long as the partners paid for their small needs in gold dust. But everybody did know that old Dick and old Tom

58

never came to Marysville together, never left Keep Cool alone. This made talk. There must be a reason; and this was the secret of Keep Cool.

I had not been long in Marysville when old Dick came alone to the camp. I saw him, a sharp-featured old fellow with white hair and beard, leading a white pack horse down the gulch. He did his trading promptly, visited here and there with friends, got a little tight, and then left for Keep Cool, setting the camp to wondering afresh. Knowing that I was a newcomer in Marysville, a gambler stopped beside me. Pointing at old Dick and his white pack horse, he said, "Old Tom'll come in next time. Funny they never come in together, ain't it?" he asked, as though he wished me to ask him the reason; but I did not gratify him. There could be but one inference drawn from all this wondering—old Dick and old Tom must have a large cache of gold dust in Keep Cool, and did not dare to leave the gulch unguarded. I think all Marysville believed this. I know that I did and that when, one morning, I heard that old Tom was dead I thought instantly of murder. But it was pneumonia that carried him off. All Marysville turned out for the funeral, and I shall always remember poor old Dick standing in the snow beside his partner's grave, his face drawn with grief. Friends tried to keep him in Marysville that night, but he would not stay. A livery team and sled took him back to Keep Cool.

"What will old Dick do now?" I asked the doctor two days after the funeral.

"Oh, he'll stay on," he said, after speaking to his team, whose restlessness kept their bells jingling. "They all stay on. He'll mine a little. But he's growing feeble. Old Tom's going has upset him terribly. I'm going up past Keep Cool. Better get your coat and come along," he added, pushing bottles of medicine into the pockets of his long coonskin overcoat. I had not yet seen Keep Cool. "All right," I said; and within a few minutes we were off behind a frisky team and singing sleigh bells.

Storms never stopped the doctor, nor the poverty of his patients. He would always go day or night, pay or no pay. And so

the people, the miners in the Drum Lummon, and the lone prospectors in the gulches far outside the camp itself came to love
him. He was inclined to stoutness even then. His jovial face,
reddened by exposure to all kinds of mountain weather was
always smiling. How I admired him for his gentle kindness!

"There are the cabins." He pointed with his whip to two snowy
hummocks among green fir trees. "That's Keep Cool."

A rushing mountain stream with snowy banks barred with
lances of sunlight and deep shadows separated the cabins. A
plume of blue smoke was curling from the fireplace chimney of
one; the other was white and still. Not a track marked the deeply
piled snow about it. I saw a blue jay flash down from a treetop in
the gulch, the blue and black of his plumage bright in the sunlight. I even heard his rasping call above the jingling of our bells
as we passed the mouth of Keep Cool. Its loneliness depressed me.

"Do you believe they had a cache of gold dust in the gulch,
Doctor?" I asked, because I wished him to talk.

"No," he answered positively, handing me the reins so that he
might light a cigar. "You've been listening to idle talk," he said,
taking the reins. "Their spare money went to relations back in
the States. Keep Cool isn't rich. Besides, its pay is pockety. It
wasn't a cache of gold dust in Keep Cool that prevented Dick
and Tom from coming to Marysville together. I stumbled onto
the reason for this. But because I've learned that talking doesn't
help in the practice of medicine I didn't peddle my discovery.

"Four years ago last October I came up this way alone. I had a
little time to spare that day so I tied my team and went over to
visit with Dick and Tom for a few minutes. Both cabins were
empty. However, I knew about where they were mining, and
went up there. I didn't like to walk in the gulch itself, so I kept
up on the mountainside in the timber until I knew I was abreast
of their diggings. But there was nobody there. The route I had
traveled had been rough. I decided I'd cross the gulch and strike
the road about where we are now. But the gulch was rather steep
just where I was. Nevertheless, I slid down, displacing a lot of
gravel that went rattling down to the sluice boxes below me.

And when I reached the boxes myself I saw that the water had been turned out of them, and that they were still wet. By this I guessed that old Dick and Tom had quit work for the season, and that they had just finished making their cleanup that afternoon.

"Then because the water was out of the sluices, and because I didn't like the idea of scrambling up the other side of the gulch just there, I started to walk down Keep Cool in the sluice boxes, looking for a good place to climb out of the gulch. And I nearly stepped into a gold pan about half full of gold. It was in the third box from the head. Of course I knew it must be Dick's and Tom's cleanup; but why had it been left there?

"I sat down to look at the gold. It was fine, no nuggets. I don't suppose there was a color in the whole lot that would have weighed four bits. And the gold had been smoothed down to a nicety. Then I saw that a fine line had been drawn with a knife straight across the gold in the pan.

"Keep Cool made a turn just there. The wind was blowing, and yet I thought I heard somebody coming. It made me feel panicky. I didn't want Dick and Tom to find me there with their gold. Without considering just what I was doing I stepped out of the sluice, and ducked into a clump of willows, wondering if Dick and Tom had seen my team. In a minute I realized what I had done, how my hiding must look if I should be discovered. But it was too late now to move.

"Old Tom, carrying a gold pan, was coming up the gulch. He came straight to the pan of gold. When he lifted it out of the sluice box and set it down on a level place, he wasn't twenty feet from me. He filled and lighted his pipe, drew a tin tablespoon from his hip pocket, and began to scoop the gold from one side of the line into his own pan. I could see it all, every move he made. If a little of the gold caved near the line he put it back, and patted it down carefully until he had transferred half the gold dust, all of it on one side of the line, to his own pan. Then he put the first pan back into the sluice box, picked up his own, and went down the gulch, the smoke from his pipe blowing over his shoulder.

"I wondered if I ought to get out of there now, and more than ever I hoped that Dick and Tom had not seen my team. Before I could make up my mind what to do I heard old Dick coming. He was talking to himself, though I couldn't hear what he was saying. He must have passed old Tom just below in the gulch. He came straight to the pan in the sluice, and without even glancing at the gold left in the pan, picked it up, and followed Tom toward the cabins.

"By now I had guessed the secret of Keep Cool. Old Dick and Tom had quarreled. Having known them a long time I believed I could make peace between them, so I followed them to the cabins. Dick talked the most, and besides I felt that I knew him best. I decided to go first to Dick's. He was kindling a fire. The pan, with the gold dust yet in it, was on the table near the window. I didn't know how to begin; and I'm afraid I bungled things. Anyhow, I told him straight out what I had seen, and what I surmised.

"I never got such a thorough cussing in my life. Old Dick was beside himself with anger. 'Get out of here, you damned pilgrim,' he ordered, pointing to the open door, his arm rigid. But when I started to go out the old man sat down on his bunk, weak and shaken. I sat beside him, tried to steady him, tried to make him see that I wasn't just a meddler.

"When he grew calmer he told me that he and Tom had quarreled. He said they hadn't spoken to each other in twenty years. He told me that they took turns cleaning up, that the one who made the cleanup put the gold into a pan, divided it with a knife, and left it on the spot until the other had taken his share. It was an awful story. I couldn't imagine two men shoveling gravel into jointly owned sluice boxes from morning till night throughout the long summer months without speaking to each other. I couldn't imagine that these two friends of mine, old partners, living alone in their separate cabins like mortal enemies, could hibernate during the winter months like two ugly bears, nursing their hatred for each other until spring. But it was all true.

62

"And what do you suppose brought on the quarrel? A ham of venison. The weather being wet and warm, Dick was afraid the meat would spoil before they could eat it. He wanted to salt and smoke the ham. Tom said the meat would keep as it was, that they could eat it fresh. And the ham spoiled.

"I tried to get them together. But old Dick wouldn't listen. Tom told me to mind my own damned business if I had any, said he would have nothing to do with the old caribou across the creek. And so it ended. I couldn't do a thing.

"That was four years ago. I'm about the only man who ever visited old Dick and Tom; and my calls were far apart, because I'm busy. The other day after I had called on Tommy Broderick up the gulch I remembered that I hadn't seen Dick and Tom for nearly a year. I went over to Keep Cool to talk with them for a few minutes. The weather was bitterly cold, the snow about the same as now.

"No smoke was coming out of old Tom's chimney. I could see that Dick had a good fire, and because I was cold went first to his cabin. He was reading a New York newspaper spread out on the table by the window. I sat down at the table myself, and we talked for nearly half an hour. When I felt that I ought to be moving I said, 'There doesn't seem to be anybody at home over at Tom's.'

" 'I ain't seen him for several days,' Dick said, glancing out of the window across the deep snow. 'He went down to Marysville last week. He's likely in bed. He's too damned lazy to keep a fire goin' anyway.'

" 'Well,' I told him, 'I'll just run over there and see if he's home, and then I shall have to be going down the gulch.'

"I wallowed through the deep snow to Tom's cabin, and opened the door. A clammy dampness stopped me short. It was dark inside the cabin. There was only one tiny window. Two of its panes were missing. The holes had been stopped with old flour-sacks, so that but little light could enter. 'Oh, Tom,' I called, groping my way toward the table.

"A groan answered me. I went to the bunk. And there he was,

63

in the last stages of pneumonia, nearly dead even then. 'I'm goin'
under, Doc. But don't tell Dick,' he murmured when I took hold
of his wrist. He died before I got the fire going.

"I ran, stumbling through the snow, to Dick's. 'Dick!' I called
when I got to his door, 'Old Tom is dead!'

" 'Yes, he is. Dead drunk, you mean.'

"I shall never forget the awfulness of his laughing. It made me
shudder. 'No, no, Dick,' I said, sternly, my hand on his shoulder,
'old Tom is dead, died just a minute ago.'

"He brushed his face with a hand that was shaking like a leaf
in the wind. His face went white; I saw his knees bend under
him; and then down he went to the floor. 'No, no, Doc. My God,
don't say that,' he sobbed.

" 'Yes, Dick, old Tom is dead,' I told him, as gently as I could.
But he broke completely down, and cried like a woman. I helped
him to his bunk and then went back to Tom's cabin. I knew that
a cry would do old Dick good, that he needed to cry. He had
mastered himself by the time I got back. I wanted to take him in
to Marysville with me. But he wouldn't go. 'No, sir, by God. I'll
stay with my partner as long as he's on top of the ground,' he told
me. And I left them there in Keep Cool until I could send
them help."

# ON THE WIDE PLAINS

# Sage[1]

### JAY ELLIS RANSOM

I want to see sage . . . desert sage . . .
Stretching to the horizon;
Silver sage in sunrise light,
Gray sage under noonday sun,
Purple sage in the purple distances
Under the sunset skies.

I want to see the prairies
Rolling away to the north,
Rolling away to the east, to the south,
Prairies extending limitless,
Rolling away to the west.

I want to feel winds
Sweeping across the plains,
From the vast horizon,
From the empty skies . . .
Sweeping across the prairies,
Bearing the breath of sage.

[1] *Frontier*, Vol. XIII, No. 3, p. 200.

# Buffalo in the Judith Basin

## PAT T. (TOMMY) TUCKER

WILD BUFFALO WERE BECOMING SCARCE on the plains by 1883 when the following incidents took place on the rich grazing grounds of the Judith Basin, almost in the center of Montana. Just three years earlier the bison had been "numbered by the millions"; three years later the herds had been almost exterminated. (See W. T. Hornaday's "The Extermination of the American Bison," *Report of the Smithsonian Institution*, 1887.)

One of the cowboys on this hunt was Charles M. Russell, whose paintings, all depicting early western subjects, are housed in museums and private collections over the country. The Montana Historical Museum at Helena has many of them, along with his castings in bronze.

In this description, published in *Frontier*, Vol. IX, No. 3, p. 227, Tucker also mentions T. C. Power (not Powers), who came to Montana in 1867 and opened mercantile stores in Fort Benton, the head of navigation of the Missouri River, and in Helena. In 1875 he and I. G. Baker, a competing merchant in Fort Benton, purchased the riverboat *Benton*, one of eight boats of the Benton Packet Line's Block P vessels plying the upper Missouri.

Tommy Tucker was in fine fettle when talking to an amanuensis. He dictated tales, among them his life as a cowboy, to Grace Stone Coates.

IN MIDWINTER OF 1883, myself and several cowboys, including Charles M. Russell, famous as the Cowboy Artist, camped on the Judith River. Those of you who have visited Montana will recall the Judith River valley, located in a huge basin about eighty-five miles across and about the same in length, the Missouri River skirting the northern boundary, the Moccasin and Snowy Mountains on the east, the Belt Mountains on the south and the High-woods on the west. The buffalo that roamed these hills came in from their different summer ranges and wintered on the long bunch grass that grew in the Judith Basin. There was always plenty of open water and good shelter in these foothills.

Our daily work was to pair off and trail through the foothills and badlands of the Missouri River to look after the range cattle, as the Indians and rustlers were at work on this range. Whenever a suspicious-looking trail or sign showed an Indian rustler had been killing or stealing cattle our orders were to report at the camps immediately. Then a larger force of cowboys would hit the trail to run down the offender.

One day in January Frank Davis, my old sidekick, and I were out trailing through the foothills. We struck Sage Creek, one of the tributaries of the Judith River. Trailing up this creek we came into deeper snow, it striking just above our horses' knees. While passing through some jack pines we chanced upon a track, which upon a second look proved to be a buffalo trail. Seeking to affirm this, and likewise to see if buffalo were still in these parts, we took up the trail, riding very carefully through the deep snow. The depth of the snow muffled all sounds of our horses' feet on the dead branches underneath. Our fear of being discovered, however, was very great, as the snow still lay on the branches of the pines where a slight jar brought down a shower of it. To overcome this we dismounted and proceeded on foot. As we had the wind in our favor no danger came from this source.

We finally came up within sight of the buffalo. They were on the edge of the tall timber, lying down. As we looked at them, we thought of the possibilities of fresh buffalo meat for camp as well as ready cash for hides. We feared we could not handle the whole herd of fourteen [sic], as our only arms were our six-guns.[1]

Returning to the cow camp we changed horses and picked our mounts with care; these particular horses had been on buffalo hunts before and could be ridden up close without showing fear.

---

[1] A few paragraphs further along he seems to have a rifle. But such a small detail would not disturb Tommy.

After cleaning our Winchester carbines, we rode out to the place where the buffs had been.

They were gone, to our despair, but we quickly trailed them to a small blind canyon, which was the source of their water supply. This box canyon had an opening about fourteen feet wide. The whole distance around was a wall of granite rock, about three hundred feet high. At the other end it was about thirty feet high, and tapered to the top. Water had at some time formed this natural deathtrap for the buffalo.

As we rode up to the mouth of the canyon we could see the buffalo about three-quarters of a mile away and quite close to the rock wall at the other end. They had seen us and were trying to climb up the wall where it was lowest.

Our plans were made at once. I was to leave my horse at the entrance to the canyon. Frank would stay there also and kill any buffalo that escaped me, as I was to sneak up within shooting distance and get what I could; so I left him there and proceeded on, bending low and keeping behind the rocks, willows, sagebrush, and other objects that would hide me from their sight.

Frank, meanwhile, kept in view and tried to attract their attention, which I believe he did, as the buffalo appeared unaware of my presence behind the large granite rocks, about eighty yards from the milling herd.

My Winchester rifle was of the very latest model and held eight cartridges in the magazine and one in the barrel. Smokeless powder was still to be discovered, and whenever a shot was fired a small cloud of blue smoke appeared. At the first crack of the rifle I dropped the leader of the herd, a magnificent creature that had done well to preserve this last remnant of a once countless herd.

This only tended to increase their efforts to climb up the wall, or to mill around. As they continued to do this, I was successful in dropping six more of their number. They then split into two bunches and bolted for the mouth of the canyon. One bunch of three went off in a direction away from the rock behind which I was hiding. The other bunch of five came almost directly towards me. So I dropped two before they ran back to their former place. The three that had bolted for the entrance were killed by Frank before they could get out into the more open country. The others tried again to climb up the almost perpendicular side of the canyon, but only fell back when they lost their foothold. In a very short time I had killed the last one as it made a final attempt to get away from my deadly fire.

After the smoke had cleared and the last buffalo had given a few dying gasps, I made my way from behind the rocks and went up to the dead buffalo. As I was looking them over, Frank rode up leading my horse. We selected the choicest of the meat, which was a three-year-old heifer, cut off the two hindquarters, tied it on behind our saddles, and rode for camp at high speed, reaching it just before supper.

Mike Ryan, the cook, was delighted on seeing the fresh buffalo meat. It meant a change for the rest of the boys, as well as ourselves, and it pleased them very much. The straight beef three times a day was not favored and a change was always desired. Getting the meat into the shack and cutting it up into steaks was left to Frank and me.

Soon the hungry cowboys were enjoying a real feed, on the choicest meat of the land. Mike Ryan, as a cook, was unequaled. Formerly he cooked on the Missouri River steamers, but cowmen traveling up and down the river to St. Louis induced him to come and cook for their cowboys. It took a good cook to keep a bunch of cowboys satisfied during the long winter months.

After this sumptuous feed, Frank and I saddled up fresh horses and rode down three and a half miles to the stageline station. The station was run by E. J. Morrison, a typical New Englander. He owned the store and furnished supplies to cattlemen and prospectors, freighters, etc., and through him we found a place to sell our buff meat. He agreed to purchase twelve of the buffalo at four cents per pound and get them from where we killed them. This was not much for him to do, as he had the ox teams and sleds. He had the buffalo dragged over the snow to where the sleds were left and loaded them on. He had no trouble in selling the buffalo meat, as it was getting scarce and the demand was great.

The buffalo hides we sold to T. C. Powers at six dollars apiece. T. C. Powers, now of Helena, Montana, controlled the fur and hide market in those days and he offered the best prices. His commercial life was given its start there.

After disposing of the buffalo and splitting half with Frank Davis, I plaited a forty-two-foot, four-strand rope. This rope was very durable and strong, made out of rawhide. To make such a rope took about a month of real work in the evenings. Other small details of repairing my outfit for the spring roundup were made about the first of March.

I had decided to go on a tour of inspection around to the heads of several creeks. I wanted to see the condition of the cattle, as March was the time when they were hit the hardest by the cold and lack of feed. Cowboys were stationed on different creeks to see that no cattle were bogged in the mud. The melting snow made the banks of the creeks very boggy, and a weak cow might very easily become fast and unable to get out. A cowboy rope was usually needed to pull an animal out of such a place, a good cow horse being able to pull by the horn of the saddle as much as a horse would by the collar. Such work kept the boys busy until the first of May.

Then the real fun and work started. All the horses were rounded up and brought in. Each rider would have from eight to twelve horses in his string for his summer use. This string was composed of both broken and unbroken horses. The broken horses did not cause much trouble. It was the unbroken ones that caused the new and untried cowboys their trouble, while it enlivened very much the life of the old riders. Each cowboy had to break his own string of horses, and a great number hit the dust before they had all their string broken.

The roundup finally started on the fifteenth day of May, when our number of riders had been increased to sixty-eight.

The captain of this roundup was an old hand at the game, having seen cowboy service in Texas. He was a cowman and knew his calling. His name was Horace Brewster, and he is still in northwestern Montana in government service. The captain of the roundup would detail the men to ride together and bring in all cattle that they could find during the day. He told each two just what range they were to ride over.

The cattle were driven to the roundup grounds close to camp. There they were held until all the calves were branded with the same brand that their mothers wore. Then they were turned loose and the camp moved farther along, and the same was done over again. An average of 1,700 calves and cows were rounded up every day, and by the first of July the work was about over.

Our last camp was on the Arrow Creek, close to Square Butte, a spur of the Highwood Mountains, and an old landmark. The roundup grounds were to be located at Lost Lake, which is within three miles of the Missouri River.

On the second day of July I had the good fortune to be detailed with Charlie Russell to go out and ride the Cottonwood Creek range. We were in the foothills and had stopped to eat our lunch. The horses grazed on the green grass and drank from the pure water of the creek. I was furnished with field glasses to enable us to see the country better. I was looking through them when I saw a small herd of buffalo farther up in the hills.

On reaching camp that evening we told of what we had seen. The next day about twenty boys were sent out in that direction to see if by rounding up the cattle and buffalo together, they might be driven carefully to the roundup grounds. This proved successful, and on the eve of July third, the night herder had 7 buffalo to watch with about 2,500 cattle.

As the next day was the Fourth of July, and the roundup was practically over, the boys had all decided to celebrate. The celebration was to consist of roping and tying the buffalo. About twenty men who were accomplished cowboys and clever with the rope were picked to go in and single out the buffalo to rope and tie them. I had the fortune, or misfortune, to be one of the cowboys picked. All the rest of the cowboys took positions around the herd to see the fun. As we rode into the herd, the buffalo bolted and started on a dead run for the Missouri River. We all took after the buffalo, twenty wild, shouting cowboys, ably followed by forty-eight more, likewise whooping and yelling, riders that would do justice to any Indian war party.

I was on the outer edge and to the left flank of the buffs, so I had an open field for running. My horse, Bunky, was an old-timer at running buffalo.

The buffalo took down a long ridge that sloped towards the river. Running at his very best Bunky was able to overtake them about two miles from the start. I rode up as close as I could, took down my cowhide rope, singled out a big bull, and shaking out a loop, I whirled my rope twice and let it fly, catching Mr. Buffalo around the neck and right front leg as he turned to go down the ravine. As I threw the rope I took three turns around the saddle horn. The rope tightened like a violin string. Bunky had sat on his haunches so that he could stop the buffalo, but there was no halt on the buff's part, and we kept on moving, against our will. Down the ravine we went, Bunky trying to hold, and his feet, plowing the ground, threw clouds of dust and rocks in the air.

I kept thinking some of the boys would run up and catch the buffalo around the legs; but no such luck. We were jerked down the ravine, while all the time Bunky was doing his best to stop the buff. His hind feet kept leaving the ground and at each jump of the buffalo the riding became rougher and faster. Thinking that we would be turned end for end any minute, I threw off the turns on the horn of my saddle and said good-by to my new rawhide rope.

The boys caught up and we all saw the buffalo jump off a low rimrock into the Missouri River and swim across. My rope was still around his neck and front leg. The last we saw of it was when the herd reached the opposite bank and the rope looked like a snake as it whipped through the grass.

The boys afterwards said that this buffalo would weigh about 2,000 pounds. That is no small amount for a 900-pound horse to stop.

Years after this experience C. M. Russell of Great Falls, Montana, who was on the grounds at the time, said that it was the only time in all his travels on the plains that he ever saw a cowboy rope a wild buffalo. A few years before C. M. Russell died he painted the picture of the tussle Bunky and I had with the buffalo bull, and I have turned down many attractive offers for this painting.

# Last of the Northern Buffalo

## Luke D. Sweetman

Luke D. Sweetman, long a resident of Montana and later of the Washington coast, came to Montana in the mid-eighties. He has written two books, *Gotch, the Story of a Cowhorse* (Caldwell, Idaho, Caxton Printers, Ltd., 1947) and *Back Trailing on Open Range* (Caldwell, Idaho, Caxton Printers, Ltd., 1951).

Sam Walking Coyote, a Pend d'Oreille Indian, captured six wild buffalo calves in the Milk River country, tamed them by running them with cattle, and in the summer of 1878 drove them over the Continental Divide by Cadotte's Pass to the Flathead country in western Montana. He sold the four calves which had survived the trip to Charles Allard and Michael Pablo. The herd finally numbered several hundred, and from it were established both the present Canadian herd and the herd, of about four hundred, on the National Bison Range at Moiese, Montana.

"Last of the Northern Buffalo" was published in *Frontier*, Vol. XII, No. 2, p. 144.

In the spring of 1883, when buffalo hunters broke camp and packed their robe hides for the long haul to steamboat landings and other shipping points, great herds of the shaggy creatures still roamed the range. The following fall, when again they resumed the hunt, not a buffalo was to be seen. What had become of them?

Many thought they left the country in a general stampede; some contended that in the stampede they plunged over cut banks, piled up, and lost their lives. That theory was not probable, for buffalo knew too well how to choose their route over

75

the rough range. However, there was one spot near the Pryor Mountains in Montana that showed signs of a pile-up. Some hunters thought the buffalo had gone farther north, into the British possessions.

It was customary for buffalo to migrate south in the winter and north in the summer. Now, being cut off on every side except the north by the advancing settlers, their instinct told them north was the way to go. There was left, however, a small remnant of the herd—125 or more—that did not choose to go with the general stampede, or in some way were left behind. This small band ranged along the divide between the Yellowstone and Missouri rivers, and as far northwest as the mouth of the Musselshell and the rougher breaks of Squaw and Hell creeks—from 75 to 150 miles northwest of Miles City, Montana. That section of the country, at the time, was seldom frequented by human beings. There, they were not disturbed until 1885, when stockmen brought in cattle from Texas and Oregon. Immediately after the coming of cattle and cowboys it was a game of chance between riders and buffalo. Odds were against the buffalo. . . .

If the cowboys had time to spare when buffalo were sighted— or if the boss had been seen going over a distant range of hills— the cowboys left their cattle to run buffalo. But if they were deep in their work—or, rather, if the boss was in sight—they only sat their horses and looked on as the buffalo left the country under clouds of dust.

In the summer of 1886 I was with the LU Bar outfit on the Little Dry. We were out on a calf roundup, branding. One day, it happened to be my duty to pilot the mess wagon across the rough badland breaks. In the distance we sighted a herd of buffalo, the main herd—about 100 head.

I had just shown the cook where to camp and was dragging up some wood for him by the horn of my saddle when suddenly I noticed other riders of the outfit, a dozen or more, wheel their horses and start on a high lope in the opposite direction. I loosened the rope from my saddle horn, left it attached to the wood, and was soon with the riders in hot pursuit of the buffalo.

It was interesting to note that when the bunch started calves were placed to the center, cows took the lead, and bulls kept outside and to the rear. This was their protective order of flight.

As we spurred our horses a drenching rain was turning the alkali and loose gumbo into deep, sticky mud. The hoofs of the frenzied buffalo dug deep into this and filled the air with mud balls, which soon likened the appearance of the riders and their mounts to that of the scenery around us. The bronco buster of the outfit was riding an outlaw horse called Sam Bass. I had given this horse his first ride the year before down in the Indian territory. He bucked considerably, then stampeded, so I headed him into the Salt Fork River and bogged him down. I named him after the famous outlaw, Sam Bass. The broncho buster was also called Sam Bass—so named because none of us knew his real name and the outlaw was the first horse he had ridden when he came to the outfit the following spring. The horse went through his usual maneuvers as Sam started him out after the buffalo; consequently he was behind the rest of the riders. He took a short cut to catch up and coming suddenly to a deep coulee, the banks of which were nearly straight up and down, he skidded the entire thirty feet or more, his horse making tracks like sled runners in the loose mud.

In the midst of the turmoil, a dozen six-shooters were re-enacting the drama of bygone buffalo hunts. Four bulls were dropped along the trail. And someone roped a calf. By this time we were quite a distance from camp, so we turned back to get fresh mounts for the afternoon circle. We skinned out a hindquarter and the hump of the bull that had fallen nearest camp. G. G. (Dick) Ingersoll had killed it, so he took the horns for a souvenir.

It was a common sight on the range to see the carcass of a fresh-killed buffalo . . . one by one they were being wiped out of existence. I had thought some of following up the straggling herds to rope young calves and start a buffalo herd of my own.

Late that fall I was riding line from the LU bar line camp, which was located along the divide between the Yellowstone and Missouri rivers. Two of us were at the camp; we rode alone each way from camp and threw cattle back to the north when they attempted to drift south. (Antelope were plentiful; we were seldom out of sight of them. We could kill an antelope for food any time we wanted, with a six-shooter. They often drank at our spring near the tent. We gave little thought to their presence, and often never looked up as they stood watching us ride by them.)

As I galloped across the head of Little Porcupine one day, towards the lead of the drifting cattle, suddenly one of the bunches that I had taken for cattle at a distance took on the resemblance of a lively whirlwind. My horse's ears pointed forward. The thoughts of cattle left my mind as we dashed towards the moving mass. It was thrilling to ride in the dust of a bunch of buffalo, across sage-covered flats, clearing sharp-cut washouts with a bound, my wiry little Texas horse as eager as I to get among them. I swung the loop of my sixty-five-foot Manila rope high over my head and dashed it over the head of a five-months-old calf. A few seconds later the rest of the bunch had put space between them and the calf. A question then occurred to me, what was I going to do with him? Thirty miles to the home ranch over a rough country to take a calf, or to ride there and bring a team and wagon back, would take time. I decided I didn't want him.

Dismounting, I went hand over hand along the rope, trying to get close enough to that lively little piece of buffalo flesh to cut the rope at the hondo. With the rope fastened to the saddle horn, my horse was doing the holding, but the calf was cutting circles around him so fast that it kept the intelligent pony guessing and changing ends to keep from being tangled up in the rope. Finally, after the calf had run the full length of the rope and thrown himself flat, I reached him and cut him loose. He scrambled to his feet and I watched him scamper across the flat in the direction his mother had taken. I decided it was a great deal harder to turn him loose than it was to catch him.

A heavy frost carpeted hills and valleys as I rode out on my line in the early morning sun of an October day. I rode leisurely to the top of a knoll, and there, in plain view, was a bunch of seven buffalo. All were lying down except one, the sentinel. Within a split second they were on their feet and headed for the highest point of the divide. The temptation was too great to be ignored. In the same fraction of a second I unconsciously dug the rowels deep into my horse's sides. I wanted to get among them before they gained the divide, if possible; but I failed—and worse, they had outwinded my horse on the steep slope. Buffalo are long-winded. When I had reached the top they were splitting the air down the opposite side. For the time I seemed to be losing ground; then my horse got his second wind and began to reach out with long strides that fast closed the space between us. After five or six miles on a down grade, we crossed the Little Dry, and I was drawing closer. A monstrous big bull guarded the left flank of the bunch. As I closed in beside, I emptied my six-shooter into him. The rest of the bunch plunged into the deep washout and out at the opposite side. I reined in my horse and sat resting with my weight in one stirrup while I watched them until they were out of sight up the steep slope of an arroyo. Their speed never slackened and they seemed to have wind to spare. In the bunch were a young calf and a yearling. As I watched them go I thought it a shame that they were not protected instead of hunted. I even regretted that I had shot the bull; he was a perfect specimen, one of the largest I had ever seen.

During the fall of 1886 a hunter of considerable note appeared. This man was W. T. Hornaday, the naturalist. He had hunted big game in many parts of the world, and was employed by the U.S. government to collect buffalo to be mounted in their natural state for the Smithsonian Institute [Institution] at Washington, D. C.

Mr. Hornaday outfitted at Miles City, Montana, with teams, wagons, camping outfit, saddle horses, and provisions. He employed men who knew the country, and in early fall set out for the buffalo range. His chief helpers were Jim McNannie and Irving Bold, both of the LU bar ranch. (I had taken McNannie's place at the line camp when he decided to go.)

79

Being thus equipped with a good outfit and plenty of provisions, Mr. Hornaday intended to abide his time and stay out as long as necessary in order to accomplish his purpose. He covered the country thoroughly where the buffalo ranged, and although the snow was deep and the winter a severe one, he followed the herd, camping wherever the occasion demanded. He did not return to Miles City until Christmas day, with his trophies of the hunt.

I was invited to have Christmas dinner at the hotel with the famous hunter, and regretted while the story of the hunt was being told that I had not been one of the party on the last real buffalo hunt.

That year nearly exterminated the northern buffalo. But until 1889 a half-dozen that had retreated to the rough breaks of Hell Creek were occasionally seen. This section of country was so rough that stockmen had to send the cowboys out with pack outfits on their roundups, it being impossible to take a wagon through.

When this last little bunch of buffalo had finally been wiped out by reckless riding cowboys, the northern herd was a thing of the past.

# Custer, Horses, and Buffalo

## PAT T. (TOMMY) TUCKER

COMMENTS ON THE CUSTER MASSACRE are almost as varied as the scores of persons who have written about Custer, his fellow officers, and the Battle of the Little Big Horn. Writers contemporary with the event had strong feelings about their versions of what took place and who, if anyone, blundered or was a fool or a coward. Major Marcus A. Reno, for example, has been both blamed (he was court-martialed) and exonerated for his part in the battle.

Tucker, on the day of the battle, June 25, 1876, was about 150 miles away on the Cheyenne River. His account, which mentions that fighting, was published in *Frontier*, Vol. XI, No. 3, p. 282, as "The Long Horns." Here the communicative Tucker displays his emotional convictions. There is no doubt about them.

He comments on Charles M. Russell (1864–1926), who, after his first sixteen years, lived, worked, and painted in Montana and never welcomed getting "off the range." Frederic Remington (1861–1909) at nineteen years of age began his artistic career in Montana but did not spend his life in the West. These two men have been considered the most able artists of western outdoor life. (See "A Few Words from Mr. Remington," *Collier's Weekly*, March 19, 1905, and Frank B. Linderman's *Recollections of Charley Russell.*)

Tucker also refers to Calamity Jane (Martha Jane Canary), who came west in 1863 and to Virginia City, Montana, in 1864, when she was twelve years of age and already a wildcat like her mother. There she "ran like a sprite with the stream of depravity and absorbed it." (See Duncan Aikman's lively account in his *Calamity Jane and the Lady Wildcats* [1927].)

Nelson Story made the first drive, of six hundred Texas longhorns, into Montana in 1866. He had made his stake in Montana gold mining.

FRED REMINGTON AND CHARLEY RUSSELL were born painters; they were both good friends of mine. They painted the West when it was in the rough; they painted the Indian, his features and actions, his squaw and papoose, his hoss and wickiup. They put him on canvas, when he was fighting, smeared with war paint; and also pictured him in his peaceful camp. They have painted the longhorn ox teams, with the long string of freight wagons, the bullwhackers, the mule skinner, who drove from eight to sixteen mules. The six-horse stage driver was painted when he was being held up.

Now I am going to say to you: Charley Russell was a born artist. I used to tell Russell a story, and within a day or two he would have it painted—man-hoss-action, everything in detail. Remington also painted my word pictures in detail.

I came to Montana in 1876. On June 1 two hoss wranglers and I trailed in 240 head of young saddle ponies that were raised in Texas, and were to be used in the United States Army. These horses were to be turned over to Generals Reno and Custer, and were to be used to round up the poor Indians.

We were camped on the north fork of the Cheyenne River, when General Custer and four hundred brave troopers were to open the battle with the Indians, then he was to get help. Did he receive help from the men who pledged their word of honor that they would be there with reinforcements when the battle began? The trap was set for Custer and his brave men by a bevy of cowardly U.S. officers, who were afraid of their own shadows. Ask me if I know; I say, "Yes." I leave it to your own judgment: would a man, knowing there were eight thousand Indians ready to go into action, willingly risk his own life and that of four hundred of his men, against those heavy odds? Custer knew how many Indians were ready for battle, and relying on Reno's promises of help, walked into the well-planned trap, where they died fighting, as only brave men can die, in a veritable hell of savagery. After the massacre, what became of General Reno? He was court-martialed and sent to Cheyenne. He has never appeared, in print, since that time.

Our outfit milled around northern Wyoming and southern Montana herding these horses for weeks, and giving the hostile Indians a few of them, now and then, to save our scalps.

Our herd was fat and slick, and we picked up some very good cavalry horses by trading with the Indians. Their horses were well broken, and some of them good animals, but thin and tired from hard riding. After running in our bunch for a short time they were in excellent condition.

The long cloudless days dragged into Indian summer, and during this pleasant season, Tobe, one of the wranglers, would often saddle his horse at daybreak and ride the highest points, to try and locate some of the U.S. troops.

Whenever he left me to tend camp I waited and watched the foothills and jack-pine ridges, fearing his old Texas horse would come loping back to camp with an empty saddle.

One afternoon while camped on Powder River, Tobe Boone and I were sitting on a high pinnacle, our horses tied to the ground. From this point we could see our herd of horses, split up in small bunches, quietly munching the late grass in the jack-pine thickets. Down in the lowlands, far below us, a dust cloud rose here and there, which told our plains-practiced eyes that the Indian scouts were on the lookout, knowing full well that the massacre of Custer and his men would mean trouble for them.

Tobe and I had been sitting on our high roost all afternoon. The sun was warm, and what little breeze there was had just a tang of autumn coolness. We had been rehearsing our experiences on the old Río Grande, when suddenly our horses threw up their heads and pointed their ears, as they always do when they sense an approach which is not yet visible.

We rose hastily and quietly mounted, ready for action. Several tense moments passed while we strained our eyes in every direction. Our horses were not to be deceived, for round a hill along a high rimrock there slowly came into view seven riders. As they trailed straight toward us we could see the glint of a bright button, and a blur of blue, and recognized them as U.S. scouts.

Calamity Jane was with them. They had been hunting for our

camp for some time, but had given up hope of finding us alive. Owing to the lawlessness, the attitude of the whole country was such as to imbue even the hardiest with a sense of alarm. The chief scout advised us to trail our horse herd across the Yellowstone and camp at the north fork of the Tongue River; and we lost no time in following his directions.

When we arrived we found that the American Fur Company was camped on the north side of the Yellowstone River.

Tobe and I packed our few cooking utensils, food, and bedrolls on our pack horses and swam our herd across the mouth of the Tongue River, then trailed them to Buffalo Camp.

Blondy Jim was captain of the buffalo hunters and a very good friend of ours, helping us stock our meager larder with delicious cuts of buffalo and venison. Big-hearted Jim, a product of the sunny south, whose friendship was genuine, and whose hospitality was without rival!

Their camp comprised twelve men, and the cook—all vigorous, husky, outdoor men, who never tired. We hunted buffalo for two months with these hard-riding plainsmen, who were all crack shots, carrying carbine saddle guns. A half-dozen half-breeds followed and did the skinning.

The hides brought on an average of $2.50 apiece, and were sold to leather concerns in the East. They made harnesses and various other things of them.

We broke camp on Milk River the last of November when the first cold winds came roaring out of the mountains. We began thinking of a warmer climate, so Tobe and I rolled our cotton, packed our provender on our pack horses, and trailed back to Texas.

We had many tales to tell the cowmen about the new country up north, of our adventures, hardships, and the long trip back home.

Nelson Story was the first man to have nerve enough to brave the new country in a large business way, trailing in the first bunch of Longhorn cattle from Texas to Montana.

This was many years ago. The Indians, or those left of them, are now on their respective reservations. The old cow trails are plowed under. The old Santa Fe Trail is drifted full of sand; and the real cowboy, with his leather-tanned face, is a figure of the past. There are a few of the old-timers left; fewer still who can neither read nor write, as youth, in my younger days, meant action and education of a far different type from what is considered education today. These few who are left can tell stories of adventure on the plains, rivaling even gangland warfare of today, true stories of trail and forest, Mexican bandits, white renegades, urging on the depredations of the lawless element, the Texas Ranger, the Vigilantes later.

# Railroad Building

## Luke D. Sweetman

THE RAILROAD CONTRACTOR'S NEED for horses in the 1880's and 1890's was great and constant: leveling ground and cutting down banks were done by horse-drawn hand scoops; filling depressions needed earth hauled in scoops or wagons; supplies for large camps, including great quantities of hay and oats, came in trailing wagons pulled by four to twelve horses. Horses supplied the power for all movement of earth, objects, and people. Trailing a band of horses hundreds of miles over desert or mountain country was all in the day's work. Finding feed and water en route required exact knowledge of the country.

The next two articles show both the hardships dealers overcame and the lives they lived. Sweetman contributed the first account to *Frontier*, Vol. IX, No. 4, p. 347, and the second one to Vol. X, No. 2, p. 143.

### I. Laying the Iron Trail in the Northwest

IT WAS IN LATE MARCH of 1887 when the first chinook came to start the huge drifts of snow melting that had been piling up since early October. This has ever since been known by old-timers as the "hard winter of '86 and '87," and as the most disastrous winter Montana has ever known. Many cattlemen who were considered rich in the fall were flat broke in the spring and were lucky if they had a horse and outfit to hire out to some more fortunate owner with which to start all over again.

In those days no one owned land, the cattle herds being ranged over the countless acres of prairie that offered their rich feed free to the cowman. This winter snow covered what grass there was as effectively as if it had been plowed under, and cattle

86

starved and froze to death by the thousands. Cattlemen's estimate of their losses was from 60 to 65 per cent of the native cattle, and in many cases entire herds of southern stock were wiped out clean. It was a hard blow to the cattle business, at this time in its infancy in Montana.

Having temporarily laid aside my plans for the cattle business, I bought a few head of horses and with one man to help drive them headed north from Miles City to the newly proposed line of railroad. This road, which was to be built through the northern part of Montana and Dakota territories, was laid out under the name of the St. Paul, Minneapolis and Manitoba Railway, and was later changed to the Great Northern. I believed there would be a big demand for horses in this new enterprise and perhaps other ways of bettering my own present depleted financial condition. So as soon as the snow had gone sufficiently to allow traveling, we struck out with our driven stock and despite our pack animals, laden with provisions and bedding, made good time. Our last camp before crossing the Missouri River was made at Sioux Pass, about fifteen miles from Fort Buford. Snow fell on us while making camp, and as a result the bacon and flapjacks we had for supper were more filling than appetizing.

The first gray dawn in the region of the Missouri River found us driving our little herd in a cold, drizzling sleet storm toward the junction of the Missouri and Yellowstone rivers. There Tom Forbes put us across on the government ferry.

After gaining the northern side of the Missouri River, we drifted eastward to where Williston is now located. This new country to me was a virginal paradise and my thoughts again turned to vast herds of cattle growing fat on the rich bluejoint grass which in sunlit places was beginning to show green. The untouched last year's growth, though bent flat to the ground by the snow, had been knee-high in the river bottoms. The low hills sloping back from the river were treeless. In fact, the only trees to be seen were the cottonwood groves that lined the river and a few straggling evergreens that throve on the rocky acres and on the clay banks of the badlands. This first picture of the untamed land remained imprinted in my mind; and it was near here on the banks of the Missouri a few years later that I staked my homestead rights.

I left the Missouri at Williston and cut across country to the Mouse River. Except for the soldiers stationed at the few forts and Indian agencies, the white men one would encounter could be counted on the fingers. For miles and miles in any direction a rider would not see a human being or a human habitation. Along the course of the river an occasional wood-hawk, who supplied fuel to the steamboats, had his dugout or log hut. No other white men had come to this region—there had been nothing to bring them.

Later on, in this same year, small herd owners from the stricken western and southern parts of Montana pushed northward to this Missouri River country where their cattle might recuperate from the severe winter. The next few years they made good money. Hay could be put up on the river bottom to insure against another hard winter and feed famine.

The railroad had been completed between Devils Lake and Minot, of Dakota Territory, the previous year. Minot, at the western end of the line, was now a flourishing young town. Here, the railroad company was daily unloading contractors with their grading equipment and pushing them westward as rapidly as possible to where their different stretches of grading work were to be done. In a short time the trail along the line of survey was a moving array of men and teams doing their bit, and, when finished, passing the others and beginning the next stretch out at the front. Soon they were moving earth over a surveyed line of more than two hundred miles in length. A steel gang followed close on the heels of the contractors, laying the track at the rate of four miles a day.

The contractors depended on the grain for their horses to be brought to the rail's end by freight and from here relayed to their camps by four- and six-horse teams. There was no hay to be had, but grass was plentiful everywhere, so the work horses were turned loose at night under the care of the night herder. Such a system was hard on the eastern horses that had always been cared for in stables with plenty of good feed handed to them. This shifting for themselves soon began to take a death toll from their numbers. Of course, they had to be replaced. I sold my entire band and wished for a nearer source for replenishing it. Not only were many horses sacrificed but many men gave their lives as well. Human tragedies were witnessed every day, and shallow graves marked at regular intervals the progress of the Iron Trail.

Where the railroad survey joined and paralleled the Missouri River, the town of Williston was taking on a semblance of permanency. So far, owing to the inability to procure lumber, it was a village of tents. Each steamboat from St. Louis brought entire families, some with their stocks of merchandise, ready to give odds for the progress of civilization. Building material was steadily being shipped in and the foundations were laid for many of Williston's pioneer business blocks of today. People hearing of the new country and sensing advantages of fortune were daily arriving in increasing numbers to swell the population and expand the frontier. The Yellowstone and Missouri rivers afforded the smoothest highway, and each boat brought in its load of home and fortune seekers.

In this growing village there were various games of chance in session at all hours of the day and night, and the usual human parasites in the gathering places of men exacted their daily tolls. There were killings, of course, but I had been in places that were better organized municipally where there were more. These little tragedies of life went hand in hand with progress and civilization everywhere.

Soon there were structures of logs and rough timber which answered the demand for stores, saloons, and lodginghouses. I remember distinctly a neat little hotel, built and operated by a Mrs. Leonhardy. She prospered, and in later years the site was occupied by a substantial brick building which was operated as the Number One Hotel for several years.

The horse market which I found so good encouraged me to

bring in more bunches of western stock to peddle along the line to grading contractors. The demand was great and the prices were high.

I remember hearing one little pioneer episode that had its tragic ending, in the camp of Leech and Francis, two Iowa contractors, where I had put up for the night. One of their men had just returned from a thirty-mile trek to the river, where he had gone to bring back a load of wood. He related an account of the death of Grinnell, a squaw man, who had got a supply of whisky from an upriver boat and proceeded to get drunk. He was at the height of his spree when his squaw, tiring of his actions, set about to pull him off his horse and put him to bed. Grinnell, not wanting to be interrupted at this period of his fun, endeavored to ride the horse over his wife. He was prevented from this only by the sudden action of his mount, which, in rearing and pivoting, unseated its rider. The squaw, seizing this opportunity, made haste to benefit by it and in so doing, clung tightly to the first hold she could find. Unfortunately for the man, he wore one of those then popular braided leather watch-guards which was suspended from his neck, and this was the woman's first hold. In the melee that followed, the knot was slipped up tight around the fellow's throat and held, thereby ending the career of one more old-timer. "You couldn't blame the squaw," the wood hauler commented. "She was only trying to protect herself."

It was on this same night that a severe storm came up and stampeded the crew's entire bunch of Iowa work horses, some sixty head in number. The night herder of this camp was a young fellow from the East, green and inexperienced in western ways. He was willing enough in his efforts to locate the missing bunch but ignorant to the first degree of common sense in hunting for the runaway horses. He rode all night and returned in the forenoon with only the horse he was riding and that one nearly exhausted. After a breathing spell for lunch and a rest for his mount, he set out again, and soon after noon he came back to the camp empty-handed for the second time. The crew, of course, were enjoying the vacation, but not so Mr. Leech. He was paying his men for straight time. I volunteered the suggestion that the night wrangler was doing his hunting in circles too close to the camp and that he would have to look farther away to find the horses. Mr. Leech asked me if I thought I could find them and I answered that I believed I could. He gave me the chance.

I figured out the direction the horses would naturally take, which was westward with the storm. I shall never forget the horse I was riding that day. He was one of a herd I had bought in southern Montana. The big brown was unusually large for a saddle horse, but the gamest fellow I have ever ridden. I was able to follow a faint trail left by the herd, and after about twenty miles of riding I saw fresh signs of it. The sun had disappeared behind the hills when I came upon the bunch, now quietly grazing. I counted them as I rode around them, herding them together. They were all there, and I headed them back toward camp. I allowed my horse a few swallows of water as we crossed a little stream and without any further halts, started the runaways at a good clip over the trail. A horse trailer's principal aid was a six-shooter to turn back those that might chance to break out from the rest, and a long rope to snap at the heels of the laggards. With these two I started the bunch at a swift pace, which I kept up through the night. With the first sign of morning, I hit the grade close to camp, and it was only a short time until I had the horses corralled and ready to harness.

Mr. Leech's displeasure at having lost so much time overshadowed his generosity, so I did not net much of a reward for my efforts. He did make up for it afterwards, however, by offering me a good contract on another bit of work. The crew had also lost some time on account of bad weather and the boss asked me to help by putting in my horses to finish the stretch. This I did and he sent me out to the end of the line, then at Lonetree, a few miles west of Minot, to fetch a load of oats. He let me take a new wagon. After loading to capacity, I put in as a lead team a pair of saddle horses that had never been driven before. This is where I had some fun—keeping the eveners off the heels of the leaders and from under the front feet of the pole team. The team was strung out nicely by the time I had been on the road a few hours, and just when I believed I could breathe safely we came to the long White Earth Hill. I set the brake and held in the wheelers and momentarily slackened the lead lines; this evidently caused the lead team, together with the sudden relief from the heavy load, to believe they were free to go to the hills; and that's just what they tried to do. When the leaders jackknifed, the wagon tongue snapped and the eveners broke, which loosened the team entirely. I had to sit and watch them tear off across the prairie as I eased the loaded wagon to the foot of the hill by gentle degrees. This is a difficult job with the wagon tongue broken. I had to temporarily patch this so the team could guide the load. Well, I mounted one of the wheelers and after much riding, rounded up the troublemakers and tied them behind the wagon. They had torn their harness to pieces and broken their eveners, so the entire load had to be drawn by the wheelers. The fifteen miles was negotiated at a snail's pace.

I stayed with the crew, renting out my teams and freighting for the camp myself, until the end of the grade reached the point on the Missouri River where Wolf Point was later built. There was an Indian agency here and that was all. The boss sent Pat O'Brien, a Montanan, and me back along the line to where Bainville is now located. This was the western extremity of the rails. Here we loaded our cargoes of oats and started back to where we were to catch the outfit. By this time they would have finished at Wolf Point and passed the other graders, going on to the front line, which would be west of Fort Assiniboine. This made a haul for us of three hundred miles, for which we were to receive a dollar per hundredweight for each hundred miles.

It was late summer now and the mosquitoes along the Missouri River and the numerous streams we had to cross were so thick it was nearly impossible to get any rest at night. Our tarpaulin had to be drawn over our heads, which kept the mosquitoes off all right, but nearly suffocated us. We nearly wore ourselves out trying to find which was the more pleasant, the mosquitoes or the heat. Our horses had to be closely hobbled, and even so we would have to tramp long distances in the morning to find them.

One night one of Pat's teams swam the river with the hobbles on. Lucky for us, the two horses couldn't find a place to land on the other side and were just swimming back when we found them.

At the Big Muddy Creek just west of the present site of Culbertson, Jakey Bowers, a squaw man, had an improvised ferry and was coining money with it. At the Milk River another ferry had been put in, but it was a poor excuse and we were delayed there a full day, getting it into a condition safe to cross on. During the day, many freighters had gathered there. We practically rebuilt the boat, and then helped each other across.

We delivered our loads and fortunately for me it was the end of the trail, for I was taken sick. The government doctor at Fort Assiniboine gave me temporary relief, but it was a case of fever and the next day after I became ill, I felt worse than ever. Leech and Francis wanted to buy my stock, so I sold to them and rode on the sick list in one of their wagons, making a trip to Fort Benton after supplies.

Fort Benton was at the head of navigation on the Missouri River and the distributing point for all incoming freight. The town was full of every character peculiar to a frontier settlement. Bullwhackers and mule skinners thronged the streets. Marvelous tales and yarns could be listened to at nearly any hour of the day from boasting miners, cowpunchers, and skinners. The skinner's accomplishment was guiding as many as ten teams with a single line from his seat on the near-wheel animal. The train was made up of a succession of loaded wagons and it was often operated over trails that took days and weeks to travel. The bullwhackers drove as many or more oxen, and walking by their side kept them in motion with the aid of the long bull whip. This whip was in itself difficult to handle; a novice might easily scalp himself with it at a single crack. These freighters kept a saddle pony with them

93

to round up their teams in the morning, and with the inevitable bedroll, a coffeepot, and frying pan were as independent as a porcupine in his skin.

Up the river from Fort Benton, Paris Gibson was planning and building a town on a beautiful plain on the Missouri River banks. This is now Great Falls. With keen foresight he was preparing for the advent of the railroad that was rapidly approaching.

I still had some fever, but I was gaining strength each day; so, with O'Brien, I boarded the next boat downstream with the intention of buying more horses to sell. At the mouth of the Judith River, O'Brien left me to go to Miles City, where I would meet him later.

The trip downstream was made without any particular incident. We were grounded all of one night on a sand bar, but escaped without mishap. We were very fortunate in having only a single misfortune of this kind, for the time of year and the prominence of the sand bars made navigating hazardous. It was three hundred miles back to Fort Buford. About the only kick I got out of the ride was watching and listening to the pilot as he stood on the prow of the boat, sounding bottom and calling out to the man at the wheel. "Four f-e-e-t; six f-e-e-t; eight f-e-e-t, N-O B-O-T-T-O-M." In addition to this pastime, there would be a woodyard to stop at, at various intervals, and the fast work of replenishing the exhausted supply of fuel.

At Fort Buford I disembarked and took the stage to Glendive, and from there to Miles City by train. Thirty-five miles out of Fort Buford we stopped at a relay station, known as the Kelsh ranch, the present site of Sidney, Montana, to change teams. That which stood out most memorably in my mind was the dinner Mrs. Kelsh prepared for us. Here, I had the first vegetables fresh from the garden that I had had in four summers. I met Major Scobey on the stage on this trip. He was afterwards appointed Indian agent at Poplar. The town of Scobey, near the Canadian line in northeastern Montana, is his namesake.

And so, in three-and-a-half months, the railroad spanned a distance of six hundred miles through new and wild land. There

94

a few years before, J. J. (Jim) Hill, afterwards known as the Empire Builder, traveled in a buckboard, and chose the route from Devils Lake, Dakota Territory, to the Pacific Coast for his Iron Trail.

## II. Early Day Horse Trailing

IN THE EARLY DAYS, when the horse business was still in its infancy in eastern Montana and the northern part of Dakota Territory had scarcely been touched, either by the stockmen or actual settlers, the building of the Great Northern Railroad brought homesteaders to this new country of endless prairies. Many of those who settled on homesteads, farms that were to be, had brought no horses or farm equipment with them. Others came across country from some distant state with covered wagons drawn by oxen, and with a breaking plow tied on back of the wagon, with which they began at once to turn over the new sod.

Owing to the inability to get proper farm equipment the country progressed slowly enough for a while. I had blazed the trail to that part of the country with horses in the spring of 1887, and could see that there would be a demand for horses among the settlers who were following the new line of railway.

So, early in the spring of '98, I bought 175 head of horses and started across country with them. I took with me a mess wagon to carry supplies and a camp outfit, and could camp on good feed and water wherever the occasion suited best. The horses had just come through the winter on open range, and while they were not actually thin, they were not slick and fat as they should be for market. With no fences whatever to contend with, and plenty of good feed and water everywhere, I grazed them towards Dakota and the market, as a man would a herd of beef steers.

By the time I had covered the three hundred miles to Minot, which was the first and only town that I came to, except Williston, then a small burg only a year old, where I camped overnight, I began selling horses right and left. I hadn't been in town twenty minutes before there were customers in my camp. Schofield and

95

Coleman, liverymen, were the first to buy. The market at Minot was so good that I peddled the entire band there rather than move on to some other point.

Soon after this I bought the entire herd of LS saddle horses, 354 head. The LS was a Texas outfit which consisted of several thousand long-horned steers, that was closing out its interests on the Big Dry, northwest of Miles City, Montana. I put in enough broncs to make 400 head, all told, and by midsummer had launched them at Minot, North Dakota. During the first two days at Minot, I sold three carloads, two of which went to Vermont and the other to the Red River Valley in Dakota. A few odd horses were sold, but there was no farming around Minot then, and the market was pretty well filled for the time, so I moved farther on east to the settlements. At Devils Lake I camped a few days. The Great Northern was building a branch line from Churches Ferry north to the Canadian line at the time, and new towns were springing up like mushrooms in the night.

I cut out 50 head of horses, left the main band at the Lake with a competent man in charge to handle the sales, and went to Cando on the new branch of the railway. The new town of Cando was under construction at the time; the main street was lined with buildings yet unpainted, and the sound of hammers came from all corners. I don't think there was a building in town completed, although a lot of them were far enough along so that stores and other places were open and doing business. There were three livery barns opening up, and the liverymen bought freely. Merchants bought delivery horses. In fact, nearly everyone in town, besides the new settlers around, wanted horses of some kind, and the 50 head lasted just two days, until I had turned them into cash. There is always liable to be a turn when least expected, and when everything was going fine there came a sudden change.

On the night of the twentieth of August that year, there was a killing frost that caught a large portion of the wheat all through the northern part of Dakota, and the farmers stopped buying almost as quickly as the frost had come. I moved on to the Red

River Valley to an older settled country where the frost had not hit so hard and between Grand Forks, Dakota, and Crookston, Minnesota, I had no trouble in disposing of the rest of the horses before snows and cold weather drove us in.

Very early in the spring of 1889, I bought the NW horses at the Prickly Pear Canyon, about twenty miles out of Helena, and trailed them to Sunday Creek, north of Miles City, a distance of between four and five hundred miles. From the Prickly Pear to Cascade on the upper Missouri River, I came over the famous old Mullan Trail.

It was at Cascade on this trip that I first met Charlie Russell, who in later years became famous as the Cowboy Artist. A partner of his happened to be riding for me at the time. The two of them had planned going to Alaska that spring but changed their plans later.

I was short of saddle horses and bought twenty head of Ben Rumney, near Cascade. After that we were pretty well mounted for the trip. It took about a month to trail them to Sunday Creek, where I left the yearling and two-year-old colts on the home range, turning them loose to mature. There I bought a band of cow horses from a cattle outfit, and trailed them through to Dakota, with the NW brand of horses. Other outfits were getting in the game, and I heard of different ones north of the Missouri River on their way with horses to Dakota, but I was on hand to be the first in Minot with a band of good fat horses. Horseback riding was a favorite pastime in those days. Often in a town like Minot a party of twenty or thirty would be out in the evening galloping through the streets. Men, women, and young folks all liked to ride horseback, so there was a good demand for saddle horses. I always had broken ones as well as unbroken ones, so could suit almost any customer.

There were times when I had two large rivers to cross, but crossing the Yellowstone with its swift undercurrent was only pastime, for the gravel and cobblestones made solid footing for the horses when they came out of swimming water. The Missouri River with its quicksand was more treacherous, and usually when I crossed at Fort Buford, where there was a ferry, I used the boat rather than have some of the horses bog down. However, I have swum it there and never lost but one, and that was when the bunch milled in the middle of the river and a mare looking for her colt got crowded under. Colts swim the large rivers as well as the grown horses do. I remember once, when I was crossing the Missouri above Wolf Point, catching a day-old colt and throwing him in after the bunch was a third of the way across, and he caught up to them before they had crossed.

In loading wild horses onto the ferry, I would cut a boatload, twenty or twenty-five head, from the main band and rush them between the two cut banks and onto the boat before they knew where they were going, never giving them a chance to look back until the gate was closed behind them, and only once did I have trouble or delay, and that was when, by some mishap, a horse turned his head, then broke back. One after another broke back between us and after several attempts at landing them on the boat, they were getting worse each time, so I had to rope and gag about half that boatload before I could load them.

Horses are usually easy to handle on the trail, but of all animals they are the worst to want to go back to their home range. So I always night-herded the first few nights out. After that, by putting them out in a good place about dark, then riding after them by the time it was light or before, I could turn them loose at nights, and never had any trouble unless a bad storm came up or the mosquitoes ran them off.

In those days in that wide-open country of high grass and small lakes and sloughs, the mosquitoes were the worst pest we had to contend with. I doubt if people of today can imagine how furious and thick they were then. Often in that country now people remark about mosquitoes. If those same people could have seen that country forty years ago, they would have something to say about mosquitoes. I have seen many a night when it took myself and the balance of the crew to keep the bunch from quitting the country altogether. It was enough to set man and beast crazy, and only when they were running could they get relief from the bloodthirsty pests. In such cases, they always ran against the wind, if there was any. It often happened that we rode hard all night and many a time my bunch has run thirty or forty miles in a single night. There were times when the mosquitoes came up unexpectedly when I had left no night herder out, and I would have horses to hunt in the morning.

Once when I had picked up the trail near Buffalo Lodge Lake, forty miles northwest of Minot, I found that they had changed their course as the wind changed. After a couple days of hard riding, I found them fifty miles to the northwest on Mouse River. Wild-duck eggs were my principal rations on that trip.

Another year when the mosquitoes got so thick one night that the night herder couldn't handle the bunch and they got away from him, I found them after a couple days' ride near Elbow Woods on the Missouri River, ninety miles southeast of Minot. At times we overcame a great deal of hard riding by smudges. Horses soon came to know what it meant and it wasn't long until they would all be fighting for the places where the smoke was the thickest. One horse in particular, my Old Paint rope horse, that I took back and forth to Dakota every year, always stood with his head over the smudge and claimed prior rights.

There were practically no corrals in Dakota. Consequently, all the roping and haltering of wild broncs had to be done out in the open, and when I sold a horse it stood me in hand to be mounted on a good rope horse with which to catch him.

As said before, I had always bought a lot of old cow horses to fill in from the cattle outfits that were gradually closing out after the hard winter of '86 and '87. Many of these outfits were from the South, and while there were no better rope horses than the wiry little Texas horses, they were broken a little differently in one respect than the northern horse, that is, the Texas roper ties his rope solid, to the horn of the saddle, and as soon as he throws his rope, his horse stops and braces himself to hold the animal, while the average northern roper takes his "dallies," or turns

99

around the horn of the saddle after he has caught the animal, and his horse keeps on following the animal roped, until his rider gets "dallies."

On one trip to Dakota, I happened to have all Texas saddle horses, and one day when I roped a bronc, the old Texas horse I was riding stopped and I lost my rope. I had to run the bronc several miles before I got close enough to the rope to pick it up. Finally I reached over and picked the rope from the ground as the horse ran, snubbed it to the horn of the saddle, proceeded to choke down the bronc, and to put a hackamore on him, as I was out there alone. I choked him a little too much, and he didn't get up again. So I went back to camp and gave the buyer another horse. When I roped this one, my old cow horse did the same thing, and I had to run that bronc thirty miles before I got him. That was the first and only horse I ever choked to death in the thousands that I have roped in the open. After that I decided that I would always have at least one or two rope horses with me that were broken my way and upon which I could depend. So the next trip I brought a bunch of big western horses from Idaho that were only partly broken. I picked out eight of the best of them for my string and broke them to suit myself on the trail to Dakota. By the time I was in the country where horse selling began I had made good rope horses of all of them.

There was one among them got to be an extra good rope horse. Old Paint, as he was known all over Dakota, was a red and white pinto, and knew his business so well that people of the farming communities always gathered around in crowds to watch the roping of wild horses and see Old Paint work. The intelligence he displayed was wonderful. I could rope, throw, and put a hackamore on the wildest of broncs on the open prairie, with only the assistance of Old Paint. After I had roped one, I could get off and leave Paint to hold him snubbed to the saddle horn at the end of a long rope, while I roped his front feet and threw him to put the halter on. When a bronc ran while thus being held, Paint always turned facing him and braced his feet for the jar, at the same time avoiding being wrapped up in the rope himself, to be jerked down. Every fall I took him and the balance of the string back to Montana for the winter, and they were back and forth on the trail so many times that they knew the country as well as I did. I kept every one of these horses until they were too old for service, then pensioned them. And they are now [1930] under a clump of cottonwood trees at the Old Ranch near the Missouri. Old Paint was twenty-seven years old when he died.

The cost of trailing in those days was nominal. With the help of three men besides myself I could handle from four to six hundred head. Wages were forty dollars a month, so the men's salaries and the cost of supplies was about all there was to it. At the present time, the cost of transporting one car of horses to and from the same points, and the additional cost incurred before they are disposed of, would be between four and five hundred dollars, and one would be lucky if it didn't reach seven hundred for a single car.

I always broke young saddle horses on the trail, many of which I rode myself. Often I would rope a big bronc out of the bunch that had never had a rope on him since he was branded, and hitch him to the mess wagon at the side of a gentle horse to provide a little excitement for the cook when we were moving camp, and in that way the time on the trail was put in to advantage, as broken horses sold best.

Every year as the country was settled by homesteaders, the Great Northern built new branches to meet the demand for transportation in the new wheat belt, until they had cobwebbed North Dakota with their new lines of railway; finally the Soo line invaded the rich territory, and all this brought the building of new towns, and there was more new country to create a demand for horses. Then came lean years, seasons of drouth, money depression, and the panic of '93.

Most of the banks in that time were only small institutions and many of them were forced out of business. Consequently, there was practically no money in the country. I was on hand with horses, as usual. People needed them but could get no money, so I began selling them on time payments of one, two, and three years. Cattle were cheap, and I traded for all the cattle I could get and trailed them back to the ranch. In that way, I was able to stay in the business, for I always knew where to get horses, and the seventeen years that I trailed from early spring until late fall yielded me a handsome profit.

# COWPUNCHERS

# Cattle Shading In[1]

GEORGE SCOTT GLEASON

Rather give me tang of leather,
Bark cloth and mud, blackened buffalo skin
More grossly, more grossly clouded
In the hoof-dust of cattle shading in.
Rather let the slavered even
Running wild music from fang-sharp guitars
Bellow over the tall darkness
Till shivered among the pioneer stars.

Horizons, horizons reach out,
Be my depth, widen my eyes by a thought
Till upon my sight the herds go
Loosened and wild, mooing to storms distraught
Hoof-trekking along old star-paths,
Wind-torn between the thunder and the sun,
Licking up an arroyo trail
Till herded hell for leather into one.

Lariats, go deep and deeper,
Fasten your coils far under, rip and bind,
Wind riders spur your horses on
Wildly across the country of my mind,
Up a raw-rock canyon coast range,
The cool well of an Alamo to win—
Not for me the brown-field plowshares,
Rather would I see cattle shading in.

[1] *Frontier and Midland*, Vol. XIV, No. 1, p. 58.

# Cowpunchers

THE NEXT FIVE ACCOUNTS, about individuals, are characteristic of cowboy times and cowboys.

Andy, inexperienced with stock owners, assumed that anyone would understand that he had only borrowed the horse. His story was written by William Lewis, of Spokane, a collector of early western materials, and first appeared in *Frontier*, Vol. X, No. 1, p. 62.

Eloise Reed recounts a handed-down tale about Jake, who came to the ranch with a past, not much caring what became of him. This story originally appeared in *Frontier*, Vol. XII, No. 4, p. 322.

A Crazy Joe, the incurable joker, was found in many a cattle outfit. "Pink" Simms wrote (*Frontier*, Vol. IX, No. 1, p. 47), "Crazy Joe now [1928] lives in a wild, isolated district near an abandoned mining town." Simms at that time was a locomotive engineer. When a cowpuncher he worked first in New Mexico for the old John Chissum (Chisholm) outfit. Then, after drifting over a good part of the Southwest and old Mexico, he came to Montana with a herd of cattle.

Cowboys often found themselves stranded when their horses got away from them. With their high-heeled boots for surety in the stirrups and their bowed legs, the men were never good walkers; but not often were they made to walk naked in the hot sun over prickly pear country. Tucker's humor is self-conscious and obvious, as was many a cowboy's, in this account which appeared in *Frontier*, Vol. IX, No. 4, p. 352. He was author of *Riding the High Country*. In telling of his experiences he made the most of them.

Invariably among cowboy tales is one about a horseman's being fleeced when journeying beyond the big corral. One of these accounts is Tucker's "The Sad Story of a High-Heeled Cowpuncher," which appeared in *Frontier*, Vol. X, No. 3, p. 235.

## I. Andy Gitchell Borrows a Horse

### William S. Lewis

FOLKS DIDN'T BOTHER MUCH with the law in early days—it was a long way to the nearest county seat. Certain general rules of conduct were established, a violation of which meant banishment, sometimes a rope around the neck thrown over the cross-arm of a corral post or the limb of a nearby tree, and in such cases the offender, often riddled with bullets, was left as a demonstration to those who newly entered the community that they must likewise conform or suffer a like judgment.

One thing that always made a frontiersman unusually peevish was to steal his saddle horse. Horse thieves were becoming a nuisance in western Montana in the summer of 1881. The *Weekly Missoulian* began to recommend "hemp stretching" on a considerable scale, and numerous necktie parties were held during the fall. A crowd of us young fellows were working at that time at Vicksville on the construction of the Northern Pacific Railroad. We had an acquaintance, a good-natured, easy-going cuss named Andy Gitchell. Like most of the crowd he gambled or threw away his money as fast as he got it. One day he told us that he was going to leave us and go on to Missoula. We asked him how he was going to go.

"Oh," he said, "there's lots of good horses around here. I'll just borrow one and ride it into Missoula and then turn it loose."

"That won't do, Andy. They are hanging cattle and horse thieves around here now."

"Oh," he replied, "that's all right. I don't aim to keep the horse. I just want to ride him."

That night Andy Gitchell took a horse that was handy and started off for Missoula. The next morning some men came into our camp and said, "If you want to see your friend Gitchell, you'll find him hanging beside the road about six miles from town."

106

## II. Jake

### Eloise Reed

JAKE RODE UP ONE SPRING and asked for a job. It was only a week before the roundup started and the boss was short-handed, so he put him on. He was a young fellow, not over twenty-five. His hair was yellow and straight and grew down to a point on his low forehead. His eyes were cold slate blue, and his gaze was always riveted a few inches above your head. His fingers were long, slender, nervous, and continually picking at something. The boys said he carried a gun in his bootleg. One of them had seen it when Jake was cleaning it and said there were two notches on the black handle. The foreman's wife, who was always curious about the history of the boys, asked him his name. He gave her one of his shifting glances. "Ramble," he said, "Jake Ramble; I go when I get ready."

When the roundup was over, Jake was given the job of herding the mares and colts. One night suppertime came and he had failed to appear. Seven o'clock, and the cook put his supper on a tin plate and set it in the oven to keep warm. Eight o'clock, and the last chore was done. The men were enjoying a last leisurely cigarette. Jake had not come. Nine o'clock, and suggestions were made as to the cause of his delay. Eyes, now anxious, searched through the summer twilight to the north. Ten o'clock, and horses were saddled. The men, now alarmed, started out seriously to look for Jake. They rode swift and silent through the hushed moonlight, each man pondering his own thoughts. They crossed the creek without letting their horses drink. They loped across the flat, thick with badger holes, and climbed the steep hills to the bench. At last they came to a small bunch of motionless horses. Little colts were startled at their approach and sprang to their feet and ran to their mothers. Then, when they had almost given up, on the top of a lone hill they saw what appeared in the moonlight to be the silhouette of a saddled horse. They spurred their tired horses on. They reached the top of the hill.

There stood a quivering horse, his body covered with sweat, caked and dried. A catch rope was tied about his neck. At the other end of the rope lay a white form. The rope was fastened to an arm that had been jerked from its socket. The body was dragged bare of clothing. The face was cut and torn. One eye was ripped from its socket. It was Jake. He had rambled for the last time.

The men dismounted and took off their hats. They covered the stark form with a stiff yellow slicker. They cut the rope from the neck of the trembling horse. Two of the men stayed as guards; the others started back to the ranch. Off on a hill a lone coyote raised his plaint to the stars. Next morning the cook, when he built his fire, found the tin plate of food. He walked to the open kitchen door and threw it into the ditch.

## III. Crazy Joe

### Harry (Pink) Simms

As I WAS AWAITING MY TURN at a service station in Whitehall, Montana, about three years ago [1925], I heard a man talking in a loud tone. His voice seemed vaguely familiar, and I looked to see who it was. I saw a medium-sized man of about fifty with a humorous face tanned to the color of old leather. I could not place him and he was gone before I inquired of the garageman as to his identity. He gave the name of a man that I had known intimately, about twenty-five years before, in the range country of the Powder River countries; although he was as mentally sound as the most of us, we dubbed him "Crazy Joe," because of certain eccentricities.

Crazy Joe was a cowboy; there was none better; he was considered to have few equals and no superiors in the Powder River country, which was a country that took great pride in the riders it bred. He was everything that was expected of a puncher at that time. He worked hard, was a peerless rider, a good roper, and he drank and fought as he worked—hard.

Joe was always performing reckless stunts for the benefit of the

108

rest of us. Of course, there were others as brave and reckless as he. The result was many sore heads and bruised bodies.

In appearance he was quite the opposite of the popular conception of what the present generation seems to think a top cowhand should look like. I judge from what I see of them on the streets and in the movies. He was of medium height, but very strongly built; he had large friendly brown eyes, a wide humorous mouth, and he was possessed of almost irrepressible good nature. His wild habits kept him continuously in rags; he paid practically no attention to his personal appearance. He was "mouthy" to a fault, and dearly loved a joke, which often caused him trouble; but Joe was weaned on trouble.

One of Joe's stunts that a good many of the boys would try unsuccessfully was finally barred by the wagon boss.[1] He would "thumb" his horse and make him buck; on the first jump he would allow the bronc to throw him and always land on his feet. Other riders who tried it were only able to perform a part of the trick, that is—none of them were able to land on their feet. Another of his stunts—a very simple one—was to ride into camp as hard as he could run his horse and drop off without checking him, taking saddle, bridle, and blanket with him. Not a hard trick to do after one has learned to uncinch the saddle on the run.

Once we had left a Powder River outfit after general roundup and found ourselves in Fallon looking for a job. We had our choice of several outfits, for everyone was short of riders; there was the CK, LU Bar, XIT, and the LAZY J, that were shipping out of there. Joe said that Mike Dodge was about the hardest-looking wagon boss that he ever saw; he added, "I'd like to work for him." Mike was running one of the LU wagons, so in time we found ourselves combing the breaks on the north side of the Yellowstone for LU beef.

With the LU wagon there was a young rider from Wyoming who called himself Tommy Day. That wasn't his real name, as we found out later. Nor was he that desperate young man by that name who ran with Kid Curry and whose career of crime was

[1] The man in charge of the roundup.

ended after the bank holdup in Belle Fourche. The Tommy Day I speak of was just a budding cowboy—I don't knew if he ever did bloom. He found in Crazy Joe much to admire; he tried to imitate him in nearly everything he did, but with very poor success, except the stunt of "cleaning" the horse when he came into camp. He couldn't handle his latigo strap like Joe, so, to make things easier, he bought a patent cinch buckle, which few cowboys used in those days.

We arrived at the Yellowstone on a cold November morning to cross our last herd. There was slush ice running in the river, and the river hands huddled up to a campfire in their underclothes. Joe, Day, and myself were among the men who were going into the river.

Day refused to take off his boots or chaps. I asked him if he still had the patent cinch buckle; he said that he did; and I told him that he had better take it off or he would lose his saddle in the river; that anyone who did that was generally gone. No man living could live long in it with a pair of chaps on. Day said, "It never has come off yet." Most of the things I knew I had learned in the hard school of experience, so I decided to let Day get his knowledge the same way. He did.

We throwed the first bunch in the boiling waters just as it was breaking day. (Cattle will not enter the water if the sun is on it.) Of course, we could not see very good. It is a wonder that Day wasn't drowned—he would not have been the first. I was working on the lower point, because I could swim; I was in swimming water when I heard a scream, several yells, and a heap of cursing. I saw a rider come plunging straight through the herd, which started to break back. It was Joe. I turned my horse toward the shore just as a black hat come floating by. I saw another dark object and grabbed at it. I got a handful of hair; it did not take me long to find that there was a man attached to it. Joe too had seen something floating in the current and had nearly drowned getting it, only to find that it was Day's fancy saddle. It was characteristic of Joe that he never let go of the saddle.

There were many savage remarks throwed at Day for not

taking my advice, some quite unprintable; one said that I should be shot for pulling Day out. The outcome was that we lost so much time that the crossing was put off till the next day.

Two days later we were on the south side and shipped all the cattle that there were any cars for, which left us with about five hundred head. We drove the herd out of town a short way and Dodge ordered us to bed them down near Fallon Creek and close to the railroad track. This was a foolish thing to do—we had a big stampede that night.

We were on cocktail,[2] Joe, Day, Tex Wilkins, and myself, and were relieved for supper; it was late, almost dark, and, as usual when going into meals, we were riding hell bent.

When we had changed horses at noon, Day had roped out a bald-faced sorrel that had been badly ring-tailed. This is an ailment caused by too much spurring when the horse is young; it causes a horse to throw his tail in a circle every time he is touched with a spur. It is almost impossible to rope from a ring-tailed horse, for as the rider starts to whirl his rope he always touches his horse with the spur and the horse throws his tail straight into the rope. Crazy Joe showed Day a way to prevent that by braiding a knot in the pony's tail and then tying the tail to one of the saddle strings. Hard on the pony in fly time, but the only way.

When we started for camp, Day was still riding Ringtail, and Joe looked down at the tail pulled tight to the saddle and tied in a hard knot and grinned. I knew by the grin that he had hell in his neck, but did not know how it would crop out. As we neared the chuck wagon Joe spurred his horse to the front. "Come on, Tommy," he shouted, "let's show them how to come into camp!" He dashed madly into camp and stripped his mount on the run as he hit the ground. Close behind came Day and did likewise; then to cap it all, he hit old Ringtail on the rump with his bridle.

That was the start of a merry evening. Ringtail was not by any means a gentle horse, and when Day hit him he jumped about ten feet, and when he lit a lump of something banged him on the

[2] The last watch before daylight.

111

heels. He kicked it and it charged right back at him. That was too much; he started out to show it to the remuda; the horses in it would have none of him and pulled out for parts unknown, followed by an irate, profane night wrangler.

The route they chose led them close to the day herd, already nervous on account of the humming telegraph wires a short distance away. In a few minutes, crazy with terror, the cattle were bellowing and running wild, with all available men in pursuit. They raced toward Fallon Creek, and narrowly missed a cut bank thirty foot high. (In another stampede that night, they went over that same bank.) They were sent into a "mill" against the Northern Pacific fence.

It was ten o'clock before we got the herd back to their bed ground. They could be left only under heavy guard for a while. The remuda was nowhere in sight, so the men who had eaten supper were sent out to find them. Shots fired by the night hawk,[3] who was still with them, showed where they were, but it was midnight before they were in. They then had to be corraled, for our night horses were worn out.

An account of the trouble we had that night would fill a novel. We were a weary, ill-tempered crew that gathered for breakfast the next morning. It had rained during the night and we were soaked—two men were hurt—our horses were all in—the cattle— they had been gathered for a beef herd—were no longer fit for beef, so they were turned loose.

Breakfast over, Mike Dodge wrote out two checks and handed one to Crazy Joe. "I'm paying you and Day off, Joe," he said. "You're a good hand, but I don't care for your playful ways. Your little playmate here," he said as he handed the other check to Day, "can go along with you; you might take him up on the reservation where there's lots of dogs—he can try tincanning them for a while, instead of LU horses."

That was the last I saw of Crazy Joe until I saw his mischievous countenance in Whitehall; and that was the manner of his parting from every outfit that took him on. His love for a joke was

---

[3] The man who herds saddle horses at night.

greater than his better judgment. It was finally the cause of him leaving the range land altogether. No one cared to hire him. That was his one fault.

## IV. Burnt, but Not Stewed

### Pat T. (Tommy) Tucker

MY BOYHOOD DAYS were spent in the Lone Star State, called Texas, where in the late sixties there was nothing but cowboys, longhorn cattle, and wild mustangs. I took to cowpunching before I was twelve years old and later on found out that I could make more silver busting broncs for the big cattle outfits.

I became interested in the tales of Montana and the northern cow country that the cowboys told when they returned from a trail drive, and decided to bid farewell to the sunny ranges of Texas at the first opportunity. I knew that if I waited a while I could hire out to an outfit driving cattle from Texas to Montana, but thought that would be too slow, so I trailed north by my lonesome.

I rode up into the Indian Territory, punched cows there for two months, then drifted up to Cheyenne, Wyoming. My silver was going fast, so I hired out to peel broncs for a big cow outfit on the Belle Fourche. After I had rode myself out of a job, I bought myself a grubstake and headed down the Powder River into Montana.

The range on the north side of the Yellowstone River looked good to me and it wasn't long before I was at work riding for a big cow outfit. Along about July, 1883, I was pointing a large herd of Texas longhorns to the famous Judith Basin country. I had never seen the Basin before in my life and when I rode into the Judith Gap I stopped my horse and gazed spellbound at the country spread out before me.

The Judith Basin is a huge rough-shaped basin, about eighty-five miles across and about the same in length. The Missouri River skirts its northern boundary; the Snowy and Moccasin Mountains bound it on the east; to the south are the Belt Mountains; and on the west are the Highwoods. As beautiful a valley as the eye could wish to look upon.

I liked the Judith Basin so well that I never left it for years. It was a cattleman's paradise. There was about 85,000 head of cattle in this valley, and about seventy-five cowboys rounded up these cattle twice a year, branded the calves, and cut out the beef steers and trailed them to the railroad.

On the roundup in 1884, Horace Brewster was our captain, and he sure knew the cattle business. One particular morning on this roundup we was paired off by the captain and given a certain stretch of country to ride on this circle. Jim Spurgen and I were told to trail up on the benchland and away from the river.

We rode due north till noon that day, then we came to the mouth of Wolf Creek, got off our ponies, and let them graze on the soft green grass. We ate what lunch we had in our saddlebags, took on a big smoke, and caught up our horses. Then we separated, I trailed up the Judith River, and Jim rode up Wolf Creek.

The water in the Judith looked mighty cooling and as it was so terribly hot I started to think of taking a dip. In those days I used to take a bath once a year and so I decided that this was an opportunity I couldn't afford to pass up. So I got down off Bunky, my cow horse, and throwed the reins over his head.

I climbed out of my clothes in a hurry and threw them on the ground, but on taking a second look at the ground I saw it was alive with ants and already the little pests had taken possession of my clothes. I snatched the garments from the ground, shook them off as best I could, and tied them on my saddle; then I turned my attention to swimming.

The water was very cool and refreshing, so as soon as my blood began to run in the right channels again, I got out of the water, climbed up the bank, and headed for Bunky and my clothes. Bunky, my good old cow horse, did not know this nice clean cowboy in his birthday suit and refused to let me near him. He knew my voice, but try as I could I couldn't get hold of those bridle reins. I kept following him around, but at last he snorted and trotted away from me and up on the bench, then turned around and looked back at me.

The sun was burning hot, and there was only one thing for me to do, and that was to take the squaw trot. I decided to camp on Bunky's trail in the hope that he would decide I was his master and not some strange animal, after all. I approached him several times, but each time he became more alarmed at sight of me; and at last he broke into a run, holding his head off to one side so that he wouldn't step on the reins.

At last I came to the edge of a large field of prickly pears or in other words, cactus, and although I searched carefully for a way to get around, I found none. My body was beginning to burn very painfully from the sun, so I blazed a barefoot trail through this prickly pear plantation.

I hadn't walked more than two dog lengths through this cactus before my feet looked like two big pincushions, but I couldn't turn back now. So I bowed my short neck like a young buffalo and kept on making tracks, with my heart pounding my ribs like a Salvation Army captain pounds a drum. But there was nobody dropping any jingle in the tambourine and here I had to fight my own salvation, and it sure was a sinful shame. Although I was a suffering cowboy, I had nothing to blame but my own carelessness, and those miserable little ants.

Between the torture of the cactus spines and the broiling hot sun I was nearly driven mad, but I managed to keep control of my senses and picked out a far landmark which I knew would bring me to the cow camp. At regular intervals I would stop and scan the horizon with hopeful eyes and each time would turn disgustedly to my painful task.

The sun began to affect my head, and I staggered on through the cactus until I fell face downward in the stickers from exhaustion. How long I laid there I don't know, but it seemed like ages before I heard a wild war whoop from some cowboys. Soon these cowboys galloped up and circled me where I lay with my head propped on a rock. I could hardly talk, for the way I was suffering was something fierce; but finally the boys got me into camp and laid me down gently where the roundup cook could doctor me.

When I came to life once more, I thought I was in heaven, and felt pretty good considering what I went through. This good old roundup cook had put under and over me, two hundred pounds of flour, so my bed had been rather soft.

The sun had blistered my body severely and my feet were swollen into shapelessness. Every move I made no matter how slight was extremely painful. All I could do was to lay still and listen to the flies buzzing around my sunshade. Finally I heard someone lope up to the chuck wagon and start talking with the cook in a hushed voice, which I recognized to be that of Jim Spurgen.

I didn't catch all that was said between the two but I did hear Jim ask the cook: "Has Tuck made his last ride?"

So I rose up out of the dough, and said, "Jim, old pard—no!"

## V. The Sad Story of a High-Heeled Cowpuncher

### Pat T. (Tommy) Tucker

I HAD NEVER BEEN BACK in the States. I had been on the dusty cow trails from Texas to Montana trailing saddle ponies and longhorn cattle.

In those good old days when the Texas boys were spreading the cow herds on the virgin ranges of Montana, we did not get much pay per month. We always got paid off in silver and gold. But as I was a puncher of good habits in those days, I had saved several hundred in gold and silver and my old buckskin money belt was giving me kidney sores. We used to ride two shifts, eight in the forenoon, eight in the afternoon, and whenever a real old cowboy threw his saddle onto a Mexican mustang he did not have a sweetheart in the grandstand making googoo eyes at him and with a lipstick in one hand, a looking-glass in the other. Wild hosses did not buck and sunfish under the shade of a tree in those good old days, but they bucked and bawled out

116

on the lone prairie, and this old cowboy of the once virgin west never got up from the ground with two hands full of dirt.

Now, my dear readers, here goes for the big loop. I was sitting on the bank of the old Missouri River at Fort Benton, Montana, meditating over the past—the long dusty trails, the midnight scares with redskins, cattle rustlers. In those days if a man did not have action he lasted quick. My old pals that trailed up from Texas with me had crossed on the ferryboat and taken the back trail for their native home, Texas. My old war hoss, Bunky, was close by taking on the big feed. All at once he threw up his head and looked down the river. Here came the old Red Cloud steamboat. I could see her smokestack as she came around the bend. The Red Cloud was the last boat that was to come up the Missouri River that fall. I slipped onto my old cow pony, rounded up my saddle hosses and my pack hosses, thirteen in all, and turned them over to a Frenchman for the winter. This old boat was stripped that night, which was bacon, beans, flour, tobacco, and whisky for the natives to winter on that was in camp for the winter. The next morning I got on this boat and as I was walking along her greasy deck the captain says to me, "Young man, take off your spurs. You can ride this old hull without spurs." I had a good time on this old boat—plenty of chow and red drink.

From St. Louis to Chicago I took the iron trail. When I got to Chicago and got off this whistling machine I ran into a stampede and a fog. I milled around for a while. All at once I could meet myself coming back, so I stopped and began to look for the North Star. Nothing doing. Corral too high. Money belt still in place, kidneys getting sore carrying all this silver and gold for three weeks. While I was standing there I felt something tickling me in the back. When I turned around there stood a big maverick that had a hair brand. He was the slick ear that was trying to horn me on his range. He says to me, "You're lost." "No, I'm on new range looking for a place to camp for the night. Where do these cattle kings camp?" I hear him say, "They roll in at the Parmer House." So I gives this knock-kneed critter, that has this silver brand on his left side, some silver and he trails me over to

117

one of these old land boats with a bell on one end, two mules on the other end. I got in and was standing in the middle of this traveling bunkhouse, war bag in one hand, J.B. hat in the other. This old pink-mustached mule skinner throwed the buckskin on these sleepy mules. They made one buck. The old bus made a noise like a rattlesnake. Off she went in a leap. I lost my stirrups, went over backwards, lit in the open arms of a well-fed white squaw. O me, O my! She bawled out, "Get off me, you dirty varmint."

Got to the Parmer House, took on two big feeds, camped at night. They hooked me for twelve bucks. I knew I would last quick at this big tepee so I trailed out to the other end of the reservation. Got feeds and sleep for three dollars a week and right there I camped and grazed all winter. Got along fine all winter. Had a good time, made lots of friends and enemies. I was out in Lincoln Park one evening and a big shorthorn was about to take my scalp. I pulled my old gat. He went to the wild buck. Then one of them fellows that has a star brand herded me down to headquarters. I slipped the judge fifty dollars for carrying concealed weapons. The next morning I bought a ticket for Kansas City. I was still three hundred dollars to the good.

And right in K.C. is where I got fleeced. I horned into the wrong place. I tried to beat the shell game, which can't be done, and I found it out. I was often badly bent but never flat broke till on this fatal day, afoot and on a strange range. I lost one year's wages in fifteen minutes. I knew I could not get a job in a bank, and I was a poor doctor, so I got a job from an old hayseed. He hauled me out to the ranch. He put me to herding an old mule in a cornfield. This mule had a plow hitched to him. This plow had two shovels and it raised hell with the sunflowers and cockleburs. Fifty cents a day, chow throwed in, 110 in the shade, no shade, and high-heeled boots. But I stuck it till I made seven dollars and six bits.

Trailed back to K.C. three miles, bought a second-hand carpet-bag—I paid six bits for same. I went to a store. I bought pins, needles, ladies' stockings. I told the clerk seven dollars was all the money I had. So he filled this old grip of mine full of ladies' junk. Then my bundle I shouldered, through old Missouri I wandered. I sold pins, needles, and stockings galore. My silver doubled more and more. But one sultry evening the lightning did crack, so I trailed to a native shack. I rapped at the door. The rain it did pour. The door it was opened and there stood before me the daughter of a cornfield sailor. And she was a humdinger for looks—black snappy eyes. I asked her if I could stay all night.

"I should say not," she said. "Dad is not home." Well, talking and moving toward the stove, for I was sure cold and wet—I did not know much about girls—I could see by her dimpled chin that she wanted to get rid of me pronto, which she did in an unusual way. Said she to me, "Where are you from?" I told her I was from Montana. Her black eyes were sparkling, her cheeks had turned to a rosy red. The frame-up had just materialized in her youthful brain. "Do the boys and girls ever jump in that country?" My answer was, "Yes, ma'am. I can beat you jumping. How do you want to bet? Five dollars is all the money I got, but I will bet I can beat you jumping." I laid five dollars on the table. She went into a side room to get her money. On the table was a big cake. It looked like it had been in a Montana snowstorm, all frosted on top. She came out with five dollars, laid it on top of mine. By this time the rain had quit. It was getting dark. She took a piece of chalk, made a mark on the doorstep. "I will jump first. We toe this mark and make three jumps." I said to myself, "Easy silver." She raised her homemade skirt, leaped out into the mud like a black-tailed deer. Then I jumped, lit right in her tracks. She jumped. I beat the second time. The third I beat her about one foot. I turned around. She had locked the door. That is what a puncher gets for being too personal.

It started to rain and got dark at once. There was a trail that went down to an old shed, so I moseyed on down to this old log shed and opened the door. I smelled cow. I struck a match. There this old milk cow lay, making googoo eyes at the cowpuncher. I struck another match, found a pole ladder. I climbed up this ladder and lay there like a maverick hog-tied. There was very little hay. I was just passing off into dreamland when I heard somebody talking. I looked out through a crack in the logs, and, say, here comes this gal and her young cornfield sailor. She was telling her sweetheart all about the bad man from Montana. They were yoked together like two young steers. The gal had a milk pail. The young buck had a lantern. They came in. He hung the light on a peg. She sat on a stool and began to pull this old cow's tits. She milked for a while, then he kissed her. I had heard the boys tell about the kissing parties in the States. I wanted to see the whole show, so I moved over into the king row. Good God, down I came on the old cow. Ho boy! The young lover stomped up the trail. He missed the door in the shack. But not me. I been in stampedes before. I slipped in the door nice and easy. Took the cake and ten dollars. Left the old grip with one pair of striped stockings in it. And guess when this slick Missouri gal got through milling around in the old cow barn and got to the shack she had a clean pair of socks to put on her feet.

# FRONTIER ANIMALS

# Coyote[1]

### H. Jason Bolles

When February drifts were deep
Coyote came and killed a sheep.
I think it was in April when
We found and dug coyote's den.
Coyote came among the flowers
In June and took six hens of ours.
One August night when stars were dim
We set a poisoned bait for him.
Next month we heard Coyote laugh
While dining on an orphan calf.
November time, among the haws
Our trap caught three coyote claws.

The year came on to Christmas day.
Beyond the barn a little way
We saw Coyote in the snow.
I raised my gun—but Dad said, "No!"
Then, "Merry Christmas, you old cuss,
Tomorrow peel your eye for us!'

That night we heard the bogy wail
Of Coyote, brisk and hale,
Arrow up the bitter air
Before we said our Christmas prayer.

[1] *Frontier*, Vol. XII, No. 2, p. 93.

# Coursing the Coyote

AUBREY NEASHAM

*Note by Aubrey Neasham:* It has been said that the coyote has more than his share of brains. Surely, his propagation in the face of an advancing civilization has been astounding, at times, and indicative of his ability to cope with the human being. The more farms and ranches which have come into being, the more opportunity there has been for him to steal his way into permanency.

There are many stories and poems written about the sagacity of the loping gray creature. Some do him justice and others tend to lessen his powers as a wizard. The following account [slightly edited], found in the yellowed pages of a leading western newspaper, is unique in its presentation of the remarkable thinking and outwitting qualities of Mr. Coyote. Taking place near Virginia City, Nevada, it could have happened anywhere in the West. The account appeared in the *San Francisco Chronicle*, March 31, 1878. [This story first appeared in *Frontier*, Vol. XVIII, No. 4, p. 244.]

IN THE ABSENCE OF DEER upon the trail of which they might legally turn their hounds loose, a number of the sportsmen of Virginia City, having succeeded in securing a trapped coyote, resolved upon having some sport with him. The coyote was placed in a box, which was put into a wagon and taken out onto the alkali plains about eighteen miles east of the city one day last week. The well-known sportsmen whose names follow procured the best mounts available and accompanied their dogs and their captive to the chosen coursing ground: Alderman Rawlings, J. S. Kaneen, James Orndorff, J. Kerr, Jack Magee, Mr. Meide, Dan Lyons, James Cheryberger, James Rock, Lewis Reynolds,

Matt. Bean, Dan S. Kerry, and nearly a dozen others. It proved to be one of the most novel and exciting day's sport ever witnessed in that part of the country. Fox hunting was dull in comparison. The coyote showed less of the vanishing speed than Mark Twain has attributed to the brute in his characteristic description, but what he lacked in speed he made up in spunk when run down. The affair is thus described by a local chronicler:[1] "The place selected for the liberation of the coyote was a sort of alkali flat about six or seven miles wide. The coyote, caged in a closed box, had been brought to the place in a wagon, and was liberated about 12:30 in the center of the flat. It was agreed to allow him to reach the edge of the sagebrush, some three miles distant, before the hounds were slipped. When let out of his box the coyote trotted off leisurely, leaving behind some eighteen or twenty hounds struggling frantically on the leash and

## Clamoring for the Run.

"It took the coyote about fifteen minutes to reach the edge of the flat, and just as he melted into the sagebrush the pack were turned loose upon the desert and took the trail in full cry, followed by a well-mounted field. The sagebrush was soon reached and then the chase began in earnest. Kaneen, who was splendidly mounted, took the lead, with Jack Magee close at his heels and the rest of the field trailing behind. The sagebrush and boulders were not the easiest things in the world to run in, but the horses, which by this time seemed to have got warmed up to the work, made light of the rough condition of the track as they went crashing through the brush or took flying leaps over the boulders. The hounds were about half a mile ahead in the sagebrush, their course marked by a continuous yelping and a trail of dust. After a run of about twenty minutes the coyote turned upon the trail and took a course leading back to the flat. Reaching the limit of the sagebrush, it shot into the clear flat again and made a beeline for the box from which it was first liberated. The hounds cleared

[1] Welles Drury, famous editor of Virginia City, was the author, probably. (Author's footnote.)

the brush but a few minutes behind, with the field not twenty yards in the rear, and at this point the chase became very exciting. The flat was as level as a floor, and when the field straggled out of the brush the coyote was about half a mile ahead and had three miles to run before reaching the box, a point for which it was evidently making. Horses, hounds, and coyote were now all for the first time in sight of each other. About half a dozen horsemen led the field, with Kaneen, Magee, Alderman Rawlings, and Jim Orndorff in the van. As they neared the box the coyote was pretty closely pressed by the hounds, but made a spurt and slid into his old retreat like a flash of lightning. The driver of the team who had brought him out jumped down and closed the door, and in a minute a pack of disappointed dogs were yelping all around it. The riders came up immediately afterward, and a hearty cheer went up in honor of

### The Sagacious Coyote,

followed by a general laugh when the utter ridiculousness of the situation became apparent. After the coyote had taken about half an hour's rest it decided to give the hounds a second run, and the snarling coyote was again turned out upon the cold charities of the sagebrush. He made off this time at a pace which discounted his first effort. It did not take over five minutes for him to reach the sagebrush, and the instant he disappeared the field took the trail. He covered about the same ground as before, but doubled more frequently and ran a good deal faster. In about twenty minutes he again turned into the flat, and "Little Martin," the driver, who was near the box with his team, concluded to go out and meet him. The coyote was doubling in fine style on the hounds, but when Martin had traveled about a mile from the box the pursued animal turned and made for the wagon. The dogs overtook him when he was yet about fifty yards from the wagon, and the leader springing forward fastened his teeth in his shoulder. The coyote turned nimbly, and appropriating a portion of the dog's ear traveled on, and gaining the wagon stopped directly under it, trotting along like a coach dog beneath

the fore axle. The hounds surrounded the wagon, yelping savage-
ly, and one would occasionally shoot between the wheels to try
conclusions with the coyote, who would generally send him
howling back with the blood streaming from his hide. The coyote
finally became emboldened with his success, and gliding from
between the wheels sprang into the center of the pack, and for a
few seconds

## Fought Savagely with the Dogs,

ripping the skin from the flanks of a couple, and sliding back to
its vantage ground again when numbers threatened to over-
power him. Little Martin, the self-constituted guardian of the
coyote, enjoyed the fun immensely, and drove the wagon straight
up to the box. The hounds, which seemed to anticipate a repetition of the first strategic movement, made a rush to cut off the
retreat but the hunted animal fought his way through, and
clearing the back of the last one in his way by a leap that must
have measured five times his length, he gained the door of the
box and was inside again in a second. The field now came up and
sent up another succession of hearty cheers for the coyote who
had made two so plucky runs and succeeded in two so gallant
escapes. At this point Kaneen saw a jack rabbit bounding over
the flat and gave chase. His horse had hardly started when his
hat went off, and the tremendous wind which by this time was
sweeping over the flat took his hat, and, turning it upon its brim,
sent it along like a wheel at the rate of about twenty miles an
hour. Kaneen followed, putting his horse at its best speed, and
the chase was as exciting as any fox run ever seen in the state. He
overtook and captured his hat four miles from the starting place.
After his return all hands took the road for home, bringing the
coyote with them, and he is now in Rock's Stable, as lively as
ever and ready for another run."

126

# Predators

ALTHOUGH ONLY A COLLEGE STUDENT when his stories were published in 1929, Richard West already knew the frontier and its men, cattle, and wild animals. He was aware that the wolf and the coyote were the only meat eaters on the plains and that bounties were placed on their hides because of the toll they took of herds of cattle and bands of sheep. As Walter Prescott Webb (*The Great Plains* [Boston, Ginn and Company, 1931], p. 40) declared, "The delight of the wolf was to cut off a cow from the buffalo herd, rip the hamstrings, and then pull the animal down at leisure."

In unsettled country, men as well as animals had to adjust to whatever befell them, for Nature made no exceptions. The men, however, were able to devise better protection.

West's story "Wolf" was published in *Frontier*, Vol. IX, No. 3, p. 231, with "Coyote" appearing on the following page.

## I. Wolf

### Richard West

THE END OF THE LOCOED STEER'S LIFE was going to be like his long struggle for existence, violent and relentless. There would be no mercy shown him. His dazed brain realized this as he faced his cruel enemy, a gray wolf, shaggy and, like himself, hungry.

When the riders had taken the cattle off the high summer range, the red steer had been missed in the brush and timber of the mountains. Since then he had led a wandering, lone life, and had sought the bare knolls where the large, white loco blossoms grew aplenty. Cold weather and a snowstorm had now driven him, weak from thirst and hunger, into a small canyon, and here he was making his last stand. A shelving rock broke some of the force of the wind, but it had caused the snow to drift into huge piles across the only entrance to his refuge.

The red steer had been locked in for three days. He had eaten the grass to the roots and grazed the bushes and even the pine needles. He could now barely stand from weakness; and the cold sapped his strength unmercifully. His eyes were sunk far into his head, and his ribs stood out from his backbone, patches of bare hide showed, and his flanks were drawn together.

The wolf did not wait. A long leap and a slash opened a twelve-inch slit in the steer's shoulder. He bellowed a weak defiance and sank to his knees. Again the wolf rushed in. This time his fangs tore a tendon. The steer's rump dropped to the ground, paralyzed. Blood ran in streams from the slashed body as the killer, closing in for the finish, sank his teeth deep into the steer's neck. The struggles of the steer became less frequent and more spasmodic. At each breath the blood gurgled out of his flaring nostrils. The eyes became gray and glazed; the death film spread over them. The wolf did not wait until the animal became quiet, but at once tore at the red flesh. His muzzle was stained and the hair on his neck and chest was dyed a dark red. Small spirals of steam rose where the warm blood came in contact with the cold air. The killer gulped down mouthfuls of half-chewed, quivering meat.

It was an hour before the gaunt wolf got his fill. When he was gorged, he lay down alongside the dead animal and licked his paws and bloody fur. When he had cleaned them, he rose on his haunches, pointed his long nose into the air, and gave a throbbing cry into the night.

## II. Coyote

### Richard West

THE CHILLING WIND that had been blowing out of the northwest all day and which had drifted the loose snow into long ridges and covered the grass and low sagebrush now began to die down. The short afternoon darkened and the sun slid towards the aloof mountains in the blue distance. The white wastes became silent and the air colder. The snow particles sparkled in the rays of the slanting sun. Stunted pines and black-barked firs that grew on the rim of the canyon were turning white with frost and a hard crust was forming on the surface. Shadows formed in the deeper places. Dark evening merged the hills into blurs.

A coyote, wild-eyed and hungry, limped out of the trees that fringed the mouth of a coulee. A hind leg swung back and forth from his hip. Blood ran from his feet and froze. The sharp snow crust cut the pads of his toes like a knife. Mange had left white patches in his gray fur and now and then bare hide showed through, like the spots on a checkerboard. The bushy tail dragged behind and the hair on his neck pointed towards the frosted ears.

His crippled leg had made it impossible for him to catch the small birds that live in the cedars or to run down any of the swifter game of the hills. His body was thin and pinched, and the proud bearing of all wild animals in the winter, when their fur is thick and long, was gone. The broken leg throbbed whenever it happened to hit a tree or stump. His sides heaved with his gasping breath; he weaved from side to side, but still struggled on. He fell over a limb on the ground; he made several attempts to get onto his feet. It was useless. The helpless leg was twisted grotesquely over his back.

The coyote lay in the snow and shivered from the intense cold. The snow that had drifted into his fur had melted and then frozen, leaving the hair matted and the hide exposed. He dragged himself a few yards towards a small cedar and stopped, with his tongue hanging far out of his mouth. A low whimper escaped him, the first noise he had made. His body slowly began to stiffen and as he thrust his muzzle sideways into the soft snow his eyes closed.

Silence settled down on the land, the trees loomed up like ghosts in the darkness.

### III. Wolf Hunt

### A. J. Broadwater

THE LOBO IS USUALLY KNOWN as the timber wolf, but it bore many names and nicknames—gray wolf, big gray, buffalo wolf, traveler, loper, loafer—and was credited with extraordinary sagacity. "Most of the large ranches keep dogs with which to chase wolves, usually the larger and swifter breeds, such as staghounds, Russian wolfhounds, greyhounds, and their crosses. Sometimes wolf hunts are conducted by drives similar to the jack-rabbit drives. . . . Where bounties are large, professional hunters trap wolves and pursue them with dogs." (Webb, *The Great Plains*, 41.)

A. J. Broadwater, a merchant in Havre, Montana, sent this account to *Frontier*, Vol. XI, No. 4, p. 382, saying: "I had some great experiences in hunting, having come to this state [Montana] when game was plentiful. I recall one in particular and am going to try and describe it. . . . This wolf hunt is an actual experience."

ABOUT TWENTY-THREE YEARS AGO I owned a pack of fifteen well-bred and well-trained wolfhounds, and kept three saddle horses, using alternately a horse and five dogs, to catch coyotes, whose pelts at that time were valueless as furs but there was a three dollars' bounty paid by the state and the same amount for buffalo hides. . . . There is no form of hunting I have ever known which offers anywhere near the thrill and excitement of having a good pack of dogs and a good horse under your knees and sighting a coyote off, say, a half a mile. No one can fully appreciate the excitement and expectancy but one who has experienced this form of sport.

The lobo, or buffalo wolf, was extremely scarce with us, even at this early date. This species of wolf is about the most formidable antagonist when cornered that I know of. They grow to an enormous size, often weighing close to two hundred pounds, and are as quick as a cat. One of such animals I have seen kill a three-year-old steer, and do it quickly and easily. They can bite a cow's tail entirely off, or hamstring them, or a horse, as they run past them, falling them almost in their tracks, after which it takes them only a few minutes to dispatch them.

My brother Harry and I started on a certain day for our regular coyote hunt. I had five dogs (the pick of my pack) and one particularly valuable dog (Blacktail by name), very fast, a killer, and a particular pet of mine, whom I had often seen kill his

130

coyote without assistance from the rest of the dogs; also a large hound called Wallace (a half boar hound and half Great Dane). Wallace had never been whipped by dog or beast. In fact, all of my five dogs at this time were of the very best. My brother also had a pack of seven good dogs.

We selected for our hunting grounds of this day a large lease tract, of about twenty thousand acres, where Mr. Simon Pepin ran his winter herd of beef cattle. We separated upon entering this lease, Harry going parallel and about a mile off my route. I had ridden only about a mile when a band of antelope arose from sage in front of me. Off went my dogs in chase of them, in spite of my efforts to stop them. I knew I had no dog in this pack which was fast enough to catch them, so there was nothing for me to do but await their return. I waited for possibly a half or three-quarters of an hour, and was finally rewarded by noting them coming back. I sighted them about a mile off, strung out in single file. I began counting them to see if they were all coming back. I counted seven dogs, and knowing this was two more than I had, I came to the conclusion that two of my brother's dogs had taken up the chase of the antelopes and were coming back to me with my dogs. I now got out my field glasses and discovered the last two were lobo wolves, following my dogs back. This was very exciting news to me. (I know of no other way of describing the sensation, other than to give an illustration.) You will possibly know the sensation which seizes a fellow when he is shooting rabbits, and a wild turkey flies up in front of him? Or when hunting deer, to suddenly behold an elk close by?

Well, I hurriedly got my dogs together, back-tracked them around a hill, and into a gorge, and there I rested them for half an hour, for a big scrap. I was reasonably sure that the wolves, when they arrived at where the dogs joined me with the horse, would follow no farther, and expected they would lie around in the vicinity for some time. Having rested my dogs up, I cut across the top of a hill directly for a point where the dogs had arrived on return from the antelope chase, and found my calculations true. I found, on mounting to the top of the hill, lying in the coulee directly under me, one of the finest and largest specimens of wolves ever seen. I yelled at the top of my lungs, "Take 'em, boys!" this being the signal for the dogs to go into action, and you can be sure they were not slow in taking up the challenge. Before that wolf had run fifty feet, the dogs were upon him. I really expected to see pieces of that wolf scattered over an acre of ground in a short time, and was sorry Harry was not there to see the fight. Well, it was some fight all right, but did not turn out as I expected. All of the dogs piled onto him at about the same time, and soon pulled him down. But he didn't stay down, much to my surprise. He was up almost as soon as down, and had grabbed one of the dogs, threw him ten feet, and was after another dog, trying to catch him. The dogs rallied again and again, but each time the air was full of dog hairs and yelps, keeping up a fast running fight all the while.

At last, my best dog, Blacktail, lay badly wounded and lacerated, and the rest of the pack whipped to a frazzle. I never got in shooting distance, it was done so quick. I had my shotgun and some bird-shot shells along, swung under my saddle skirt, thinking I might run into a bunch of sage hens on the trip.

About this time, Harry came up with his fresh pack of dogs and renewed my hopes; but Mr. Wolf polished this bunch of fresh dogs quicker than he did mine. He ran off about half a mile, and stood watching us from the sky line. I looked at poor Blacktail, think I shed a few tears, but the anger I felt gave me an inspiration. "Harry, you take Blacktail on your horse down to Milk River, wash his wounds, and wait there for me. I'm going to kill that wolf or crack a rib."

I was riding my top horse, Babe, half-breed Hamiltonian and cayuse, who had done a quarter in twenty-six seconds on track, and I knew was good for sixty miles at a gallop. The wolf proved very accommodating, and waited until I was within a quarter of a mile of him before starting to run. There was a long flat of seven miles in front of us, without a coulee or break. I let Babe take it rather easy for a time, and gave him his head. He knew exactly what I wanted him to do. For the first two miles, his wolfship wasn't the least worried, only occasionally looking back over his shoulder; but as I begun to draw closer and closer, he put on all the speed he had, his long tongue lolled out of his mouth. But Babe gained steadily. I noticed in the distance some badlands, and made an extra effort to finish the race before we came to these, but without success. I raced up within thirty feet of him several times, and tried to shoot from the running horse, but don't think I came within many feet of hitting him, at any of my shots.

I have heard and read of this feat of people who killed their game from a running horse. This stuff is all the bunk. The man never lived who could hit a target as big as an elephant, thirty feet away from a running horse, with a rifle or shotgun, either. They might handle a revolver with some little degree of accuracy, but I doubt it.

My wolf made these badlands before I could head him off. There is where I should have pulled up and stopped, but it never occurred to me to do so. By the very greatest of good luck I rode through a mile of these badlands at breakneck speed, where every jump of a horse was courting death. I recall at one place an almost perpendicular descent of one hundred yards and a short rise of ten or twelve feet, at the top of which we ran right into an old crater about twelve feet across. I could see no bottom. We were directly on top of this, running at full speed, before I discovered it. There was no possible chance to stop or turn the horse. I recall throwing my feet out of the stirrups, thinking I might grasp the edge of the crater when the horse fell into it. I thought this would be my last wolf chase; but that game little horse cleared that twelve feet of space as easily as I could step three feet. I knew of a water hole a short way off, and supposed the wolf would make for this. When I was within twenty steps of the water hole, I slid from the saddle, and ran up to the bank, looking down into the water hole, to see the wolf just quitting the bank on the far side. I gave him both gun barrels. The only effect was to turn him a cherry red in rear, and make him bite himself.

I now had to race back to the pony, as my only hope was to

head him off before he reached some very formidable badlands, where no horse could go. Babe was equal to the occasion. I ran by the wolf just before he reached the gulch. I ran the horse about forty yards past him, and slipped out of the saddle, shotgun in hand. The wolf stopped dead-still, gave me a look-over, rolled his lips back from his teeth, laid his ears down to his head, and charged straight at me, his mouth wide open. I was waiting for him to come within ten or twelve feet before firing, as I knew if I missed he would soon finish me off. But he never came that close. It was all a bluff. He charged to within twenty feet and stopped again, started to veer off around me, and I fired. The charge almost tore his head off. I did not take the measurements of this animal, as I had nothing to do it with, but I had often loaded 175-pound buck deer on this same pony, but try as I would, and I certainly worked hard and long at the try, I could not load this wolf on the pony. So I skinned him, or rather her, there. The pelt was almost as large as a yearling calf. I presented it to Dr. J. H. Irwin, who is now practicing medicine in Great Falls, Montana.

# Strange Comrades

## FRANK B. LINDERMAN

IN ANY BOOK ABOUT ANIMAL HABITS, strange associations like those in the following accounts are to be found. They were published in *Frontier*, Vol. VIII, No. 2, p. 83, as "Two Anecdotes." Linderman, a stickler for fact in all his writings, wrote: "In a magazine that came to my home the other day I read an article dealing with strange comradeships among animals and birds. It recalled to my mind two very exceptional examples of association between natural enemies."

### I. Bear and Pigs

BACK IN 1869 JOE HENKEL, now of Kalispell, was employed as night watchman over the store and warehouses of Durfee & Peck at old Fort Belknap, Montana.[1] In the spring of the year that Henkel began his nightly vigils for the company, a Blackfoot Indian brought two cub bears to the post and traded them to Abel Farwell, the manager of the store. The cubs thrived and, always playing together around the post, became favorites of the engagés and the steamboatmen who came up the Missouri River from St. Louis.

One day in the summer when a band of Indians were trading at the company's store, Clubfoot Tony borrowed a bow from one of them and shot an arrow straight up into the air. When the arrow came down it struck one of the cubs and killed it. The other, lonely now, took up with an old sow and several growing pigs, and began at once to live with them in the bastion of the old fort. They became inseparable, the bear, knowing herself to be

[1] On the Milk River near Harlem, in north central Montana.

135

the wisest, assuming leadership over the strange company that ate and slept together.

The steamboats brought many strangers from the States to Fort Belknap, and one night the company's store was entered by way of its front window. The glass had been broken out of the sash, and the ground beneath littered with its pieces. Henkel had heard nothing in the night, and when confronted the next morning with proof of the burglary could only say the thing must have happened while he was eating his midnight lunch. "I'll charge you up with everything they have taken," declared the irate manager. "All right," agreed Henkel, duly meek under the circumstances. "I'll pay."

But nothing was missed from the stock in the store. The mystery grew until one moonlight night in the late fall, past midnight, when Henkel, seated on a crockery crate in the deep shadow of the store building, saw the bear coming up from the bastion. The post was deserted. There were no sounds in the stockade except the rippling of the river, and an occasional ribald shout from the camp of some rivermen downstream. The bear was the only living thing in sight. She stopped in front of the store and sat up on her haunches to look craftily about, as though she intended studied mischief and feared interruption. "Woof-woof!" she snorted, evidently smelling Henkel, but uncertain of his position. Down she dropped to all fours, walked a step or two, and stopped again. She was a little worried.

Henkel sat very still. Every movement of the now nearly half-grown bear was easily discernible in the bright moonlight that shimmered on the store's windows. Once more the bear sat up, head turning, nose lifted so that the faint night breeze might tell her if her plan was feasible. It brought her no weighty warning, and dropping again to all fours she shuffled hastily to the window, smashed the glass with one blow of her heavy paw, and disappeared into the store. Henkel, in great glee, ran to the sleeping quarters of the manager. "Wake up! Wake up!" he panted. "That feller's in the store again right now!"

The manager called another man, and the three ran to the

136

store. One stopped by the broken window, one at the back door, and the other, Henkel himself, who knew he had only to face a pet bear, unlocked the front door and entered. The two outside waited, with their rifles ready. Henkel, inside, struck a match. His companions saw the small flame flicker through the windows. "The fool," they thought. "He'll be shot—killed!"

But instantly there was a terrible racket. Things began to tumble, glass to jingle, and out through the broken window bolted the bear with a small wooden keg fast to her head. The keg had held cookies; in her greed to secure the very last one she had wedged her head so tightly into the keg that she could not get it out again. Blinded by it and terrified, she ran to the safety of the bastion and her friends.

Of course, she would have to be killed now that her bad habit was formed. The men waited for her to come out of the bastion. But she didn't come. And strange to relate, not even a pig showed himself for two whole days and nights, in spite of feeding calls. She would not permit them to leave their quarters. It was as though she knew the men had sentenced her to death and believed that like punishment would descend upon her companions because of their association with her. The bastion was besieged until the morning of the third day, when the bear herself, yielding to hunger, came out alone, and was shot. Somehow, during the siege, she had rid herself of the keg.

## II. Deer and Cat

THE ANATOMIES OF THE COMMON HOUSE CAT and the cougar, or mountain lion, are almost identical. Size is about the only difference. The cats, all of them, are natural enemies of the deer. Everybody knows that the mountain lion is the greatest destroyer of deer; and I believe a full-grown lion will each year account for from twenty to fifty. But not everybody knows that the smaller varieties of wildcats sometimes kill deer. I have myself seen a lynx spring from a spruce tree upon a deer. (And I killed the lynx.) Often when I was a young man I found deer I believed had been killed by bobcats; and many times I have trapped a bobcat at such a kill, so that, naturally, all members of the cat family must look somewhat alike to a timid deer.

In 1888, when the forest reserves were new, Link Lee of Big Fork, Montana, was appointed ranger with quarters on Tobacco Plains.[2] The government had not yet set up its forestry stations, and the one on Tobacco Plains was established temporarily in a cabin built and owned by a squatter named Mike Petery. The Petery cabin stood on the edge of a meadow near Edna Creek, and was jointly occupied by Petery, N. M. Dudley, and the newly appointed forest ranger, Lincoln Lee, who had trapped with me in the earlier eighties.

When Lee took up his quarters in the cabin the only pet about the place was Petery's cat until Lee, one day, caught a fawn in the meadow and brought it in. A young deer tames very easily, and within a day or two the fawn was given its liberty. It soon learned that the men would feed it, and it always showed up at mealtime, greedily lapping condensed milk from the same pan as Petery's cat. The cat and deer were friends from the start and never quarreled over their food, even when the men tried to make trouble between them. When the pan was emptied the fawn would lick the cat while the latter relicked the pan and purred contentedly. After the meal the deer would slip away into some willows that grew at the lower end of the meadow and sleep until another mealtime arrived. He seemed to know the exact time to return to share the men's bounty with the cat.

When fall came the deer had grown husky and more playful. His spots were nearly gone, and his coat was "short blue." Now he and his friend, the Petery cat, made a game which they played together for nearly a year. It gave both opportunity to display their natural instincts; and the most astonishing feature about it was its demonstration that both players perfectly understood their unnatural relationship. The trail out of Tobacco Plains passed the Petery cabin over level ground. On the far side of the

2 Tobacco Plains, in the extreme northwestern corner of Montana, was so called from the old Indian tradition of gathering kinnikinnick for smoking.

trail from the cabin door was a grindstone set in a frame, which permitted a person to sit upon it and by peddling with his feet grind an ax or other tool. The deer and the cat made good use of it, and their daily performances were watched by many a man besides those who regularly occupied the cabin.

The cat, after purring a proposal to the deer, would spring upon the grindstone's frame and crouch. Her claws would prick nervously from their cushions, her body grow tense, her tail tip twist threateningly, like that of her big cousin, the mountain lion, when he is crouched to spring upon his prey in the forest. The deer, thus challenged, would trot up the trail a little way, then turn to face the cat. Planting his sharp hoofs carefully, he would move them often to better positions, the fine muscles of his shapely shoulders alive and dancing with excitement. There was much preparation by both. It was a part of the game itself. There seemed to be agreed signals between them. It was as though the deer asked, "Are you ready?" and the cat replied, "You bet!" Then the deer would race past the grindstone, and the cat would spring, reaching out with clawed front paw to strike, just as a lion strikes a deer. But she always missed. The deer was too cunning for her. She could never land on his shoulders, probably because he could see her, and knew what was going to happen. Her countless failures did not lessen her love for their game, however, and she was always ready to try once more. Determined to win, she would spring again and again to the grindstone's frame, go through the same old preparation of pricking out her claws and twisting her tail tip, while the deer, as though laughing at his friend's lack of luck, would turn to race back. This went on every afternoon until the following fall. Then, when the October moon was full, the young buck slipped away into the dark forest where he was killed—or found better company and forgot to come back.

# ON THE FRONTIER

# Pioneers[1]

### H. Jason Bolles

Barbers hearkened across the prairie;
Lawyers squinted beyond the years;
Doers all, uprose the merry
    Pioneers.

They crossed their streams in a miller's hopper,
They built their roads with a farmer's hoe,
They fought their foes with a butcher's chopper,
And hung their thieves with a latigo.

They cast their bullets of tinker's metal,
They nailed their houses with cobbler's brads,
They panned their gold in a brewer's kettle,
And drove their drifts with a cooper's adze.

They have served a writ on the bare, bright acres;
They have shaved the mountains behind the ears—
Heroes, adventurers, doctors, bakers,
    Pioneers.

1 *Frontier*, Vol. XII, No. 3, p. 211.

# A Wisconsin Youth in Montana, 1880–1883

## John R. Barrows

John Barrows had an unusually accurate memory and was an excellent teller of tales—a peer, really, of Frank Linderman and Charley Russell. Barrows was sixteen years of age when he came to Montana; nine years later, after studying in a law office in Helena, Montana, he practiced law and became a representative in the first Montana state legislature (1889) and, later, in the second. After long residence in San Diego, California, he returned to Montana to ranch on land left by his father in the Judith Basin country. There, when nearly blind, he dictated this account, published first in *Frontier*, autumn, 1927, and later incorporated into his book *Ubet* (1934).

Ubet, once a busy stage crossing, is now a railroad signpost. John's father had given the place its name; when asked if he could suggest a good name for the post office, he responded, "You bet."

The last stage of our journey from the Sawmill Gulch was about thirty miles, but we were traveling light with a tough little team of cayuses and a lumber wagon almost empty. The day was bright and warm and our course lay over thinly grassed uplands, dipping into an occasional small watercourse. Early in the afternoon, from the top of a sterile hill west of Daisy Dean I beheld my destination—an insignificant huddle of diminutive log cabins at the foot of a low hill near the confluence of two small streams. We were at the head of the Musselshell Valley. Mountains fronted and flanked us, mountains naked and snowy, mountains rounded and green, and old mountains revealing rocky vertebrae. From the contemplation of these encompassing heights the eye turned incredulous to the little smudge of civilization in the midst of untouched wilderness.

I presume that the greater part of an hour was consumed after arrival in renewing acquaintance with my mother and younger brother and sister, after which I took steps to explore my new surroundings. The settlement was housed in a four-room log cabin, L-shaped, with dirt roof and floors. One end room was the trading post. Next to this was the bunkhouse where the regular employees and transients slept, called "the ram pasture." The corner room was our family bedroom, and connecting with it, forming the short end of the L, was a combination kitchen and dining room. This room was distinguished by having a board floor. There were two other log buildings—a stable which would accommodate about four animals, and a dugout storehouse and root cellar.

The door of the trading post was so low that, perhaps without necessity, I ducked my head on entering. I had no sooner entered than I felt that the place was crowded. A card table surrounded by four poker players took up almost every foot of available floor space. The game must have been interesting or I must have been uninteresting, for almost no attention was given to my entrance. This inattention to myself was in no sense reciprocal, for the emporium with its meager display of merchandise was ignored while I studied the men at the table. Facing me was Antelope Charlie, a tall, well-built young man with long hair and the mustache and goatee so much affected by the scout. His legs were under the table but there was visible above it a gorgeously decorated buckskin shirt of Indian manufacture. At his right sat a famous frontier character, carrying easily the name of Liver-eating Johnson. He was a broad, burly man, unkempt and abundantly bearded. His flannel overshirt as well as his red flannel undershirt was negligently unbuttoned. His hairy arms and big hands suggested the sailor. Opposed to him I saw my first specimen of the squaw man, Jim Carpenter. In this brotherhood, Carpenter had taken the highest degree, for he was not only allied to a squaw but he had modified both costume and ap-

144

pearance to conform almost as nearly as possible to the savage standard. He was a smooth-faced, middle-aged Missourian. His rather scanty hair was worn long with side braids hanging before his ears attenuated and ludicrous with their decorations of fur and trumpery ornaments. He wore a fancy buckskin hunting shirt and leathern belt, which with its dependent knife sheath was heavily decorated with brass studs. Sitting with his back towards me was Frank Gaugler, the owner of the establishment. It was some time before the rigor of the game relaxed and my advent was noticed, whereupon I was accorded words of welcome and an opportunity to study my future employer.

He was a man of medium size with a face that showed benevolence and inefficiency. He was bearded, like Johnson, but unlike him his beard seemed to indicate no aggressive quality. It was such as one might expect on a bearded lady. Above his chin, hairy but not masculine, were a loose mouth and watery eyes—a man honest, kindly, slack, and nerveless.

The room was small for its purpose, not more than twelve by sixteen feet. Across one end was a crude bar or counter and piled upon rough shelves behind this was a scant but varied showing of the general stock. A few bottles of Hostetter's and Angostura with one or two cordials were tucked on a shelf within view, but of the most active commodity, whisky, no advertisement was necessary. Strictly speaking, the stock display was inartistic. Some showy trinkets for Indian trade hung from nails and the shelves were tightly packed with "sourdough" clothing.

For something more than two months I took a minor part in the life at the forks of the Musselshell. The tide of emigration from settlements in the older valleys west of us was commencing. There was considerable travel and life was active and full of business. At first I had no regular employment although I made myself useful in the trading post, especially at those times when the proprietor was incapacitated by liquor. I took a kindergarten course in horsemanship and was able to ride to our post office, Martinsdale, something more than a half mile distant, and make a safe return. In the absence of any other help I assisted my mother in her kitchen work and rapidly accommodated myself to the new environment.

We had for visitors at this time a family of Red River half-breeds who camped near us for a month or so, and I became quite intimate with the son and heir of the clan. Moses Wells was about my own age. Beyond the fact that he could ride and shoot, was an accomplished hunter, and could speak English, French, and three or four Indian languages fluently, he was uneducated. After one hunting trip with him I sat at his feet and confessed myself ignorant of everything essential. We started early one bright morning for the mountains some twelve miles distant, each mounted on a reliable saddle horse, and cantered over the smiling prairies until we were within a couple of miles of the timber line. We were upon the high ground between Daisy Dean and Mud creeks and here a careful survey of the foothills discovered to Moses a large band of black-tailed deer. After considerable difficulty I managed to see them too.

Up to this time I had assumed that this hunting expedition was a joint affair. I now accepted gracefully a subordinate position which I never lost. The trained eye of the half-breed instantly discovered the weakness of the position held by the deer and we left our eminence and galloped in a devious course through coulees and over low ground until it became necessary to change our mode of travel. Tying our horses to some stunted willows, we hurried forward on foot, then on all fours. I remember that this part of our approach was through the snowy slush of a ravine. Next, prone on our faces in the grass, we wormed our way to a position behind a prostrate tree. Here I was informed in a subdued whisper that there were fifty black-tailed deer quite close to us and I meekly complied with the suggestion that we should exchange guns. I had the better arm.

I was directed to get ready and fire at will as soon as my companion had fired the first shot, but when I lifted my head so that the game was visible, I was stricken with a virulent attack of buck fever and fired but one shot. (The bullet may be found by anyone who chops down the right tree and splits it into kindling

146

wood.) But the hunt was not a total failure, for the uneducated half-breed with twelve cartridges in the magazine of my '73 Winchester had killed nine large deer. Our unequal achievements, together with the fact that my horse bucked me off on my ride homeward, had a tendency to reduce my self-esteem to proper proportions. I made one more excursion with Moses, but on this occasion we flagged antelope and I was the flag. I took a position directed by my comrade and there, lying on my back, I waved my legs in the air for what seemed an interminable time. The antelope were attracted by my ridiculous behavior and three of them remained as testimonials to the skill of the sixteen-year-old half-breed. . . .

My inconsiderable part in the events of this period was preparing me for my first real adventure, and this adventure was moving slowly and relentlessly in my direction. It had the shape and substance of a herd of cattle on the trail to new pastures in the buffalo country. In an effort to fix the time of its arrival, I recall that on one day early in August two men with the cradles known to our ancestors, went into the field of oats, full three acres, to harvest, and were driven to shelter by a violent snow squall. I had hardly ceased marveling at this display of Montana climate before one of the DHS herds reached our settlement shorthanded, and I accepted a position as cowboy at thirty dollars per month. There was a wild scramble to get together the equipment available for my new role, and that afternoon I was happy in the humblest position behind the drag of a herd of fifteen hundred stock cattle.

There were about twelve of us in the party. Besides the foreman, there was the cook, who drove the mess wagon, two night herders, who slept in a very primitive Pullman bed suspended from the bows of the calf wagon, where beneath, in the bottom of the wagon, was the nursery for those inopportune calves dropped in the course of the day or too tired to follow the herd. This combination was hauled by a dignified and solemn yoke of oxen and was in the charge of a lank youth who was much in-

147

clined to follow the example of the night herders and sleep in his seat. The post of honor was held, of course, by the two men who on opposite sides directed the head, or point, of the herd. Next in importance was the pair working perhaps a quarter of a mile in their rear on the flank, and three or four of us followed in the rear, urging along what was called the drag or drag-tail, the discouraged or unambitious dregs of the herd—old bulls, the footsore and weary, and young calves. All this I learned within five miles of travel. We camped for the night at Daisy Dean.

My joy in the new employment was somewhat tempered by the consciousness that I was considered in my true character—a tenderfoot, a pilgrim, a kid—picked to fill as nearly as possible a place made vacant by the retirement of a cowboy who was devoting his present energies to recuperation following a stabbing affray. I had to hear how many knife wounds he had received and be assured by the man who had inflicted them that they all were in his back and not at all dangerous. Liquor was the excuse for his inefficiency. I discovered that camp fare was bountiful but not elaborate, and that my bed was hardly as comfortable as that to which I had been accustomed. Much I had to learn and some of this knowledge was only to be acquired after years of effort, but the fundamentals were easily understood. I was to get up promptly when called, to dress with alacrity, to roll my meager bed into a compact bundle, tie it securely, and deposit it in the mess wagon. I was automatically penalized if I left anything lying loose when we moved camp. It was part of every man's duty to assist in taking down the tent and stowing it properly, as well as in all other work not within the cook's jurisdiction. There was also a horse to be caught and saddled. Much of this was done in the half-light of dawn and before breakfast.

On this particular morning, the cattle had left the bed ground and were strung out along the road to be traveled for nearly a mile, grazing in the anxious and hurried manner usual at that time of day. Our route almost to our destination lay along the disused Carroll Trail. For nearly forty miles I was returning over ground covered on my journey from Fort Benton, but there was a new interest in the experience. I was appraising my companions and being subjected to some measure of scrutiny on their part. I learned their names or nicknames and collected information more or less reliable concerning their histories and antecedents. We could be called cowboys by courtesy. There were four or five men somewhat experienced in handling cattle, two or three glorified farm hands, and the rest were like myself, green boys or casual laborers. . . .

One hot day the foreman and our straw boss had gone ahead to look for water, leaving us with an inert and immovable herd on a dry benchland. One of the boys found a soldier's overcoat in almost complete disrepair and this garment was modishly arranged upon a large calf. When the surprised animal was released he was entirely changed; from one of the slowest of our deadheads he was transformed into something demoniac. With elevated tail and protruding tongue, giving voice to the most astounding bellows, he charged through the center of the herd transmitting to them, by some strange alchemy, his own fervor. In a moment some of us were undergoing a new experience. We were riding pell-mell after a stampeded herd; and thus we rode for a mile or more, the ground trembling, the air filled with thunderous bellowing of frightened cattle, until the maddened herd poured over the brow of a steep hill into the deep narrow valley of Beaver Creek. This was a wonderful sight to see, but no more wonderful than the celerity with which our foreman and his right-hand man mounted on their horses and fled from the impending destruction. The herd was checked in the valley, and after milling for twenty minutes or so the innocent cause of the stampede was removed and the herd settled back to comparative quiet. Then began the search for two perfectly good pairs of boots and socks, for our superior officers had been surprised while enjoying a foot bath. To this day who put the coat on the calf remains a mystery.

No reasonable complaint could be lodged against those in authority in our party, but rebellion is latent, and anything that tended to the discomfiture of the boss was more or less openly welcomed. On one dark and threatening night there was some uneasiness in the herd, and the boss, moved by some natural anxiety, left his bed, lighted a lantern, and leaving it hung in the tent went outside to listen. After he had been gone for some moments, one of the boys blew out the lantern. Presently we heard a shout, which remained unanswered, only to be followed by more shouts, growing fainter but intermixed with language growing more pungent. A cold rain set in and was still falling at dawn when our dripping and exasperated superior found camp. How the lantern went out became another of those inexplicable mysteries of the early days.

Near the site of Lewistown we left the Carroll Trail and crossed Big Spring Creek, not far from a trading post conducted by a Frenchman. The next night we camped on the high ground between the Judith and Snowy Mountains and I nearly perished from lack of bedding. On the following morning we descended from the country of sparse pines to one of the branches of Mc-Donald Creek, and turning northward drove our herd over many hills, crossing many streams. Here we narrowly avoided a small war with some bullwhackers who were "doubling up" on a steep hill. As we crawled slowly past them we urged our herd with the usual prolonged shouts of "*Oh*-ma-ha" and "*I*-da-*ho*-oh." The well trained oxen responded to our urge by stopping whenever the emphasis was placed on the "o." We passed with a consciousness of mischief well performed and also some more or less authentic information about our antecedents and our final destination.

This day at noon camp we were visited by three hungry Indians. The word hungry is perhaps surplusage, for Indians are always hungry. Donations of food were prohibited by our foreman, and those of us who were soft-hearted suffered under compulsion of eating a hearty meal under the wolfish eyes of these savages. There was some retaliation, however, for the Indians almost in our camp killed an antelope and sat down to a nauseating feast of raw liver and entrails, garnished with brains and cracked marrow bones, and when they had finished there remained little of the antelope and less of my compassion.

The following day was devoted to branding calves born during the exodus, and signalized my introduction to calf wrestling. I nearly fainted from horror when the hot iron was applied to my first calf, but I revived with a whiff of the acrid smoke and a sharp prod from the immature horns. Our work was done in a corral close to the clump of quaking aspens, within a hundred yards of the site of Giltedge, later a flourishing mining camp.[1]

When we were under way on the morning of the next day, we met with an example of Indian vigilance. Upon the top of a rounded butte two or three miles ahead there rose a lone Indian, who with his blanket made many semaphoric signals and then faded from view. This was wireless advice to his camp, perhaps three miles distant, and resulted in a visit from fifteen to twenty Blackfeet, crudely commercial and sociable. We were within sight of the new buildings of Fort Maginnis and within a mile or so of the DHS home ranch when we said good-by to our bovine companions and left them, no longer to be harassed by us, but to face the perils of a new range, hungry wolves, and Indians and a desperately hard winter.

The home ranch of the DHS was on Ford Creek. Black Butte, the eastern buttress of the Judiths, was at our north, and the Judiths proper, like an encircling arm, constituted our western and northwestern horizon. This location was an open, fertile, well-watered valley. The streams were bordered by a dense growth of willows with occasional cottonwoods of good size. Near a beautiful spring there had been constructed a commodious log cabin, L-shaped, and near it a stockade corral of heavy logs, formed in part by log buildings—quarters for the men and horses. The buildings were provided with loopholes for defensive purposes and were so placed that all sides of the corral were commanded. The massive hewn doors swung on wooden

---

[1] Now a ghost town close to old Fort Maginnis, about twenty miles east of Lewistown, Montana.

hinges and could be firmly fastened by heavy wooden bars. We soon made ourselves at home in the men's cabin and scraped acquaintance with earlier arrivals, exchanging experiences on the trail and apocryphal anecdotes of personal history. My sojourn at the ranch was extended for some reason to two or three weeks—the busiest leisure of my life.

Quite near us was a camp of fifty lodges of Piegan or Blackfeet Indians under Chief Running Rabbit. They were near the eastern frontier of their vaguely defined territory and somewhat apprehensive of their savage neighbors. Their camp was so attractive to me that I could hardly be relied upon at mealtime in the cookhouse. I was interested in everything I saw—the decorated tepees of tanned elkskin (the old ones begrimed with smoke and travel-stained, with faded effigies and symbols, the new ones spic-and-span and glaring), the domestic occupations and home industries—tanning of skins, making of pemmican, preparation of winter clothing, plain and ceremonial, the painting of buffalo robes for personal wear—every sight was a new page in my book of experiences. . . .

I formed a close alliance with two Indian boys of about my age—Meetah and Tsipah. I fed them surreptitiously but bountifully, and to this day I am not ashamed of my pilferings. I taught them a few useful words of English and in turn acquired an equal number from their vocabulary. They were fleeter of foot than I, but less successful in wrestling bouts. As their guest I visited their portable homes, but managed to resist dinner invitations. The typical tepee was a conical lodge of specially tanned elkskin stretched over a framework of perhaps twenty-five slim poles of peeled lodge pine. The bottom of the tepee was held down by stones. The door was a slit opening, covered in bad weather by a shield-shaped flap. Within this circular interior with its ever-present smoldering fire and simmering kettle, the tent wall was ingeniously wainscoted to a height of three or four feet with tanned buckskin held in place by willow wands tied to the lodgepoles. Tanned robes served as beds, and the lord of the lodge reclined luxuriously upon a back rest covered with a selected pelt.

I found very much to my surprise that the unspoiled Indian at home was not the taciturn savage of romance. The camp was alive with merriment. There was much skylarking and laughter, innocent practical jokes were the rule, and a good deal of hilarity seemed to be based upon a play of words. This unconscious air of gaiety and good-fellowship would be thrown off instantly and the whole camp take on a dignity and solemn stateliness upon the arrival of unexpected or unwelcome guests, as the visit of an officer or unsympathetic civilian. The squaws would cease their crooning songs, the play of the children would come to an end, the bucks would become wooden and frigid, and one could almost say that the papooses felt the change in the camp atmosphere. From this I am inclined to generalize and assert that our ideas of the taciturnity of the primitive Indian are misconceptions.

Thus far we had been favored with ideal weather. There now came a young blizzard from the north and with it the Irish lord and his party.[2] This personage, who hunted big game in the Rockies for several seasons, was an heir of the Jameson family, distillers. His name has had its prominence on two occasions in Africa. This scion of a wealthy house was an undersized, alert, and affable individual, crippled in a steeplechase accident, and hardly able to stand up against the recoil of his rifles. He was a game sportsman, well liked by his guides and hunters. These supernumeraries were discharged at our place and the expedition broken up. The trophies were packed for shipping to Ireland and the three hunters, "Pomp" Dennis, Bob Carpenter, and Sam Elwell, arranged to winter in a comfortable cabin which my father had built in '79 at the head of Mud Creek. They were pretty well provisioned by their former employer. When they invited me to pay them a visit about three weeks later, I accepted with great cheerfulness. By this time winter had settled. There

[2] This person cannot be the Sir George Gore who conducted a two-year hunting trip in Montana in the mid-1880's.

153

was almost no snow on the ground, but the prairie soil and the small streams were hard frozen, and there was a consistent chill in the air, ignoring the bright sunshine of our shortened days.

Father's cabin was a cozy log structure with a practical fireplace at one end, a ditto door at the other, and one window, ten by twelve inches, in the east side. My friends had constructed an upper and a lower bunk in the corner next the door and improvised four crude stools and a table. The cabin stood in a deep and narrow gulch within twenty feet of a bubbling spring. One corner was stacked full of provisions. The pines in the neighborhood were veritable Christmas trees, hung with winter meat, elk, black-tailed and white-tailed deer, antelope, and bighorn. A snowstorm setting in about noon the day after my arrival had no terrors for me. We gathered firewood and sat around our cheery fire in our snug cabin with the feeling of satisfaction that every normal individual finds in defying the elements. While the cold wind howled and the snow sifted from the peaks above us, my hosts, busied about the evening meal, delighted me with stories of their frontier experiences; nor was I sated when a comfortable bed invited me to sleep. Next morning we rolled out when we felt like it. (There is no doubt in the world that this is the right time to get up.)

While the fire was being kindled, I took the water-bucket and started for the spring for a supply of fresh drinking water. But I stopped when I opened the door. In front of me was a blank wall of snow. My surprise was extreme, but my companions regarded it as quite natural. A considerable quantity of snow had to be shoveled back into the cabin before we could dig out into daylight. We contented ourselves with melted snow for our immediate needs and after breakfast, with some labor, dug a tunnel to the spring. This was considered better than an open cut, which would drift full day to day. Later, we managed to wallow through snow like amphibians to the steep slope to the east, where the snow was no real impediment to progress, and there amused ourselves gathering firewood. The floor of the narrow valley was filled to the depth of at least ten feet. The cabin had disappeared, and for more than two weeks, during my entire stay, I never saw the roof. The chimney, projecting perhaps a foot above the snowy surroundings, smoked like a miniature volcano.

It was an era of high living. The choicest cuts of the choicest game were roasted in the coals, and our naturally good appetites were stimulated by imported relishes and condiments donated by Jameson. On warm days our door was left open to give light and air. For me this was a period of pure delight. Two of my companions had served in the Confederate and one in the Northern Army and I was treated to many stories of army experience, invariably humorous. We played cards and checkers by the light of a sputtering candle of buffalo tallow or looked over back numbers of the *London Illustrated News* by the light of the open door. Here I learned to smoke, using a frontier mixture of plug smoking tobacco and the dried leaves of the bearberry, *l'herbe*, this hot and fragrant blend consumed by an Indian pipe which had belonged to the famous chief, Red Cloud. We were not in the least interested in the temperature, buried as we were in the snow, and when genial weather came, indicating the time for my departure, I left the camp with sincere regret, carrying with me one of the most pleasant memories of my life.

And now, before settled spring weather, with the hills barely showing green through the old grass, our Flathead friends visited us on their return to their homes west of the Divide. Their coming was like the advent of the circus—a few scouts in advance followed by a long procession of riders, ponies with lodgepoles or travois or packed with the winter's spoils, the whole cavalcade wearing a general air of prosperity and well-being. Near the tail of the procession came a herd of loose horses, many bearing packs. I remember one cantankerous mare that carried an Indian packsaddle with a light load. On one side in a rawhide pouch there were three well-trained pups, on the other side an equally well-trained papoose. The old mare was loose and seemed to think that her purpose in life was to discipline the other horses, for she ran from one to another, biting and kicking as the case

155

seemed to require, but her cargo was never disturbed. We had a lively trade for a day or so, and I had occasion to air my knowledge of Chinook and sign language, which I had picked up during the winter months. We invited one Indian to come behind the counter as interpreter and house detective. This individual was at once conscious of his elevated and important position, helping himself to stick candy, dried apples, and crackers until I was sure he would die, but he lived through it and was really of great service to us. Our special friends were again invited to sit at Mother's table, where they behaved with more real gentility than many of our Caucasian guests. Their visit was profitable and would have been wholly pleasant if unscrupulous whites had not furnished them with liquor.

With the party were two Pend d'Oreille Indians who had been with the Flatheads during the winter hunt. To relieve the tedium of buffalo hunting they had gone on a successful horse-stealing expedition into the Crow country on the Yellowstone. But the Flatheads, mindful of the adage that a man is known by the company he keeps, would not permit the stolen horses to be taken west, leaving them with us upon our promise that the Crow agent should be notified and the horses returned. After the main party had left out place, the two Pend d'Oreilles came back, drunken and defiant, and took their booty from the corral. They had hardly proceeded a quarter of a mile before they were met and halted by young Charlo, son of the Chief. We were the distant witnesses of the altercation, which ended in the killing of the young chief and the flight of the suddenly sobered murderers. They left their victim in the greatest possible haste and rode to the protecting timber along the south fork of the Musselshell, emerging shortly upon the hill south of the stream. A loyal Flathead Indian, delayed at our place, made a hurried demand for a "big gun." He was given a '76 Winchester and a handful of ammunition. The distance was about eight hundred yards and there were no obstructions. We could see the spiteful little spurts of dust where the bullets struck the dry hillside just under, just over, just behind the targets, but the fleeing Indians lashed their horses into a frantic burst of speed while they resorted to the Indian style of making their horses' bodies protect their own. They were soon out of sight as well as out of range and the young chief was buried unavenged. . . .

The cattle which tenanted the foothills and prairies so recently vacated by the buffalo were somewhat nondescript in character, of diverse origins, and not at all uniform in physical characteristics, as were the Spanish cattle of the south. They were of good size, red, white, and roan, with some brindles and a few blacks and duns. According to modern standards, their horns were too large and long for any popular breed, although to distinguish them from the longhorns of Texas they were called shorthorns. The name was applied with no great impropriety for they were in reality grade Durhams. Their ancestors had followed the trail behind the prairie schooners of the Mormon or Oregon settlers or that great migration to California after the gold discovery. The pioneers of western Montana found their little herds grown to unmanageable proportions and gradually the increase in native stock filled one by one the valleys east of the Rockies. Large herds trailed through the welter of mountains from Utah, Oregon, and Washington, to new pastures in the buffalo land, and at the time of the range-cattle industry some herds were driven up from Texas into our country. The descendants of Blossom and Sukey, the family milk cows, in their new freedom, where they fought for their lives against the wolves and coyotes and saw their enemy, man, but twice a year, reverted to the feral state. Timidity was their characteristic, changed to reckless ferocity when they were much harried.

The most real and vital accomplishment of the cowboy was completeness of his knowledge of bovine psychology. We studied their modes and habits, and we watched their movements for indications of their mental states. We listened in the dark for sounds expressive of herd opinion, and in the form of song we made our plea for conversation during the long night. It must never be thought that the cow has a good ear for music. If this

were true the herd would be stampeded by our efforts. The cowboy sang at night in order that the animals might be conscious
always of his presence and to avoid startling them by un-
announced approach. Talking was as effective as singing, but no
sane man will talk to himself for hours at a stretch.

My first real work on the home range began with the fall roundup, in which we also gathered beef. I had more than the usual
interest in this roundup since it was arranged that I should go
East with the beef shipment and spend the winter at school.
Shorthanded as we were, the work of branding calves and
gathering beef in one operation was slow and sufficiently labor-
ious, but when the day came on which we were to leave the range
and hit the trail for Miles City, we had a great plenty of riders
and horses to make up the trail crew, and the two hundred miles
we were to drive were justly regarded as a pleasure trip.

There was much of routine about it. I was usually selected to
ride ahead of the herd and scare away straggling bands of buffalo, so that their behavior might not startle our beef cattle. This
does not mean that the country was overrun with them, but a
small band of stampeded buffalo could disturb the equanimity
of fourteen hundred head of fat beeves, and one little run would
run off a dollar's worth of tallow from each animal.

We made two or three dry camps before reaching the Yellowstone. The country traversed was naturally arid and hardly a
drop of rain had fallen since the spring deluge. We managed,
however, to find water for our cattle every day but one. This day
found us on the dry uplands known as Bull Mountains and we
bedded down our tired herd within five miles of the Yellowstone
after driving from daylight to dark. The cattle were unquiet, as
was natural, and extra men were on herd. About one o'clock
everything was reasonably quiet—it was a bright, starlit night—
and we were congratulating ourselves that we would have no
further trouble, when a slight draft of air from the south brought
the scent of open water to our thirsty herd. It seemed that every
animal was on foot in an instant, and there was a low chorus of

that kind of bovine talk which cannot be described to anyone who has not heard it and to him who has it needs no description. We managed to keep our herd under some kind of restraint for about three hours, when with the first streak of dawn they went beyond control, heading in the direction of the desired water. The leaders were belly-deep in the Yellowstone when the drag was still two miles away. It took a long time for every animal to satisfy his thirst.

This operation was about concluded when from the cliffs on the opposite side of the river came the reverberating reports of a dozen blasts of dynamite where the Northern Pacific construction crews were making ready for their day's work. Our herd left the immediate vicinity in such haste that we lost two miles before they could be stopped. From this point we drove one hundred miles down the river, and every day when we put the cattle into the water we were compelled to handle the inevitable stampede as soon as their thirst was satisfied and association of ideas had time to operate.

One day when I was waiting for the recurrence of this phenomenon I noticed a prostrate cottonwood log from which the bark had fallen. On its smooth bleached surface were carved the names of two members of Custer's Seventh Cavalry and the date—a day in June, 1876, about two weeks prior to the massacre.

The progress of our drive was one day interrupted while we paused to examine a curious evidence of the precarious character of life on the Yellowstone in bygone days. A conical mound dominated the area of grassy bottom land and the mound was surmounted by a squat log structure with a heavy dirt roof. This equivocal erection was about eight feet square, and its walls stood no more than two feet above ground. The heavy logs of which it was built were pierced with loopholes, but there was neither door nor window. Fifty yards away on the valley floor was a ruined log cabin. The little citadel on the hilltop was accessible only through a tunnel from the log cabin.

After drifting our cattle down the Yellowstone for nine or ten days, we reached the crossing place selected, about five miles

159

above Miles City. We had been favored with pleasant weather from the time of leaving the home range, but now the air turned cold and we endured one of those indeterminate fall storms, neither rain nor snow. Early, very early in the morning we brought our herd to the riverbank and began the rather perilous task of crossing the icy Yellowstone. Our cattle had roamed over a range where only small streams were to be found, and they had now to cross a broad, rapid river, clear and cold—a stream that had carried its fleet of steamboats. Preparing for this event, each man had selected the horse he thought best suited to the work, but the best judgment was not always displayed. Some of the boys picked their fleetest or most spirited mounts, and these were invariably poor performers in the water. I prevailed upon Tex, the only member of our party who could not swim a stroke, to ride one of my horses whose capacity in the water I had tested upon occasion during the summer, while I rode another animal worthless for most purposes but as steady in the water as a ferry-boat. Most of us shed unnecessary gear, such as six-shooters and belts, chaparejos, boots, and spurs, but Tex wore his entire regalia, remarking philosophically that he could swim just as well with his six-shooter on as off. Our discarded apparel was loaded into the mess wagon which was to cross the river on the Fort Keogh ferry, a few miles below.

The cattle went into the water with considerable reluctance, but the crossing was well chosen, and we kept crowding them until the leaders were carried off their feet by the current and the depth of the water. Instead of striking out boldly for the opposite shore, these swimmers would return to our bank of the river, and we were getting nowhere rapidly. At this tide in our affairs Perk Burnett undertook to set an example by swimming his horse across in the hope that the cattle would follow. We watched his progress with considerable interest. There was swift current and swimming water for about one hundred yards, and all went well with him until he was nearing the opposite shore, when his horse began to flounder and Perk left the saddle, or rather he attempted to leave it, for his stirrup leathers and tapaderos held the foot imprisoned. For a few moments it seemed as though the treacherous Yellowstone was about to claim another victim, but man and horse eventually reached the shore at some distance below. Whether or not the cattle were encouraged by this leadership, we soon had them strung out, and a very interesting spectacle it was—fourteen hundred head of beef cattle, unaccustomed to broad water yet swimming with unerring instinct, their bodies entirely submerged—only heads and tails visible—clogging the river in a long diagonal towards the opposite bank. The last steer across, we urged our mounts, willing or otherwise, into the chilly waters. Being a good swimmer and having recommended my horse, Baldy, to Tex, I kept in position during the swim just below him, and with unfeigned admiration perceived that his cigarette never went out of action.

When we emerged upon firm ground we were hardly picturesque. Most of us had carried all superfluous clothing turbanwise on our heads. We were all drenched to the armpits, and our wet underclothing was a long time in warming and utterly failed to dry, for a drizzling rain kept us in an uncomfortable state of sogginess. We had considerable difficulty in getting our cattle across the railroad track—one big steer in fact going into open revolt. There was only one lasso in the party and only one man with boots and spurs, but despite adverse conditions the recalcitrant was finally roped and dragged under a trestle, and we moved our herd on slowly to the west bank of the Tongue River, where we expected to meet the mess wagon with all the comforts of home. The mess wagon, however, was in difficulty. At the ferry landing the four horses had escaped from the nerveless grasp of the cook, and a rider sent out in search of our ambulatory home returned at dark with an ill-assorted lot of provisions carried behind the saddle and the news that the horses had not been caught. We had built a rousing fire around which we stood and steamed in the cold drizzle, relieving at short intervals the miserable pair who were holding the herd. This performance was continued during the night. . . . The storm abated towards morning, and the air, keen and crisp, warmed slowly under the autumn sun. By nine o'clock our mess wagon reached us and we soon forgot, or tried to forget, the hardships of the night. In due course our cattle were loaded into cars, and I accompanied the shipment to Chicago, afterwards returning to my old home in Wisconsin to attend school that winter. . . .

The spring of '83 found me again employed on the DHS Ranch, where I was beginning to feel much at home. In Granville Stuart, part owner and manager of this outfit, I had found a man who so commanded my respect and admiration that his influence upon my character and conduct was profound. A Virginian by descent, one of the earliest of Montana's pioneers, an instinctive gentleman, self-educated, well-read, fearless—a man who had married a Shoshoni squaw who held her place in his household as a loved and respected wife and mother—he needed no other qualities to make him my ideal. Under the mud roof of his log-cabin library there were housed several thousand volumes of good books, and in this library, whenever opportunity offered, I obtained my substitute for an education. Such friendship as is sometimes shown between a veteran and a youngster existed between us. My hours in the library were not always devoted to reading. A rack of firearms, obsolete and modern, was the starting point for many vivid accounts of pioneer experiences dating back to 1857, when the flintlock was the common arm of the Indian and Colt's muzzle-loading revolver the latest thing in firearms. In explaining the mutilation of a Hudson Bay "fuke" he gave a dramatic account of the first buffalo chase he had witnessed on an early visit from western Montana to the plains country. A small hunting party of Blackfeet was running a herd of buffalo and shooting with such rapidity that Stuart was sure they were armed with some kind of repeating or breech-loading rifles, but he found that the untutored savage had devised a method for converting his crude flintlock trade gun into a rapid-firing weapon by an ingenious but simple process. In order that the long, clumsy musket might be used in one hand, the barrel was filed off, reducing its length nearly one-half. The stock was similarly amputated and

162

the result might be called an immense, clumsy horse pistol. To avoid the necessity of opening the pan and priming it at every shot the touchhole was reamed out to a generous size. With horse at full gallop the possessor of this remarkable weapon poured into the muzzle an unmeasured charge of powder, and upon this haphazard explosive he spat, from a supply carried in his mouth, one large, round, leaden ball, which fitted so loosely in the generous bore of the musket that it settled into place without aid of a ramrod. The gun was carried muzzle up during all this performance and until the moment of discharge, and primed itself through the enlarged touchhole. Thus prepared the Indian hunter had only to urge his horse to the approved position alongside the running buffalo, when the weapon was pointed and discharged in one motion. There could be no possibility of missing, but there was an ever-present chance that the gun might burst.

# Lousy Hank

FRANK B. LINDERMAN

AFTER YEARS OF PROSPECTING Thomas Cruse discovered the Drum Lummon vein of gold, naming the mine after his parish in Ireland. The town that formed overnight near it in 1876 he named Marysville for one of the first women in the camp. A few years later it numbered about five thousand people. The mine was sold to an English company in 1882 for $1,600,000. Its total production has been estimated at $20,000,000. Today Marysville is a ghost town. See Linderman's "The Secret of Keep Cool" above for other comments on the town. The account of Hank appeared in *Frontier and Midland*, Vol. XV, No. 3, p. 230.

ONE MAY DECLARE that there is no such thing as luck, and yet if he recognizes the eccentricities of fortune he will feel the need of some such term. Management may play a part after fortune has dealt her favors, and not before. To fall headlong on a mountainside and skin one's nose in contact with a hitherto undiscovered outcropping of rich, auriferous ore is pure luck. Management, good or bad, follows the fall. Fate, destiny, fore-ordination may sound heavier and more learned than luck; nevertheless, they are equally vague and more or less synony-mous. Luck is common, may bed down with anybody anywhere, and yet, with all her freakish cheating, luck was Marysville's patron saint. We knew that she might suddenly visit the camp in any guise. More than once she appeared in Marysville as dire misfortune, and then when her ruse had tricked us all she un-masked to smile warningly at the weakness of our faith.

When the pay gravel in Cave Gulch petered out, Marysville gained a citizen. Nobody knew anything about him, excepting that he was known by the name of Lousy Hank and that he had loose habits in both dress and deportment. Perhaps, upon his arrival in Marysville, Lousy Hank might have commanded more attention if the camp's citizens had not been so worried about the new drifts in the Drum Lummon. The new station had been cut, and drifting pushed for more than three months, and yet no pay had been encountered on the new level. Could the great lead have pinched? Was old Marysville to become a ghost camp? One did not ask these questions, and yet they were uppermost in everybody's mind. It was even whispered that merchants were canceling their orders for goods, and we knew that already a number of miners had left the gulch for other camps, so that when Lousy Hank came to Marysville nobody noticed him.

If Hank heard the rumors which were disturbing all of us, he gave them no thought, and immediately took up with Steve Decker who hadn't a care in the world. Decker was well connected, so Marysville believed, probably because his brother owned a street railway in an eastern city, and the Piedmont mine in Marysville. Anyhow, Decker's habits were such as to attract Lousy Hank, and the two became inseparable. There was no real harm in either of them, and yet neither would work, and both would drink. Hank was tall and heavy. Decker was thin and short. Hank hadn't a cent to his name. Decker drew a monthly salary from a position he held in the office at the Piedmont mine. His position was in reality a sinecure, but neither Decker nor Lousy Hank was sensitive about such matters. Decker's credit was good in Marysville, so that he and Lousy Hank got hilariously tight the night they got acquainted. Sometime before morning the two got themselves up to the Piedmont, and there Hank went to bed with Decker. They were so wholly unreliable, so utterly improvident and so perfectly congenial that Hank remained at the Piedmont with Decker. This arrangement proved beneficial to both, since it afforded Hank a needed haven and enlivened Decker's days at the mine.

The tramway from the Piedmont mine to the mill was long and somewhat rickety. In its center, high above the ground, there was a diamond switch where the loaded car coming down from the mine to the mill passed the empty car going back to the mine. The diamond switch did not always work as intended. Sometimes the loaded car would be derailed at the switch and dump its ore to the ground beneath the tramway. This was annoying to the industrious topmen and millmen, but not to Lousy Hank and Decker. These worthies found both excitement and refreshment in the eccentricities of the rickety tramway and its crotchety switch by betting drinks on the trips of the loaded cars. Decker would wager that a car of ore coming slowly down from the mine to the mill would spill at the switch, Hank would bet that the car would land safely at the mill. And the outcome was always satisfactory to both, since win or lose there was a drink in sight for both whenever a loaded car left the mine. All that was required of the loser was to uncork and pass the bottle of whisky—and Decker furnished the liquor. Meanwhile, Marysville's troubles were multiplying. By now everybody knew that the owners of the Drum Lummon had met adversity on the mine's lower level and that Drum Lummon stock had fallen to nearly nothing. But these ominous tidings did not agitate Lousy Hank and Decker, who spent their days betting on the cars on the Piedmont tramway and their evenings in the saloons in Marysville.

But one day when they were sitting in the office window with their bottle between them, the Piedmont cars came down the tramway so often that there was but little time between drinks. Both Lousy Hank and Decker got drunk, and in reaching for the bottle to pay a lost bet Hank fell out of the window to the rocks twenty feet below and broke his leg.

The doctor had him taken to a house in Marysville where he could be given attention. He banned liquor and forbade Decker to visit Lousy Hank. The house belonged to a Cornish miner who had worked in the Drum Lummon for years as shaft boss. The

166

man's wife and daughter were natural nurses, and Decker agreed to pay them for their services. There was but a single flaw in the whole arrangement—the house was the gathering place for several Cornishmen who worked as miners in the Drum Lummon, and sometimes they held parties there talking, and drinking, and singing over their beer until a late hour in the night. However, it was the best the doctor could do, and Hank got along amazingly.

But things were not going so well in Marysville. The Drum Lummon mill first hung up twenty stamps, then fifty stamps, and finally shut down altogether for want of ore. Whole shifts of miners in the upper workings were thrown out of employment; and there was no pay on the lower level. The big Drum Lummon lead had pinched out. Already there were many houses for rent in Marysville.

However, the doctor appeared to be busier than ever. Perhaps the general state of mind in the camp made extra work for him. Anyhow, he was always driving about the gulch and over the hills. One day when he had to go up Penobscot way I went with him. Upon our return to Marysville the doctor stopped to call on Lousy Hank. "Come in," he urged me. "He'll be glad to see you."

I could scarcely recognize the man in bed there as Lousy Hank. He had lost much flesh; and, cleanly shaven, he looked neat, well-bred. His face, whitened by confinement, seemed intelligent, and yet there was something disturbing about his eyes. They looked wild, feverishly excited, as though the man suffered mental torment. I spoke of this when we were again in the buggy.

"Yes, I know," the doctor said, turning the team. "There's something wrong with Hank besides his broken leg. It's a mental condition, and I can't understand it. He's naturally phlegmatic. Nerves are things Hank never heard of, and yet he's fretting fearfully about something."

"He wants to get out and get drunk with Steve Decker," I laughed.

"No, sir. No, he doesn't," the doctor declared emphatically. "He never asks for liquor. I expected he would, and that I'd have trouble about it. But he has never asked for whisky, and I know he doesn't get any. His condition shows that he doesn't get liquor. He's doing fine."

The doctor was always serious about his patients. "Too bad Hank didn't break both his legs, doctor," I said jokingly. "If he had you might have made a man of him."

But he paid no attention to this. "Something besides Decker and whisky is troubling Hank," he said, half to himself. "I've tried to talk to him about it," he went on, speaking to me. "He told me that he has to go east, wants to raise money for clothes and railroad fare. But his reasons for going east aren't good. Once he told me there was an estate to settle back there, and next day he said there was some family trouble back in the States. I thought he might be flighty at first, but he couldn't have been."

The doctor stopped the team in front of a log house. "Hold the reins," he said. "I will not be long here."

When the door of the house opened to admit the doctor, a little girl came running out. She was a pretty child, with long, golden curls. Climbing into the buggy beside me, she begged for a ride, and to please her I drove up the road a little way. I saw Steve Decker coming down the road when I turned the team to drive back to the house. He called to me, and I waited for him to come to the buggy.

"Will you please give this to Hank?" he asked, handing me a letter in a long envelope. "They will not let me see him," he added, spitefully.

"Yes," I promised, putting the thick envelope into my inside coat pocket. "Hank is looking fine," I told him, and then drove on, because I saw that the doctor was waiting.

"Be careful of it; it's important," Decker called. I waved my hand to show him that I understood.

The doctor had recognized Decker. I told him about the letter, and he drove back to the house where Hank was confined so that I might deliver it without loss of time. The next day I went to Helena where I had been called for jury duty. I did not return

168

to Marysville for ten days. "How's Lousy Hank?" I asked, when I met the doctor.

"Oh, he's gone, vanished the minute I let him out," he said. "He bought new clothes at Rider's, and took the stage for Helena. That's all anybody knows unless it's Decker, and Decker pretends to know nothing more."

The mystery of Lousy Hank's disappearance would have held our interest at any other time. But there was now talk of pulling the pumps out of the Drum Lummon, so that Hank was forgotten. The mine that had produced millions was dead and was to be abandoned. A few miners, all of them Cornishmen, and, some said, pets of the Cornish manager, were still drifting on the mine's lower level, but they found no pay.

Two miserable months passed, and still the rumor that the mine's pumps were to be pulled persisted, and still a little smoke came daily out of the tall stacks at the shaft house up on the mountain, and daily the mine whistle blew, summoning the tiny shifts to the lower level where there was no pay in sight. And then one morning, after the stage had brought the mail to Marysville, the doctor, with a dozen men behind him, came running into the drugstore. "Look, Tom! Read this!" he said to me, spreading a Chicago newspaper upon the counter, and pointing to black headlines that read:

New Management For Drum Lummon

American Mining Engineer will take charge of famous gold mine in Montana. Has just returned from England. Declares he will put the big mine back on dividend-paying basis within thirty days. Says bad management to blame for falling off of gold production.

Then I read the man's name and looked up at the doctor. I had never seen him so excited. "It can't be," I said, incredulous.

"Bet you a box of the best cigars in this camp it's Lousy Hank," the doctor said, folding the paper.

I took the bet—and lost it. It was Lousy Hank who came to Marysville to manage the Drum Lummon. And he did put the mine back on a dividend-paying basis within thirty days; yes, and kept it there for more than twenty years.

There was no magic about it. When the doctor had Lousy Hank taken to the miner's house in Marysville, he unwittingly beckoned both fame and fortune to attend him there. Lying in his bed, Hank overheard the Cornish miners talking, boasting, over their beer. He learned that they were willfully driving the drifts on the lower level in the Drum Lummon alongside of rich gold ore and were timbering it up as they went ahead. More than this, he learned that the Cornish manager had ordered this to be done, and that he was buying Drum Lummon stock on the market and giving a few shares now and then to his miserable confederates.

No wonder that I saw excitement in the eyes of Lousy Hank the day I visited him with the doctor. As soon as he could walk, Hank went straight to London, and without exposing the ruse managed somehow to interest the dissatisfied board of directors of the English company. And from that day until he died no Englishman would put a dollar into mining property in the United States until Lousy Hank had examined it and pronounced it good.

# Reminiscences of a Pioneer Woman

## MRS. T. A. WICKES

MRS. WICKES TOOK REPRESENTATIVE FACTS from the lives of her friends and herself and blended them into the sketches that follow. Although she probably wrote these sketches about 1930 when she was in her eighties, her memory was clear and her honesty complete.

Her husband, with John Vawter, ran the general store in Wickes, founded in the mid-1870's. Wickes had the first lead-silver smelter in Montana, and near the town were several rich mines, such as the Alta, with a reported production of $32,000,000.

Mrs. Wickes herself was, one surmises, the pioneer woman who carried gold to Helena. J. X. Beidler, who "always got his man" and whom Nathaniel Pitt Langford, in *Vigilante Days and Ways* (1912), termed "a modern Haman," was a deputy United States marshal, a man prominent among the Vigilantes of Virginia City, Montana.

"The Pioneer Woman of Montana" appeared in *Frontier*, Vol. X, No. 4, p. 337; "The Robbery at Wickes" in Vol. XII, No. 1, p. 62; "A Frontier Picture" in Vol. XI, No. 3, p. 277.

## I. The Pioneer Woman of Montana

I FOLLOWED THE PIONEER WOMAN up the Missouri River fifty years ago last August, in 1880. The river was very low. We saw the sun rise in the same spot three times, and between Bismarck and Benton, we drank that muddy river water for forty days. But the pioneer woman was cleverer than I. She strained that muddy water through the seat of a cane-bottomed chair, for she told me so.

We saw General Miles on the Missouri, still chasing "hostiles." The wife of the chaplain of Fort Assiniboine (as they'd have military escort, when landing at Cow Island) offered to take my baby, Bessie, with them until I could send for her in safety, and would adopt her as their own should I be killed by the Indians, on landing at Fort Benton. But the Indians had fled.

On arriving in Montana, the pioneer woman unpacked her belongings, set out her apple-tree slips, and unrolled the tent. The campfire was made for her, and she cooked the meal. She was always cooking meals. Her husband cut logs, she helped lift them, she mortised them, shingled half the roof, cut the stove-pipe hole, climbed down, and fried the venison for supper.

With meals at $1.00 she started a boardinghouse. Indians peered in at the windows and stayed to dinner. Sooner or later they always paid. Not so all the whites. A dying Indian sent a man five miles to pay her for his last meal with her—for she told me that, and also that she had never lost a dollar from an Indian.

Later, after the Virginia City gold rush, flour was $100 per sack, three apples for $3.00, a bunch of grapes a gift to be remembered for a lifetime. Each lady in Wickes mining camp received one from the owner of a mule-team freight load brought from Ogden, Utah, but there were only three ladies, and over a hundred men to buy the luscious fruit. People lived out of tin cans largely in those days.

Near Missoula, before that, leaving their first home, holding one baby in her arms, and another a bit older at her side, on a high spring seat, above their valued effects in the wagon, the pioneer woman traveled night and day with her husband and the hired man past burning cabins and massacred settlers to find safety from pursuing Indians. Overtaken by the shouting hostiles the hired man turned back and met them. He, too, was an Indian and of their own tribe. A conference was called. That intrepid woman sat on a stump with the two babies and watched the cruel faces, as she could not understand the Indian jargon, while the hired man told of the kindness of the family to him and the love he felt for the little children. He won the day—they were saved.

In their new home her seventh Montana baby was one day tied

in a high chair and neglected, for the harvesters were coming. It had cried all the morning. A stern-faced squaw, working in the garden, entered the kitchen, took the child—the frightened mother knowing it unsafe to protest—and with reproachful look at the mother bore it to the potato patch, where the contented child cried no more that day.

Once the pioneers went to a little mining town, twenty-four miles from Helena, where was a heavy payroll, and the woman's husband cashed the checks. Helena banks lent the money. There was a hitch one day among the officials as to the date of the payday, which had been postponed. The money had arrived and was bearing interest; delay meant not only expense, but danger, indefinitely, outside bank vaults. The stage had refused to carry funds out to the camp. The husband would be spotted and held up if he went to Helena. So the little woman volunteered to take her pony and buckboard, as no one would for a moment think she had her valise full of gold, silver, and bank bills. She went ostensibly to the dentist's office, and said so, to a group of friends who were idly standing in front of the store.

Some miles from home, standing across the road, a saddled, bridled, riderless horse, a man running towards her saying, "That dog is killing chickens in the field. Are they yours?" "No, I do not live here." Was it a ruse for identifying her, she wondered? No, the innocent rancher trotted his horse behind her for three miles and then took a crossroad. Covertly she watched him. Within two miles of Helena she discovered a wheel had set and wouldn't turn; the horse was laboring, sweating. Tying the wheel with a piece of rope found in the road she lightened the vehicle, for, taking off her heavy buffalo coat and donning her beautiful otter cloak, trimmed with sealskin, reins in hand, she walked like a teamster by the side of the outfit down Broadway to the back door of the old First National Bank, deposited the few thousands she carried, and sent a message to her husband: "All is well!" At home again, when dusting the mantel, the pioneer woman put a dingy paper, full of dirt, into the fire! But not a reproachful word was spoken by the husband, who thus had lost two months' pay in gold dust.

173

As time wore on, family gold dust became more plentiful and the pioneer woman took a trip, with two of her children, by stage to the States. Her husband, before buying her ticket, saw to it that no treasure box, with messenger, was to go. But ten miles out from Helena, at a cabin door stood a messenger, with treasure box (it was X. Beidler, the famous guard) to take the journey. Mr. Beidler expressed his regret that children were along and instructed the mother, should sign of highwaymen appear, to hold them close to the floor of the stage. Night came and darkness. A plunging and stumbling of the six horses, a rocking of wheels, bouncing in mid-air, shouts of the driver, ceaselessly cracking the whip, but not a shot fired, for the ambush had failed. The road had been tied across in many places by heavy ropes. They had been saved as by a miracle—and also the $125,000 in gold dust.

## II. The Robbery at Wickes, Montana

THE LITERATURE of the western mining camps has other tales of men being lured into robbery by the apparent ease of staging a holdup. That lure exists today, but the protection afforded money now is manyfold what it was in early Montana. In this tale no protection was provided for the large payroll; taking it at gun point would be, in the jargon of the day, "as easy as pie." However, similar tales tend to end in hangings.

A MIDSUMMER DAY in the Rockies! The sun climbing over the mountains sent its insistent glare on the mining camp and the mercury climbing in the thermometer. There was no humidity— dry heat. The soft billowy clouds that constantly float in Montana skies noticeably absent. A hot day. The Alta payday.

Not a zephyr in the scrub pines on the hillsides, nor a flutter in the bunch grass on the bar; scarce even the whir of the grasshoppers, as they rose and then sank back into stillness. Even the train was caught by the inertia of all things, apparently, for it droned out its screeching whistle and arrived at the hillside depot at 10:30, a half hour late.

At the First National Bank in Helena that day the assistant

teller, John M. W., had been packing the treasure box to go on the train to Wickes. The box measured two feet in length, eighteen inches in width, and twelve inches in height, was made of steel, and was a heavy lift for one man. Shoving it along, where it would be convenient to him, and whistling softly he shoved in the piles of silver dollars, when after a moment's reflection, the young man went to the cashier's desk and addressing by the familiar abbreviation the gentleman seated there, said: "Mr. Klein, we have such a lot of silver on hand, that although the $4,000 is in the box, could I add, in silver, another thousand?" He received an affirmative answer, and it was but a few moments before John came again to the cashier and smilingly said: "Mr. Klein, we have *such* a lot of silver, can't I go ahead and put in another thousand still, or even more?" With a preoccupied air, the cashier gave his consent. By the weight of the precious coin, $17,500 in the box was ultimately saved from disaster, thanks to the young man who packed it.

The railroad tracks of the Great Northern followed the low line of the foothills from Helena, gradually rising to the tunnel, but stopping trains at the hillside depot at Wickes, quite a way above the bar, which in turn was quite a way above the town.

For two or three days Dad Nixon had gone with his one-horse wagon up to the depot for the delayed payroll; and as he stood waiting for the slow-coming train, his eyes rested on the half-mile stretch of bar below him. Once the gorgeous, yellow blossoms of the arnica plant had made it gay with color, but the fumes from the beehive roasters had blighted every blossom, the plants were dead, and there was no vestige of prickly pear or sagebrush. At the far east end of the bar were the neglected graves of four men, who, at various times, had died with their boots on; and at the west end, its depot road, down which he would soon go, passed by the schoolhouse, the doctor's home, and an empty shed.

He did not notice the fellow sitting on a log near him, whittling, nor reflect that the loafer had been there for three mornings, nor did he feel surprised when, after the box was loaded,

175

the young man climbed to the seat beside him to ride down the hill. Nor did he guess that in so doing, he gave the signal to two men in the empty shed that the money at last had come.

Almost as soon as it takes to tell it, those men, with masks over faces, one of them with a gun, ordered the driver, but without a spoken word, off his seat, took possession of the outfit, and departed down the bar.

About a half hour before this, Mr. Jim S. with his light, fast team and shining top-buggy had left the town and taken, as usual, his morning drive on the bar. Dad Nixon had watched him out of sight when he drove down into the gully that separated this first bar from the second.

The second bar, which was two or three miles long, extended by a long steep slope into the timbered hills of the Cataract mine and country, and the road, reversing its direction, went directly west again, through Murphy and Neil's Gulch. Crossing this second bar was a tiny mountain stream, which at times was only two or three feet wide, spreading out close to the road, and trickled and sang in harmony with the loneliness of the way. It was an unfrequented road, but on this eventful morning had on or near it at least eight men, who were working out their road tax while machinery at the Alta mine was being repaired.

The robbers had reached the gully and by some coincidence found Mr. S. there before them. What conversation transpired none will ever know, but Mr. S. went back to town with the wagon, the thieves hurriedly began the ascent of the second bar with the buggy, urging the team to its utmost speed, and were met by two boys hauling a load of wood to town. Harry M. and his younger cousin, Glenn, knew the horses and the buggy containing two men with black handkerchiefs over their faces. The team was streaked with sweat and appeared exhausted.

In the distance the miners saw the thieves climb out and push the buggy. The heat and the grade and the load, and perhaps a partly set wheel, impeded their progress. To transfer the weight of the box by horseback was impossible. Reaching the summit and the timber, they threw the harness upon the ground and turned the horse loose to graze, leaving the buggy standing by. The thieves disappeared!

But what more easy for them than to drop down the steep mountainside into Wickes, only a mile or two away? The road over which they had come was a long loop from their starting point. What easier than to take their riding horses, picketed on the slope close to the town, and go quietly back into the village?

Out of the stillness of that sultry July morning in 1890, forty years ago, in the Wickes camp, came the excited and profane cries of men, the whinnying of horses, the adjustment of saddles, the jingling of spurs, the swearing-in of the sheriff's posse, and all the running to and fro of restless women and children, where from lip to lip, spreading news as no telegram could have done, the words flew up and down the gulches: "The payroll, the payroll is stolen!"

Dad Nixon had lost no time. Running to the hotel, breathless, he had phoned to Boulder to the sheriff (Dan McNeil), who got the story and hurried to the scene of action. But Boulder, the county seat, was ten miles from Wickes, over a range, and on horseback took at least an hour to travel.

At the far west end of the town a lady sat picking the stems from a pan of gooseberries preparatory to making a pie. Hearing the news, she started to tell a neighbor, looked across the street, and saw two young men leading their riding horses into a barn, evidently going to join the posse. Hurrying over to them (she knew them both, one having been her boarder for years), she called out, "Boys, have you any guns? I have one over at the house you can have!" B. W. did not answer.

Coming closer, three times she put the question to him, noticed he was trembling so that he could hardly adjust the saddle on his horse, got no reply; but M. S. called out, "I have a gun," and so she went over home, thought of her pie. She glanced at the clock; it lacked ten minutes to twelve. But there would be no haste for dinner, now; and the neighbor called to her, "The men say those robbers looked like B. W. and M. S."

"I bet they're right!" she exclaimed, and thoughtfully went

into the house. "Ten minutes to twelve, from ten thirty, for the circuit of the loop, ample time!" she thought, her intuitions confirming her suspicions.

The miners agreed one man was heavy and the other light, with the slimness of youth. They had worn no disguise of costume, just regular overalls, such as all the men wore, and their faces had been hidden. B. W. was a general favorite, social, kind, and of good habits. Not a man would say he could swear to his identity.

When Harry came home with the wood and his father from working the roads, and the hot gooseberry pie was on the table, B. W. was still absent, having been among the first to join the posse to hunt the robbers.

"Harry," said his mother, "did you know those men when you saw them?"

"No, Mother, I didn't, but when Billy said afterwards—"

"Never mind what others suggested to you," sternly replied his mother.

In the meantime, on rode the pursuing posse, until they reached the grazing horses and the empty buggy.

Puzzled, they began searching the bushes, when inadvertently a man stepped on a tuft of grass which sank beneath his weight and dropped him into a hole twenty-four inches by eighteen inches by twelve inches, or a little larger. But it had no treasure box in it. Doubtless it had been deposited earlier on the way. Every inch of roadside was excitedly searched on the return. In the little stream had been cut a pocket twenty-four inches by eighteen inches by twelve inches and in it was the treasure box, the contents undisturbed.

Later, when the grand jury met, both mother and son were subpoenaed as witnesses. But the all-important question, that of the exact time of day, was not asked of the lady; and she could not and would not volunteer it.

And Harry? A hush fell on the courtroom as the other witnesses were sent from the room.

"Harry," solemnly said Judge Parker, for he had heard the

boy would not tell what he knew, "Harry, has anyone told you how to testify?"

"Yes, sir."

"Who was it?"

"My mother."

"What did she tell you to say?"

You could have heard a pin drop in that room.

"She told me, sir, to tell the truth, the whole truth, and nothing but the truth."

A smothered cheer went up from around him.

"Did you know the men, when you met them?"

"No, sir."

Needless to say, the case never came for trial in the district court.


### III. A Frontier Picture

THOUGH THIS TALE READS LIKE FICTION, it is factual. The very awkwardness of the telling verifies that. Mrs. Wickes, now deceased, would probably have told an inquirer the real names of the persons in her story. Romance then, as now, is tempered with practicality. Seldom, however, does it carry the twice-blessed fortune enjoyed by Isabelle.

FIFTY YEARS AGO, and to be exact, in September of 1880, Wickes, in Montana Territory, was booming. Some five hundred men were employed at the Alta and other mines. Concentrators had been built, the smelter was reducing ores, and families were moving in, for the fame of the temperance camp, in the midst of lawlessness, had been widely published.

The camp stretched out like a giant hairpin. Two long gulches sloped down and converged at a center, where stood the post office, the store, the butcher shop, and the Concannon Hotel. Opposite, on the mountainside, intervening between the gulches, was the concentrator for iron pyrites, reached by a difficult grade. Here teamsters held conversations with their mules and deemed profanity indispensable. Over toward the sunrise, towering above the smelter and "the works," rose another hill, grass-

179

covered, but crisscrossed to the very summit by long-since-unused paths, trails of departed buffalo, resulting now in squares of freshly fallen snow.

At night from its sparse patch of tamarack and spruce could be heard the whir-whir whine of the mountain lion, as he lay in ambush watching the crimson glow of the furnaces, and the smoke, taking form in the crisp air, above the never-ceasing noise of machinery.

On this early September morning, leaving unlocked his rather pretentious cabin of four rooms at the far end of the West Gulch, steadily trudged a middle-aged Welshman, the boss of the smelter, in unusual attire. Freshly shaven, in his best brown suit, and shoes shining, a new brown felt hat, and a fur coat over his arm, he hurried past many cottages, but still attracted no attention, for at that hour, every man in town was at work; and the three (and only three) women in camp were washing their breakfast dishes. No one had guessed that he was boarding the Salisbury coach to bring home his bride from Butte the next day.

But trust a mining camp for gossip!

The furnace fires had to be maintained day and night, to prevent what was known as "freezing," and the substitute necessarily placed in charge couldn't resist telling the news at noon, and the next evening when the stage arrived, with a burst of speed horses love at the beginning and end of a long line of travel, a goodly crowd had assembled to see the new woman—ostensibly for many other reasons.

Men were there expecting the *Helena Independent* and the *Butte Miner*, with territorial news, men expecting letters from the States. Black earringed swarthy men were there expecting no mail, having left their names, as well as their crimes, beyond the sea. Men were there to buy fruit from a freight wagon, en route to Helena from Ogden, Utah, which had arrived that day. Men, leaning against the outer wall of the hotel, tipped back in kitchen chairs, smoking. Close by, a row of young men were dangling their legs from the hotel platform where the stage would disgorge its contents. The faces of this waiting crowd were very different, but the swinging legs were much alike, swathed in gunny sacks, encased in German socks and lumberman's rubber-soled shoes. The owners looked expectantly, waiting for orders to be sent to Bonanza Chief or the Alta mine. Thus all intent, for various reasons, on the incoming stage.

In a moment, sacks of mail were pitched from the coach, while dropped from roof and sides its customary load of a dozen or more laborers, each with his roll of bedding, who walked rapidly away. The body of the coach was bouncing and rebounding with the change of weight on its leather springs. Apart, with one large foot on a front wheel of the coach, stood a burly Norwegian, his pipe in the pocket of his mackinaw, his six-mule team around the corner still hitched to two empty ore wagons. His face had the full, deep-red glow that marks climatic exposure in the Rockies, his features large, heavy, and unattractive; his pale blue eyes, unblinking, showed him honestly and eagerly scanning the wedding party, as it alighted from the stage.

Erik Monskagen was looking with a purpose. The boss was helping down a portly, rosy Welsh woman of middle age, followed by two girls, who bore no resemblance to each other, and were not, in fact, related. The younger, the daughter of the boss by a former marriage in Wales, was smiling and tossing out grips and paper bundles, right and left, and lastly extending a crutch to the other girl, who seemed not the least interested in the groups around her. She was the only child of the widow, who had left all her hardships and cares behind her to become the wife of the well-paid boss of the smelter at Wickes.

Laden with luggage, they started cheerfully for the long walk up the Gulch, except Isabelle who, with bowed head, trudged laboriously along, leaning on the crutch. Her hat had been lost on the journey, but in spite of fresh sunburn and disheveled hair, and notwithstanding the dust, with which all were covered, she had a dainty look. A bunch of kinnikinnick was pinned to her jacket, and its red berries rivaled the color in her cheeks.

Thus equipped, the party walked up the long gulch, crossed the tinkling brook, to find the house of their destination lighted with a carbon-oil lamp, and a table mysteriously but opportunely spread with a workingman's supper. The keen air had furnished the workingman's appetite. Nor did they heed the fact that those furnishing the surprise were peering at them from the cracks over in Bachelor's Row.

Erik, in the meantime, found, unconsciously, that his purpose had speedily developed into a firm decision. Still neglecting his tired mules, he drew from his wallet a five-dollar gold piece, and two silver dollars from his pants' pocket. He reached over the sideboards of one of his wagons, dumped his new shoes onto the floor, and presently in the shoe box (number eleven, the shoes) were placed, from the Ogden freight wagon, four apples (representing four dollars), and the balance of space filled with grapes in heavy bunches.

Surreptitiously, later, they were conveyed to the doorsteps of the strangers' home, shoe box and all, and were the first of many gifts that followed later.

The gift had nerved Erik also to make an early call next morning when his shadow fell across the open doorway of the smelter. "Say, boss," he stammered, and paused for a moment, watching the puddling of the silver ore. "Say, boss," he repeated rapidly. "I want one of your girls."

"What's that? Need a cook?" came the leisurely question of the man with the long iron ladle, lifting into the light the bubbling, glowing stream of metal.

"I want a wife," said Erik very simply, and waited.

"You do? Which one?" quickly responded the busy worker of the silver ore.

"The lame one," came in hushed tones from Erik.

"Well, that's all right; better talk to her mother. We can't spare Nettie, but Isabelle will decorate your cabin with white buckberries and stuff while you go hungry."

"Then I'll get her a Chinaman," said practical Erik.

The boss raised his eyes at this extravagant speech, for the Chinese cooks demanded forty dollars in cash, their keep and sometimes that of their various cousins.

Not long after, Isabelle's mother was informed of the situation, and without waiting for preliminaries, she adroitly began singing Erik's praises to Isabelle. Belle gave her mother a prompt rebuff. With rising color she informed her mother that the nice fellow in Butte, Welsh, too, and a beautiful singer, had long since asked and received her promise to wait for him, until he could make a stake in this new land. He was young, he was handsome, and ———. With a finality of tone but with an arm about the girl's shoulders, the mother gently said, "Yes, I liked him, but he's no good, hasn't a penny, has no pull, and you'd better forget him. Erik owns his mules, gets twenty dollars a day hauling ore, has a nice cabin, and they say he has an undeveloped mine in the same drift as the Alta."

Continual dropping will wear even a rock, it is said, and although Belle kept a tintype of a stalwart youth under her pillow, she hid it in the daytime and watched daily when the Comet ore team went by the house, and sighed.

Soon she and Nettie joined the Good Templars lodge, the only social organization in the village. They met a lot of new people. The next Saturday night Erik joined the lodge and took the two girls home on a hand sled.

One day, Erik, having been to town (Helena), brought home from Bailey's jewelry store an oval pin for Belle, a large carbuncle in it, set with pearls. Without a thought of unsuitability in so doing Belle gladly accepted it.

Only the finest goods were placed on sale, in the early days in Helena. Freight was as heavy on a tin dipper as on a silver ladle; white silk flannel not so heavy as outing, and far more to be desired. If in the market at all, the best could always be had. So soon Isabelle's pretty wrists wore the longed-for bracelets, and almost before she knew it a ruby ring was on her forefinger, and she was betrothed.

The marriage, when it came, was a prosy affair. A stage ride into Helena, Nettie and Belle's mother the only witnesses; Belle in a ready-to-wear brown silk, bought with Erik's money; a minister found who would take the responsibility of marrying two

183

strangers, for no licenses were issued in Montana until a much later date. It was Jewish New Year's Day. The ceremony over, they had a wonderful dinner, served by Mr. Zimmerman in the old Cosmopolitan hotel, famous for its Columbia River salmon, its venison, wild fowl, and city guests on that anniversary day.

Back in an unexpected snowstorm to the new home, close to the hillside, where today speed the trains through the Great Northern tunnel. New dishes, new carpet, and a rocking chair went with them on the coach.

On the mantel, over the open fireplace, Belle's mother had placed her wedding gift, two beautiful blue-and-white china teacups of ancestral date, brought from Wales across the sea, each cup and saucer in the famous willow pattern, with its birds, its lovers, and its rustic bridge. On either side stood a huge specimen from the concentrator, ore in brilliant red and yellow upon snow-white, deadly poisonous but exquisite iron pyrites to grace the home.

Harder than ever to realize that far-off wedding day, when one of those teacups, outlasting its owners, is today placed on the table where this sketch is being drawn.

Time passed on.

Ever, even after a year or two, Erik's pocketbook was cementing the affection of that home in a homely, helpful way. Isabelle had a sewing machine, a wringer, and later on a baby carriage with a silken spread. New joys and new tenderness were in the cottage, but the golden-haired baby that brought the sunshine came only to leave it within a few short months in deeper shadow.

Never to be forgotten the music of that Elkhorn band! Back from the memories of those far-off years comes again the funeral music of that band of Welshmen. The wonderful dirge, the low, sweet, true minor notes of Welsh harmony so loved and mastered by that people, as by no other.

No liquor was allowed in camp in those early days. Occasionally, a vinegar jug or a kerosene container with intoxicating contents found its way into the bunkhouse beyond the Reading Room.

Erik, too, had a quart can labeled "axle grease" that he carried from the Comet in his ore wagons, whose contents flushed his face and made him rough and rude at home, more and more frequently.

Life for Isabelle grew lonelier, day by day.

One wintry day, the men who did the loading at the Comet were for some reason unable to attend to it. Erik had it to do, or go without his load and his pay.

Overheated, and driving more slowly than usual, on account of an icy road, he went with brakes locked down the slippery grade, chilled to the bone and facing the north wind all the way. Pneumonia followed. In a short week he was gone.

There was a ready purchaser for the outfit, mules and wagons, but six months passed before the samples of ore from the undeveloped mine were sent to an assayer, and now again the unexpected happened. The mine was valuable, was sold, and as Erik had no parents living and no brothers or sisters, by Montana law it all went to Isabelle. Stranger yet, she knew what she would do with the money. She would buy beautiful clothes, a sealskin cloak, more jewelry, and take a trip "across the pond" back to Wales, and show her faraway kindred her resplendent presence.

The trip across the sea was taken, and excursions into the mountain fastnesses where for a thousand years Isabelle's ancestors had resisted invaders, until, at last, Llewelyn's title had been given to the heir of the English throne. Isabelle loved the land where she was born, but the lure of the mountains of Montana ever carried her most loving thoughts, the land of white-capped peaks, far away.

Soon it was springtime in the Rockies. When a letter came with a Montana postmark, Isabelle went where she would be all alone to read the pleading words from the Butte lover of long ago, who had ever loved and waited for her and now begged her to return to him and happiness. The eager journey was soon taken, with its felicitous conclusion. Life, sometimes, as for Isabelle, has its compensations.

185

Silent the old smelter is today, in that busiest of early camps in the Rockies; no smoke drifts from its tall chimney; hushed the crunchings of the slag pile; gone the deafening din of the crusher, the whistles, the shouts of the drivers; and as still, as silent, the voices of all those intimately associated with this sketch, for they sleep their last unbroken sleep beneath Montana skies.

# A Child in Virginia City, Montana, in 1863

FRANCES E. ALBRIGHT

IT IS INTERESTING TO LEARN what a child's mind seizes upon and later recalls, especially if the childhood has been spent in a raw and rough community. Aside from the Tendoy incident in these recollections, life in the tough mining town of Virginia City was, for a child, probably very like life in any small, active town in the United States in 1863. In spite of the lurid doings of the Plummer gang and the hangings by the vigilantes and the roistering deeds of Jack Slade, the Jekyll-Hyde of the town, this writer recalls schoolteachers, parades, sleigh rides, and dried fruits. The recollections appeared in *Frontier*, Vol. XI, No. 3, p. 280, as "A Pioneer Child's Story."

In the same year another little girl, known as Mollie Sheen (Mary C. L. Fitzgibbon, later Mrs. Peter Ronan), came to Virginia City and subsequently dictated her memories to her daughter, Margaret Ronan (*Memoirs of a Frontier Woman*, a master's thesis in the library of the University of Montana). She recalled bull trains and the twenty-four-horse teams pulling three or four wagons hitched together, the "fancy women," the learning of the names of wild flowers and wild animals. She knew one of the Plummer gang, Jack Gallagher, later hanged by the Vigilantes, for he was a boarder in her home—Jack, "courteous and soft-spoken." She recalled the first Mass, the first wedding. She told of herself and a companion scraping the sluice boxes of the miners after they had left for the night and of coming home with gold dust, perhaps a half-dollar's worth, until her father objected.

And at the same time a little hellcat, Calamity Jane, was in Virginia City, soaking up the town's wickedness. Even gentle Mollie Sheen saw the grief-stricken Mrs. Jack Slade as she came into the hotel to see her husband's body, cut down from the hangman's rope and carried inside.

I WILL NOT TELL YOU anything of the wild outlaws, as I never knew or saw any of them, and their deeds are well told by Judge Callaway and other speakers on early days. Rather, I will tell you of a pioneer child's recollection of life in this old town.

On our train from Fort Bridger were ten men, a mother, and a three-weeks-old child and a little girl. We came in September, 1863, and lived in a large tent, as the weather was very mild, until our log cabin was finished, in Spring Gulch, Pine Grove. We moved down to Virginia City in the spring and lived in a two-room cabin with a dirt roof, no floor, and no glass in the windows. We had robes and furs on the ground and a fireplace for cooking and were as comfortable as could be. The beds were built against the walls and were called bunks. The only chairs we had were round blocks of wood with three legs, called stools.

The first thing I remember was the creek which runs through the town. It was much larger than it is now, as there was no irrigation or city water taken out of it then. Father had a partner, Tom Smith, who had a big Newfoundland dog which could be ridden by a little girl. He also had a sack of candy, some apples, or nuts and would call to me to come over. Although I was forbidden to go near the creek, I always forgot. The man went inside to get the treat and just got back in time to pull me out of the water as there was only a board to cross on. Mother got there about the same time. And I got what I deserved. It seems funny to think of water being peddled in this town; but I have watched a man fill his barrels at our spring for a long time. Every man had a well, and of course with so many people here and no sewer system the water was not pure. Many died with mountain fever, but I am sure it must have been typhoid, as you never hear of mountain fever now.

School was my next recollection. The first one was in a log cabin next to Mr. Emslie's stone house and in the library grounds. Here I learned my letters, or A, B, C's, as they were called. This was a private school taught by Miss Royce. Next I went to the public school, also a log house of two rooms, which stood where the Callaway house is now. The small children went to a Mrs.

188

Eldred. Here we were taught "reading and writing and 'rithmetic to the tune of the hickory stick." She gave you about half a page of spelling, and every word you missed she gave you a slap on your hand with a large wooden ruler. The other studies were taught the same way. After we were promoted to the higher grades, the teacher, a Mr. Marshall, did not slap us with a ruler. He had a strap for those who disobeyed the school rules. I can say very few were so punished. However, he would throw pieces of chalk at you if you whispered. He was an expert, almost always hitting his mark. Then he said, "Bring that chalk here and stand on the floor."

Oh, I had a wonderful time at school! We had speaking and singing every Friday afternoon and spelling bees once a month, when the town folks came to spell with the kiddies. Every one who went took a tallow candle (as there was no other kind of light), a lunch, and a tin cup. We always took a lantern with a candle in it when we went out at night. I went to school to Mrs. Mary B. Elling, who had a private school one summer before she was married. I also went to Mrs. Mary Bennett and her father, who had a church school.

One of the main business streets was from Vicker's corner up towards the gulch. It was a toll road after you left the city. You had to pay to get to Summit on it, even people on foot. There was a large hotel, picture gallery, several dry-goods stores, a Catholic church, a hospital, a Good Templars hall on this street. The side where the Banderbeck house is also had a big store, warehouses, and another hotel. Most of the dances were held in this Good Templars hall. Here was where I learned what little I knew about dancing, at the tender age of ten years. The Ortons, a family of musicians, had children's dances from seven to ten o'clock at fifty cents' admission.

Another thing I remember was the freight trains, the only way we ad to get groceries and dry goods. They surely were the covered wagons! The freighters had three or four big wagons trailed together and drawn by twelve to fourteen yoke of oxen. They could only make two trips during the summer as the nearest

railroad was at Corinne [Utah], 360 miles away, and oxen travel
very slowly. I don't think I will ever forget the poor oxen, so
tired and weary, with those heavy oaken bows on their necks,
straining and pulling those heavy loads, and the driver with a
big whip that he would crack like a gun. Fresh fruits, apples,
peaches, and plums were very scarce, as they had to come by
express; so our fruits were the dried and canned ones, or the wild
raspberry, huckleberry, gooseberry, and chokecherry, which we
gathered ourselves. These berrying trips were considered pleasure trips, as the men fished and hunted the wild grouse, ducks,
and sage hens; and we camped out several days at a time. Our
early vegetables were raised in hotbeds by two French women,
who peddled them as they did in Brittany in panniers on the
backs of donkeys which they led by a halter.

Another thing that was of great interest to me was the sleigh
riding, mostly in two-seated cutters; the horses wore strings of
bells around their bodies and necks, and as each bell was a different size or tone, they were quite musical. Father had a large
bobsled painted green with a name in gay colored letters,
"Gambarinus," on the sides, which was the name of the man who
first made beer. With a lot of buffalo robes in the bed of the
sleigh, father would let us gather our little friends for a ride.
Many times the big flakes of snow would be falling down. We
surely had a lovely time. This sleigh was very popular for moonlight rides. Even the governor's wife did not object to a ride in
it. I remember when Governor B. F. Potts first came to the town.
The citizens wanted to give him a welcome, so they brought the
cannon out in front of our house and fired the national salute of
thirteen guns as he was coming over the Bozeman Trail way.

You may think I was a cruel little wretch, but a funeral was a
wonderful sight to me. In those days the lodges came out in full
regalia and had one or two brass bands playing funeral dirges
and marches. The processions were from town to the cemetery.
I also recall a Chinese-Masonic funeral. It surely was very
wonderful—three or four hundred Chinamen marching and

throwing little sheets of red paper, burning joss sticks, and fire-crackers to keep the devils away; they also had a band playing their strange music. Some of them had beautiful silk clothes, and each had a white sash over his shoulders, and all wore wooden shoes. There were many flags and banners, also several wagons of hired women who wailed and turned around to laugh.

I remember the building of the present schoolhouse and court-house. I also went to school in this one to a Mr. T. B. Gray, Mr. R. B. Hassel, and A. A. Leonard, and several others.

I don't remember the date of Tendoy's visit to Virginia City with his five hundred warriors, squaws, and papooses; but I remember that the town was guarded by scouts on all the hills, and every man who had no gun was given one from the arsenal and plenty of ammunition. The cannon was placed in a good position and all were told to be ready at the first shot. However, the chief said he was friendly and liked the white folks; so they took a big lot of beef, flour, sugar, coffee, and blankets and made a treaty of peace with him; but everyone kept his gun handy until they moved on. The Indians all over Montana were on the warpath and were killing and burning out all the isolated farmers. We went up one Sunday to his camp and he put on a war dance for us. The Indians had on their paint and feathers and strings of scalps. They gave their war whoops and beat on their tom-toms, flourished their tomahawks, and danced so fast and furiously I was afraid. The chief asked why more did not come and seemed to think that we did not trust him.

Politics was another thing that had great interest for me, as they had torchlight processions, bands, and speeches, as well as having the windows of the houses lighted with rows and rows of candles. Although I did not know what it was about, I thought it a grand time.

Virginia had a theatrical troupe who lived here and put on Shakespeare plays twice a week. I remember Hamlet. When the lady drowned herself, I surely screamed until mother said a fisherman had caught her and pulled her out. These shows were partly vaudeville, as they had singing, dancing and clowns. They had a real circus here one winter—trained animals, riders, and horses. Sleight-of-hand and musical shows came real often, so we had some fun in those old days when I was a child.

# Sky Pilot Tales

## Joyce Donaldson

The Reverend John Hoskins and the grandson of the Reverend William King told these accounts, published in *Frontier*, Vol. XI, No. 1, p. 69, to a college student, in 1930. Mr. Hoskins came to Montana in 1884 as the seventeenth Methodist minister to enter the state; Mr. King had preceded him by two years as the thirteenth. Mr. Hoskins' first charge was in Virginia City, Montana, a quiet and much diminished town from the roaring days of the 1860's.

Tales of clergymen in the early West proving their mettle to the rough men of the camps and towns are numerous. Ministers preached in saloons, a miner taking up a collection largely in gold dust—this is perhaps the favorite theme, followed by that of the brawny preacher who whipped a braggart or an insulter. The most widely known preacher in early Montana was W. W. Van Orsdel, who arrived in the state in 1872 and was loved as Brother Van. He was active until his death in 1919.

## I. The Reverend John Hoskins

In 1885 I had charge at Townsend, Montana. One day as I was walking down the main street I was stopped by a man whose appearance told me he was a miner. "Say, Parson," he began abruptly, "are you too proud to come up to Diamond City and preach to us placer miners?" I answered, "I'll come any time arrangements can be made." The next Saturday I saddled my horse and started out for Diamond City, which lies by the way of Confederate Gulch. The road I followed was the stageline, which at that time ran from Helena down through the Missouri River bottom at Winston, through Diamond City, and on to White Sulphur Springs.

When I arrived at the mining camp, Mr. Allan, who owned the hotel, took charge of my horse, while his wife and daughter took charge of me and my saddlebags, which contained my Bible, discipline, and several hymnbooks. That evening I strolled down to the cabins of the placer miners. Some of the miners were working, and others were in their cabins. Those dwellings were the cleanest cabins I had ever seen in a mining camp. The tables and stools were homemade and had been scrubbed white—real white.

I announced that services would be held in the hotel Sunday morning from eleven to twelve and in the afternoon from three to four. Sunday morning between ten and eleven the miners could be seen wending their way toward the hotel, each carrying a homemade stool or chair, as it was necessary to improvise pews. At eleven o'clock the bar in the hotel was closed and the services commenced. At the close of the service the bar was opened for refreshments, but I was given refreshments of a different character in the other room. At three in the afternoon the miners again appeared for services, and the bar was duly closed. At the end of the service the miners expressed the desire to have a social time with the dominie. The bar was opened again, but none, however, invited the parson to take refreshments.

One grizzled old miner stepped up to me and said, "Dominie, don't we take a collection?" I said, "That's if you please." So he asked Mr. Allan for a sack, which proved to be made of chamois leather about one inch wide and about four inches long. "Could you also lend me a spoon?" queried the miner of Mr. Allan. Rising to his full height, the instigator of the collection said in a dignified tone, "We will now take up the collection." Turning to Mr. Allan, he said, "Will you use the spoon first?" The hotel proprietor stooped down behind the counter and dipped his spoon into a bag. When he withdrew the spoon it was full of gold dust. The spoon was then passed to each man, who in turn scooped a little of the precious dust from his bag into the chamois-leather sack. After the bag, which took the place of the more conventional hat, had been passed all around the room, it was handed to me with this pointed question, "Do you know what to do with it?" I answered, "Well, I think so." I was then warned to "be sure and tell the man at the assay office in Helena where you got this, for he's apt to arrest you for robbing sluice boxes."

Upon arriving at the assay office in Helena, I was greeted by a smile, which indicated that someone had already told the assayer about my collection. He took my dust, weighed it in a sack, and dumped the contents out onto a marble-topped table. Then after mixing it thoroughly, he shoveled up a little and weighed it again. The next step was to put the dust into a crucible, where it was soon boiling over a hot flame. The assayer skimmed off the dirt and poured it out into two little molds, where it was allowed to cool and harden. After the gold had hardened, he weighed it and turned to me and said, "Well, how much do you think your collection amounts to?" After I had made several futile guesses he said, "Well, Parson, you earned forty-five dollars by preaching to those miners."

When I lived in the Deer Lodge Valley, around '84, the Indians were just getting their first taste of civilization. The Montana Union was an independent Montana railroad which ran from Butte to Garrison, where it connected with the Northern Pacific. Along this line at any point where the train stopped there were certain to be several Indians who would climb on just before the train started. Having no comprehension of a ticket, they would coolly ignore both the ticket agent and the conductor. They never got any farther than the steps of the train, and there they would ride until some whim beckoned them off at one of the numerous stations along the route.

A wedding thirty miles away in the eighties didn't mean a half-hour ride. Getting up about seven o'clock, I hitched my horses and started out for the place where I was supposed to make two people happy for life. Between five and six in the afternoon I saw that I had reached the end of my journey, for I saw a log house with three tents pitched around it. I was later informed that the tent at the rear was for the babies, the one on the south side of the house for the men, and the third tent was for the women. After I had performed my part of the ceremony, one of the men a little bolder than the rest suggested that I lie down. He sent me up a ladder to the second story, where I was supposed to go to sleep. After time had been allowed for me to get to sleep, the fiddle commenced, and I could hear them dancing until three or four in the morning. As I hadn't slept any, I dressed and went downstairs, after they were through dancing, and asked a young man if he would feed my horses while I got a cup of coffee. It was four-thirty when I started; I arrived home about one that afternoon. I went to bed immediately and slept until five, when I was awakened by my wife's shaking me, saying, "John, get up. There's a man who wants to get married." "Where?" I drawled out sleepily. "Up Paradise Valley about five miles away," was her reply. Seven times during my ministry I had two weddings, a funeral, preached twice, and attended Sunday school, in the same day.

In the year 1888 I was the pastor at Glendive, Montana, the seat of Dawson County. Dawson County at that time was bounded on the east by both North and South Dakota and on the north by Canada. Seven counties have since been taken out of this county. I was the only resident pastor in the county. One evening an Indian scout rode up and informed us that Sitting Bull intended to drive all the whites out of Dawson County. The five hundred people who lived in Glendive at this time began to prepare for defense. A message was immediately dispatched to Helena for ammunition as there were not over a dozen cartridges in town. At night the women and children were put in the brick schoolhouse, while the men, two by two, went on sentinel duty. Before the ammunition arrived, we heard that Sitting Bull and his band of five hundred Sioux Indians had left Poplar and gone down to Sidney, where they had crossed the Yellowstone and had made their way into Dakota, from where they went down into Wyoming. When we heard this our fears were allayed, but we felt even safer when news reached us that Sitting Bull had been killed.

One of the funniest sights that I have ever seen was in the Deer Lodge Valley in 1884. At the small town of Stewart the railroad had sunk a well so that the railroad might have a water tank. A hydrant had been attached to the tank in order to supply water for the depot and the community. One day about noon a group of Indians got off the train. They approached Mr. Kinney, who owned the post office, restaurant, grocery store, and rooming house, with the usual request for food. Mr. Kinney filled a dishpan full of pieces from the table and scraps of meat and led the Indians to the hydrant, where he showed them how to get water. To see those Indians eat the meat with their fingers, meanwhile turning the faucet on and off in an effort to fathom its source, was as good as any curiosity show I ever saw.

## II. The Reverend William E. King

ONE DAY AT VIRGINIA CITY, a woman whose drunken husband had threatened to beat her came running into the Methodist parsonage. My grandfather was absent and the woman found only my timid grandmother to offer her protection. Just then a step on the porch signaled the approach of the enraged husband. With her baby on her arm my grandmother grabbed a revolver and pointed it at the drunken man, who at the sight of the gun backed off the porch. The revolver proved to be unloaded, but the man was later heard to remark, "The parson's wife drew a gun on me, and she'd have shot, too."

When the King family arrived in Virginia City, the mother was sick in bed with rheumatism, while the family was faced with poverty, as the charge was several months behind in salary. Winter was coming on and the three small children were in need of winter clothing. Mr. King, however, was able to secure some new but moth-eaten army coats free of charge from a local store.

Taking his two-year-old son in his arms, he laid him on the table on a piece of paper, marked around him, and thus secured a pattern with which to make a suit from the army coats.

My grandfather was an exceptionally strong man, having at one time been on a life-saving crew on Lake Michigan, in order to earn his way through Northwestern University. His physical strength combined with his moral fearlessness contributed to his successful pastorate. The boast was made in Virginia City that every new parson had to take a licking. Upon hearing this Mr. King rolled up his sleeves and offered to take on any man who cared to fight. Curiously enough, the size of his muscle seemed to hold back any opponents and from that time on the parson was treated with the utmost respect.

However, a man who had whipped his wife and was reprimanded by the minister threatened to "get that parson." The minister's friends, knowing the man, warned the minister to keep off the street. The next day this man was in town, the minister, undaunted, made it a point to walk through a crowd of men where his enemy was standing. Farther down the street, within eyesight of the man who had threatened to get him, a group of men were demonstrating their physical prowess. Mr. King joined the group and, in his turn, bent his leg at the knee and held it rigid behind him, then invited the men to take turns standing on his leg. Whether or not his enemy saw the demonstration was never known, but he was never to make another threat against the minister.

In the early days each pastor had several appointments besides his regular charge to fill. These appointments were often scattered within a radius of sixty miles or more in different directions. While driving to one of his appointments in Madison Valley, Mr. King came to a swollen stream, which was too deep to have the horses ford. He was proud of his boast that he had never missed an appointment, so he swam the stream and walked the short distance to his destination. He preached in a puddle of water, made by his dripping clothes.

# A Frontier Divorce in the 1860's

## WILLIAM S. LEWIS

AH, YES, the pioneers took life as it came, acted, and, as this account illustrates, made the best of the result. And what, in this situation, would have been as good a solution? The story was first published in *Frontier*, Vol. XI, No. 1, p. 68.

OLD STEPHEN B. HOWES was a Kentuckian. He was born on a farm near Lexington, about a hundred years ago. When I first met him he was already a man well along towards his nineties and a great, original, unexplored source of frontier history for the whole region from Illinois to the Pacific Coast. In 1863, the year of the great Sioux massacre, Steve wintered at Denver. Early the next spring along with another man named Lutton, a jayhawker from Kansas, he set out from Denver with wife and family and headed for the placer gold mines of the Montana Territory. Each of the two men had a team of horses and a prairie schooner into which they loaded their chosen worldly possessions, their respective wives and children.

There were no roads and they traveled cross-country without even an Indian trail to guide them. Along the way they encountered many trials and misfortunes. Finally, in going down a hill one of the wagons was so badly wrecked that it was impossible to repair it and it had to be abandoned. A halt was now made. Each family selected the most necessary of their goods. Leaving the rest beside the wrecked wagon they loaded the meager remainder into the single wagon and proceeded on their weary way.

Hardships and misfortunes continued to disturb the harassed emigrants. In the close proximity of the single wagon the two families did not now get along well together. Weary and forlorn the two women began to nag their husbands and grew acrimonious towards each other. Each day the situation grew worse and it finally developed into a most violent quarrel between the two harassed men. The two wives now took sides against their respective husbands, who finally came to blows. Realizing that their situation had become very serious and that if they continued any longer together they would finally grow so desperate that one might kill the other, and being thus no longer able to travel together, the little party finally halted way out there on the plateau hundreds of miles from nowhere.

In desperation the men unloaded the wagon, grimly sawed the wagon box in two, separated the running gear and fashioned two crude little two-wheeled carts, with square box bodies, out of the single remaining wagon. As owner of the original wagon, Howes took his pick of the improvised carts. Each man then loaded his few remaining possessions into his little vehicle and hitched up his team to it. When it came to the families the breach between husband and wife had widened too far for any reconciliation. Howes's wife angrily refused to go with him, and chose to go with the other man. Lutton's wife in turn deserted her husband and cast her lot with the harassed Howes.

The children were likewise divided. Howes's little daughter was taken by her mother. Lutton had three children, a boy and girl about grown, who cast their lot with the father, and a little boy, Walter, who was taken by the mother. Howes's wife and daughter stolidly climbed into the cart alongside his erstwhile friend and, without a parting word or a backward glance, stolidly drove away to the South, headed for California. Howes, with the other man's wife and little son, proceeded on to Montana. As old Howes used to say, "There wasn't any divorce courts handy on the plains thereabouts, so we did the best we could at the time."

Howes, with his adopted wife and son, eventually reached Montana where, along in the summer of 1864, in company with old Jim Simpson, Howes, according to his own statement to me, built the first house ever erected on the site of the present town of Bozeman, Montana. Old Howes used to tell me that he was entitled to assert several claims to distinction: that he was the first discoverer of gold on Crow Creek, now Broadwater, near Radersburg; that he dug the first mining ditch in that vicinity; and that he had participated in the first divorce proceedings in the whole Territory. He died a couple of years ago [*ca.* 1928] at Coeur d'Alene, Idaho, with no known heirs or further estate than this tale bequeathed to me to be released on his death. Howes's name and exploits have escaped the notice of Montana historians; the only historical reference to him is the obscure mention that a man named House was associated with Colonel Bozeman in the founding of the town of Bozeman.

# The First Funeral in Valley County, Montana

## Jessie Mabee Lytle

This account was told by an old frontiersman to Jessie Mabee Lytle, a teacher of English in Helena, Montana, and was contributed to *Frontier*, Vol. XII, No. 1, p. 64. Similar material has served often for western humorous fiction in various guises. In such stories the body is usually "planted."

Well, sir, the ranks of the Montana frontiersmen are shore a thinnin' fast. I was a ridin' last herd with old Jim Betts today. I and him was to the fust funral ever helt in Valley County and them days Valley County covered as much territory as the hull of New England. I've heerd it was the biggest county in the United States before Sheridan, Daniels, Phillips, and Roosevelt counties was cut off'n it. I was a thinkin' of that fust funral today whilst I was a rollin' along in the percession behind that gorgeous plumed contraption that helt all that was left of my old pard, and a wishin' he was alive to see hisself travelin' in such spangup style with half the countryside trailin' behind him along down Main street, past all the fine brick buildin's with plate-glass winders into 'em and cement sidewalks in front on 'em; got to travel back a long hard trail to the Main street of fifty-odd year ago and that September day when Jim and me both rode in the hearse.

As I fust remember the street there wasn't but a few scattered log buildin's, half-a-dozen at most. Bill Williams had a drugstore and post office in one on 'em, though he wan't bothered much with mail the stage comin' so irreg'lar like; and there was a general tradin' post and a sort o' restaurant in another, the rest on 'em was saloons; nary a sidewalk, a few split logs laid side by side and end to end kept folks up out o' the gumbo when it rained; that, and a couple log hitchin' posts was about all the conveniences we could boast.

The day of the funral the road was plum dry and the dust was a flyin' in a cloud behind Pete Cobb's rickety spring wagon as he drove into town. Pete had a ranch 'bout four mile east and oncet a week he'd hitch up his ornery pinto cayuse and come in with fresh meat to sell.

He used to pass a couple of log shacks on the east end of the street before he come to the beesness district proper; McVees lived in one on 'em and Harleys lived in t'other. When Miss Harley see Pete a comin' with the canvas he used to cover the meat a flappin' out in the wind behind the cart, she run to the door and hailed him.

"Hi, Pete, I want a hindquarter today."

Pete was a lookin' straight ahead and a mite deef into the bargain, so he kep' right on a goin' and the old lady knew doggone well if ever he got down to Tim Kinney's restaurant with that fresh meat she would likely be eatin' salt side fer quite a spell longer, so out she run a wavin' her apern and hollern' to the top of her lungs, "Peeeete, I say, I want a hindquarter today."

When Pete see the woman he stopped and sez he, "I ain't a peddlin' no beef today, Miss Harley."

"No beef!" she sez. "What's that you got under that canvas?"

"Nothin' to speak on," sez Pete, oneasy.

That roused the old girl's curiosity and she steps around behint the cart quick and takes a peek. Pete was a tellin' us he never see a woman so flabbergasted in all his born days. She told some of the women thet she spleened agin beef the hull winter. Anyways, she never stopped to ask ary questions, but made tracts for the house pronto, and Pete he slapped the reins on old Paint's back and druv up in front of Stub Bliss's saloon, where most of us fellers hung out them days, and he lets a yelp out of him that brought us all pell-mell lookin' fer Injuns er prairie fires er both to oncet.

203

"Lookit the cache I got in this here wagon," sez Pete, disgusted.

Some feller jerks the canvas off careless-like and sez he, "My God, Pete! Where ya git it?"

"I see the magpies a circlin' aroun' over by the creek bank and thinks I it's mebbe that red heifer I lost a while back, so I hitches up this ole spotted limb of Satan and goes over for a look-see. Found this —— carkis."

"Ain't it that ole bum we run out o'town last week?"

"The same," agrees Pete. "What you fellers aim to do with him?"

"It's yore find, Pete," some smart-alec ventures.

"Yeah? Well, I ain't settin' up no undertakin' joint and I reckon it's up to the leadin' citizens o' this town to plant this bo."

"Pore seed," sez another, jokingly.

"Plant him where the soil is rocky so's he can't take no root."

"No, ya don't," sez I. "If I have to do any diggin' we'll plant him down by the river bank where the soil is loost."

"Jokin' aside," sez Ezry Hilter, "we got to bury this feller fer the good of the community and the sooner the better."

So we rustled up a couple spades and a half-dozen of us boys clumb in the back of the wagon along with the corpse, sittin' on the edge of the wagon box three on a side, right where them plumes waved from today, and we set out.

A little piece down the road we met up with Father Champlain, an old-time Missioner among the Injuns, and he had it all doped out that it wan't more'n right he should go along and say a word fer the pore soul, and nobody offerin' no objections, he clumb up 'longside Pete and the cavalcade perceded.

Up to the time the Father jined us and called our 'tention to't we hadn't none of us saw the pitiful side of the thing, the pore chap dyin' all alone and far away from all his kin like he done, and we shore wanted to do the proper thing, fer as we knew; so when one of the fellers suggested singin', we talked it over and decided on "The Cowboy's Lament," bein's 'twas the only thing we all knew clean to the end. We sang it hearty, if not so tuneful, to the accompaniment of the rattle of the wheels. We figgered we might's well get it off our chest as we went along to save time later.

We selected a nice green spot down by the river and had it all hollered out when who should come tearin' out from town but old Louie Hoffman. He was a spurrin' his hoss and wavin' his arms as fur off as we could spot him and we sort of helt up perceedin's to hear what he had to say.

"Stop it! Stop it!" he yells, as soon as he come into earshot and Lord only knows how long afore that. "This here is my propity and you ain't goin' to plant no stiff right where I aims to set my house."

We tried to argy with him and tried to talk him into settin' his house a mite to one side, but he swore a blue streak it wouldn't make no manner of difference, 'cause his wife would always remember it was there ever' time he wanted to come up town after dark. O' course we see his side o' it right off, and we heaved the bo back into the wagon and pulled over agin the hill.

This time we hadn't got more'n fairly started to diggin' when Ezry recclected we was right where Sid Willis had staked out a homestead claim the day before and he mightn't take kindly to us fellers doin' the fust plantin'. We hadn't went down fer yet and was plum willin' to be reasonable accommodatin', more especial as Sid was inclined to be a bit hasty hisself.

Havin' tried both extremes we decided to strike a happy medium and selected a spot in the exact center of the valley. We was just unloaded and ready fer action when a young chap comes abustin' out o' a tent clost by and sez he, "What do you birds think you are a doin' here, anyways? Can't you see them there stakes amarkin' the progress of civilization? This here spot is the future roadbed of the Great Northern Railway. This ain't no place to start a cemetery."

Ezry scratched his head and grinned round at us friendly like he always done when we got in a jackpot together.

"Boys," sez he, "I dunno how you feel about it, but these here hindrances we've met up with look to me like the workin' of Providence tryin' to learn us pore ignoramuses that we can't go round plantin' people promiscuous-like. 'Tain't right, so to speak, and 'tain't decent. Sposin' 'twas some kin of ourn, how do you spose we'd feel then, huh? What we gotta do is stake out a bonofido buryin' ground and when that there railroad goes through this valley there won't be ary acre of land that ain't valleable to somebody. What do you fellers think of stakin' her up there on the bench? That hain't nothin' but grazin land and pore at that."

Ezry should a knowed fer I and him had rode it many a time fer stray dogies when we was both workin' fer the Bar B outfit. So that's what we done, and we buried that hobo right where yore Hillside Cemetery stands today. I see they've made out to dig a well and got some fair-sized trees agrowin', but what struck me all of a heap was the prosprous farms and well-cultivated wheat fields that clean surround the place and stretch out as fer as eye can see on that tract of land we thought was plum wuthless. That's the Progress of Civilization, I s'pose, but it's crowdin' too clost fer us old-timers and we're movin' over the border into unexplored country, like Jim done, one by one."

# Theatricals at Fort Shaw, Montana, 1874–75

## Agnes B. Chowen

WHEN SHE SENT THIS MANUSCRIPT to *Frontier* (Vol. XII, No. 4, p. 303) in 1932, the author wrote: "I got my material by living it, being one of the six [Boll] children, the youngest of the girls. My sister Hermine, my brother Theodore, and I attended our first school at Fort Shaw." Her book, *Living Wild*, principally for children, tells of the sojourn of the Boll family in the West.

Fort Shaw was an infantry post established "as a military post protecting travelers on the Mullan Road and settlers in the Sun Valley from Blackfeet raiders." It was on the Sun River, which the Indians called the Great Medicine Road to the Buffalo. It became "the social center of a large area; the first professional stage performance in Montana was given on this stage" in a building 125 feet long. (*Montana: A State Guide Book* [New York, The Viking Press, 1939], p. 268.)

ON A PRETTY STREAM in the foothills of the Montana Rockies slumbers old Fort Shaw, at one time one of our country's most important frontier posts in the West, built on the historic Helena-Benton stage route to protect settlers from the Indians, and especially to protect from lawless white men the big shipments of gold and the hundreds of thousands of valuable furs that were hauled to Fort Benton to be sent down the Missouri River to St. Louis.

Fort Shaw was named in honor of Robert Gould Shaw, colonel of the Fifty-fourth Massachusetts, first regiment of colored troops from a free state that was mustered into the United States service. On anniversary days the colored people of Boston carry floral offerings to the Shaw memorial on Beacon Hill, a relief bronze

207

by Saint-Gaudens, over which the sculptor is said to have lingered lovingly for more than fourteen years. More impressive, though, to the westerner is the memorial almost across the continent in the shape of this isolated fort, fast fading from the sight and memory of man.

Fort Shaw was established in June, 1867, under Major William Clinton and was named Camp Reynolds. Two months later the name was changed to Fort Shaw. To General John Gibbon, in command from 1870 to 1878, is due the great improvement that raised the fort to its highest point of beauty and efficiency. His irrigation ditch, brought from Sun River, about seven miles above the post, gave the yellow-gray monotone of fort site and environment flower gardens, green lawns, beautiful trees, and many acres of luscious vegetables.

One day the wife of General Gibbon was returning after a visit to Helena, and being obliged to stop in the Prickly Pear Canyon for ambulance repairs saw a house which she had not noticed before and went to it to ask for a drink of water. The lady of the house opened the door, and Mrs. Gibbon, with her first glance at the woman and her long-haired, smooth-faced doctor-husband, who was painting local scenes in water colors, realized that they were people entirely out of their natural sphere. The conversation soon revealed that they were actors of European birth who had been persuaded by a relative to come to Montana during the gold rush. They hoped to return to the States the next summer. There were six children, the oldest a girl in her teens and a clever actress.

Fort Shaw had a theater in which the soldiers amused themselves and the settlers of the surrounding country, with minstrel shows, variety performances, farces, and an occasional drama. Before her call was half over Mrs. Gibbon had decided to bring the Boll family to the fort for at least one season of professional theatricals, realizing the advantage of having real women in the plays instead of pretty-faced soldiers who spoke in falsetto when wearing the petticoats.

The Bolls were overjoyed at again having what was meat and

208

dessert to them, and the visitor was hardly out of sight continuing her journey before Mr. Boll was unpacking a trunk into which he had thrown a few plays and costumes while packing to leave Chicago for the West. At the time they had laughingly remarked that the properties might serve at least to stampede buffaloes or hypnotize Indians. And the fact that during the Seminole war a band of Indians had captured a company of strolling players, killed some, appropriated their costumes, and, arrayed as Othello, Macbeth, Romeo, Iago, and others, rode in high glee back and forth in front of the fort where the surviving actors found refuge, did not in the least deter the Bolls from joyously embracing the opportunity to act in the wilderness at the very time when Sitting Bull and his cohorts were in the ferment of hostility that culminated in the Custer horror.

True, the Bolls never had acted in English, but that fact brought no pause. Mr. Boll began at once to translate some of his best German plays, hoping to have one, starring Ida May, ready for the opening performance.

Letters brought by the regular stage kept them informed of the progress of their dwelling, which was being built against one side of the theater and was to consist of two spacious rooms, like the theater proper built of slabs and other rough lumber hauled from a sawmill on the Missouri River thirty-five miles away. The officers and soldiers were doing their utmost to further the scheme. In due time the ambulances from the fort came and conveyed the Bolls and their belongings to the new home.

This frontier theater was a great barnlike structure, 125 feet long, with a stage measuring 24 by 35 feet. It was unfinished, unpainted, and unfloored, but had this advantage over the early theaters of Shakespeare—nowhere was it open to the weather. All the front seats and two additional rows to the right were reserved for officers and their guests. Before every performance fresh sawdust was sprinkled in front of these seats and in the main aisle from the door to the stage. Kerosene lamps, large and small, with reflectors, furnished the light. The footlights consisted of flat lamps set in a row where they lighted the orchestra as well as the proscenium. When melodramatic dimness was needed a signal was given the leader and the entire orchestra rose like one man and turned the wicks down to the blue. In the same way light was restored.

The price of reserved seats was one dollar; other seats were four and six bits, and were sold to the soldiers on credit, the first sergeant of every company keeping a list of those in his company who attended the performance and, when the paymaster came, deducting the amount due the theater from each man's roll and giving it to the manager.

The music, in charge of the post's bandmaster, was excellent, he being one part German and three parts music—German music at that.

The Boll's living room, which led directly to the stage by two low steps, served as dressing room for the women and Mr. Boll, though the latter did most of his dressing in the kitchen.

Fort Shaw was at the height of its well-being in 1874, and on their arrival the Bolls found the theater managed by a man of superior stage knowledge, having in his youth been under the personal training of the famous Lydia Thompson.[1] He was now "premiere danseuse" and "leading lady" of the organization, which was officially known as the Fort Shaw Dramatic Association. He and all the others gladly ceded to Mr. Boll the leadership and received him with open bottles.

Every evening directly after supper the living room began to fill with actors and other satellites of the profession until not a foot of seating space could be found. Everybody sang, regardless of voice. The songs in vogue then were "Annie Laurie," "Mary of Argyle," "Shells of the Ocean," "Come All of Ye Young Drivers," "The Dreary Black Hills," "The Cold, Chilly Winds of December," "Good Old Colony Days," darky songs, and others. The cowboy had not yet arrived. Jokes and riddles were extreme-

---

[1] A British actor-manager, noted for her beauty and her daring costumes. In New York her chorus girls began interest in leg shows and her company started American burlesque. (Bernard Sobel [ed.], *The Theatre Handbook and Digest of Plays* [New York, Crown Publishers, 1940]).

ly popular. When tattoo sounded, the visitors departed, for a little later all lights had to be out in the fort.

The Bolls were the first professional actors to appear at the fort, and their coming was heralded by word of mouth and handbills, distributed all over the territory. Mr. Boll could not complete the translation of his favorite play in time, so "Ingomar, the Barbarian" was selected for the opening performance.

Everything possible had been done to make the first performance an outstanding affair. Early in the day the heterogeneous collection of rigs from plain and mountain began to encircle the theater premises like flies round spilled molasses, and at night the house was packed to overflowing.

As expected, the music was unusually good. Mr. Boll as Ingomar was in his element, and Mrs. Boll looked very pretty as Parthenia, wearing a white Grecian garment of flowing folds, a bunch of scarlet flowers on one shoulder, and a broad white bandeau holding her dark ringlets in place. The slight foreign accent added interest to the text. Many plays were later put on in which Ida May vivaciously played the ingenue or soubrette parts until the tragedy of her first love-romance saddened her. Many of the soldiers were in love with her.

Among the odd people who attended the first play by the Bolls was a nondescript individual who probably never before had seen a theatrical performance. "Ingomar" moved him ecstatically. He was bound to give Mr. Boll a token that would make the giver remembered always. It happened that his one earthly possession was an ordinary mule with an extraordinary bray, that started with a long-drawn breath as though he were going to sneeze, then changed to the wail of a steam calliope, and ended in wet, human sobs. This creature the man humbly presented to Mr. Boll—handed it over the footlights like a laurel wreath, as it were. The recipient became greatly embarrassed. But the actors about him were equal to the occasion and accepted for him with cheers, then straightway named the animal Ingomar. The donor went wild with delight and took the whole male cast of the play out to celebrate.

Ingomar became the pet of the fort, the soldiers taking turns at caring for him. He wallowed in crusts of bread from barracks kitchens, and in potatoes and other food, varied by an occasional surreptitiously secured measure of oats, depending on who was on duty for the day at the government stables. While all delighted in feeding, currying, roaching, and otherwise ornamenting Ingomar, no one presumed on Mr. Boll's right as owner, much to the latter's sorrow; for Ingomar the Popular became the bane of the Boll family and might have been returned to his owner had they known where to find him or even his name.

The wily beast knew perfectly well who was responsible for him at the post, and when the messes at the barracks were closed for the night, or he had been emphatically ejected from the premises for helping himself to unguarded provender, he wandered disconsolately around the theater building for hours, and on reaching the open windows behind which the Bolls were reposing opened that terrible bray duct of his. He had a trick of lifting the cover of the water barrel, and his persistent rubbing against it often made Mr. Boll spring up and look for a whip, which he never had. The hogsheads used for household water were the erstwhile containers of whisky, and for a long time retained a strong odor of the liquor, giving a piquant flavor to many things cooked in it, and almost making a highball of the drinking water.

When the water barrel was finally hopelessly closed to Ingomar, he developed a fondness for the parade ground, because the little gardens in front of the officers' quarters were not always well guarded at night, and the recently planted trees around the parade ground had luscious grass springing up near them. In the daytime the soldiers on duty did their quickest to get him out of sight before he should be seen, but Ingomar was hard to manage, after being so much favored. In despair the guard would hasten to Mr. Boll and inform him that his mule was on the parade ground again, and Mr. Boll, as distressed as the soldier, would lead Ingomar for miles into the hills. But always on his return he found Ingomar at the fort ahead of him, making

212

straight for the forbidden spot. It did no good to picket him, as he was wise about untying himself and gnawing the rope or pulling up the picket pin.

One Sunday afternoon when the elite of the fort were congregated on the porches, in holiday attire and atmosphere, to listen to the band concert on the parade ground, Ingomar unexpectedly appeared on the scene and marching straight to the flagstaff began to rub his bites. That was the last of his offenses on the parade ground.

In spite of all rules and prohibitions, the soldiers could always get whisky at one or the other of two places in opposite directions and about five miles from the Fort. Their credit was good for the amount left after their legitimate debts were paid. So when Mr. Boll decided to put on "Ten Nights in a Barroom," there was some hesitation among those who knew that though the Seventh Infantry had won titles of "crack" regiment, "gallant," "warring," it was also noted for its "fighting" members, and "Ten Nights" was a strictly temperance play. However, it was considered high-class melodrama by rural audiences in the East, and Mr. Boll put it on for its possible moral effect.

His daughter Minnie, the most talented of the Boll children, played the part of Mary Morgan. Besides her talented acting she had a sweet singing voice, and her hair curled naturally.

The house was filled to capacity, and Mr. Boll experienced the surprise of his career when he saw this gathering of fighting men, coming red-handed from an Indian battle, sitting soundlessly absorbed in every word spoken in the play. There was little applause, so intense was the attention, and the silence gave Mr. Boll and Minnie better opportunity to bring out the strong points of the play.

She sang "Father, dear father, come home with me now"—one verse just before her entrances in the first three acts. When, at the end of the third verse, she staggered onto the scene with blood covering her face after having supposedly been struck by the bottle hurled at her miserable father, a concerted move of ominous sound sent a tremor of apprehension through the actors

213

and spectators, and Mr. Boll with a simple but imperative gesture quelled it and proceeded with the play. A decided snicker was audible in response to the swift ducking behind the bar of Slade.

But when the next scene revealed the interior of Mary's home with her lying on a white little bed and having a white bandage around her forehead, the silence was so absolute that one could hear Ingomar rubbing against the water barrel, and it remained so until she whispered, "Come nearer, father, I don't want mother to hear—it would make her feel so bad. I am not going to get well, I'm going to die." Then came unrestrained sounds, like the closing notes of Ingomar's bray, and Mr. Boll beamed with satisfaction and relief.

The next day the sutler did a tremendous business in dress goods and trinkets, and from every building, be it barracks, stable, bakery, tailor shop, or officers' quarters, came the subdued verses of "Father, dear father, come home with me now." Soon the whole Boll family, except Mr. Boll and the oldest boy, Theodore, blossomed out in new calico dresses all alike, for the soldiers, unknown to one another, had bought dresses for Minnie from the same bolt of material, because it was the brightest in the store.

The oft-repeated declaration of Sitting Bull that he would not stay on the reservation, that the government had no right to interfere with him, that the country belonged to him and his people, and that he had the right to go where he pleased and do what he pleased, had so inflamed his followers that white people were being molested to a degree where the government had to take drastic measures. This resulted in the first retaliatory move against these Indians that opened the terrible Sioux war.

Early in the spring the Sun River valley was thrown into a ferment of excitement and fear, for the Piegans and Blackfeet lost no time in harassing the settlers, who were ordered to form a protective association and be in readiness to flee to the Sun River crossing where the fortifications were being strengthened and enlarged.

When General Gibbon and three-fourths of his men departed

for the battle front, the Bolls realized that they must leave for the East if leaving were still possible. With a small escort they reached Fort Benton, where they soon secured passage to St. Louis on one of the Missouri River steamboats, and made the trip without interference from Indians.

The Fort Shaw soldiers reached the scene of the Custer disaster the day following its occurrence. The field was strewn with stripped and terribly mutilated bodies of their fellows, which they buried as quickly as possible. The body of Custer was not stripped or mutilated. He was found lying fully uniformed, his hands folded before him, his hat drawn low over his face. There were two bullet holes in his body, which was sent to Bismarck and later to the military cemetery of West Point.

Years later Ida May realized the dream of her life—to visit the scene of her youthful romance. Unknowingly, she chose the unfortunate time when Fort Shaw had been abandoned as a military post and the government had not yet made use of it otherwise. She went by automobile from the nearest town and was plunged into a spell of bewildered pain. At the crossing she began to strain her eyes for the flag floating from the tall pole over a square of pretty buildings surrounded by trees.

"That can't be Fort Shaw!" she exclaimed, as, at the foot of the well-known bluffs, she beheld a group of low, gray buildings huddling together like a band of sheep in the rain.

"It sure is," the chauffeur replied.

"But—but where is the theater—with the little house attached? It was the largest building at the fort, and the first to be seen when coming up the road."

"Oh, that! It was burned several years ago."

Before she could say anything more, the car came to an abrupt stop, and the man exclaimed, "Here we are, on the parade ground. Do you want to get out?"

Dazedly she nodded, repeating, "The parade ground! The parade ground!" She alighted and turned around several times, glad that no one was by to witness the bitterness of her disillusion. Not a sign of life anywhere; fences and buildings torn away and the prairie entering. And this was Fort Shaw, the very center of her universe when those dismal buildings across the southern border of the parade ground were neatly painted and well-kept quarters of officers, having airy porches and pretty flower gardens to tempt Ingomar; when the popular boardwalk, especially at evening, was animated by beautiful women modishly gowned, and distinguished-looking men resplendent in uniforms with gold lace, gold cord, and epaulets, as they went to a ball in the long building beside the school, or promenaded in the direction from which, through open windows, came sounds of laughter, lively conversation, music, interspersed with clink of glass, china, and silverware, foretelling a gay function.

Now, more than one-half of the boardwalk was missing, the remaining part broken and disintegrating; the porches were out of shape and sagging to the ground; portions of fences were strewn about, and the gardens had left not a reminder.

The barracks opposite the officers' quarters were heartbreaking—lumber torn away everywhere, roofs caving in, adobe falling out of the cracks and mingling with the general devastation usually wrought by range cattle and horses. The buildings that had lost their doors and windows looked at Ida with hollow, questioning eyes, as though asking why she had come. She, too, asked whether that urge through the years had persisted just for this.

The bandmaster's neat cottage had completely disappeared, as had also McKnight's sutler store, which was post office and stage station as well. Germania Hall, beside the theater, where the band used to practice and give concerts, gone as though it never had existed. After reflecting on the past for half an hour, Ida May told the chauffeur to take her to the cemetery. There she strewed the graves of remembered ones with wild flowers and read inscriptions that made the tears come.

On returning to the city she passed again through the fort. The smoke-reddened sun was sinking rapidly in the limitless benchland stretching northwest, its last beam momentarily illumining the ghost of Fort Shaw, already drawing night's gray blanket across its feet as though to hasten her departure. At the foot of the bluffs a shadowy coyote was pausing, listening wistfully to the plaintive cry of a curlew skimming low till the broad bow of its wings dissolved into nothing. Then all was still save the talking night wind, hurrying up the valley.

# HOMESTEADERS

# Clearing Sagebrush[1]

## Irene Welch Grissom

It stood alone, the crude low shack,
Tarred paper walls, a blot of black
Against a vast and tawny plain
Men called *The Place of Little Rain*.
The dusk was shot with crimson light
From piles of sagebrush burning bright.
The man who watched, with eager gaze,
The flaming sparks and purple haze,
All day had torn the fibers strong
And raked them into windrows long.
The acrid smoke was prophecy
Of wondrous changes soon to be.

He did not see the arid land
With weary miles of desert sand,
The scanty grass and prickly pear,
That fought to hold a footing there.
He caught the flashing silver gleam
Of ripples dancing on a stream,
Now gaily winding all about
Through fields of green, then in and out
Of nodding grain; and everywhere
The water went the earth was fair
With growing things . . . The embers died . . .
The barren plain was dark and wide.

[1] *Frontier*, Vol. IX, No. 3, p. 219.

# Homestead Days in Montana

## Pearl Price Robertson

THIS ACCOUNT portrays the hardships early settlers met and, with indomitable spirit, overcame. The Robertsons were living on a ranch near Ronan, Montana, when in 1933 Mrs. Robertson sent this manuscript to *Frontier* (Vol. XIII, No. 3, p. 215). For contrast with a ranch-woman's life only a quarter of a century later, see Mrs. Glenn's "Journal of a Ranch Wife, 1932–1935" below. It is striking even though the later account is of depression days.

YES, WE LIVED ON A HOMESTEAD ONCE, not so many years ago. Back in 1910 it was—twenty-three years ago in March—that we made our grand adventure by coming west to live on one. We were young then, Alec and I, and life was full of promise. We had been married four years, but somehow had never been able to reconcile ourselves to the bread-and-butter sort of existence led by the people in our native state—so smug and safe and comfortable, the same yesterday, today, and tomorrow—you know, just being born, growing up, living and dying, all in the same cramped space. There must have been an adventurous streak in the make-up of both Alec and me. Anyway, a restlessness of spirit made us both long to get away, though neither of us ever quite admitted that longing.

At the time of our marriage, four years before, there was nothing we wanted so much as a home and a baby. We had no capital other than our love for each other—very much of that—youth, inexperience, unshaken faith in the future, a willingness to work. The home always came first in our plans and was as beautiful as any dream home could be, with wide lawns, gardens, and orchards, great barns and fertile fields—a farm built up out of the raw land by the work of our own hands, a place to create beauty, to build projects, to change visions to reality; a haven and a refuge never to be completed throughout the years—we did not wish ever to come to the place where we could sit down with folded hands, saying, "It is finished; there is nothing more we can add."

But somehow things did not work out the way we had dreamed them; in three and a half years we had three pink-and-white, golden-haired babies; and our only home was a rented one—a little farm which we tended faithfully, partly from sheer joy at digging in the soil and watching green things grow, and partly for means to provide baby shirts and little shoes and other things so necessary to the proper bringing up of the cherubs.

When we learned, somewhat by accident, of Uncle Sam's free homestead land in Montana, it seemed such a happy solution to our problem of acquiring a home of our very own that we decided to avail ourselves of the opportunity at once. But well-meaning friends and relatives had heard many lurid tales of Indian depredations, of outlawry, and of a rigorous Montana climate, and tried to dissuade us from so rash an undertaking. My own ideas of Montana had been gleaned from much that had been written of "the wild and woolly West," and, I must confess, I myself had thought of it as only a barren waste covered with cactus and sagebrush, inhabited by rattlesnakes and blood-thirsty savages. But the more we investigated Montana's home-making possibilities, the more enthusiastic we became, so that in the end nothing could deter us from our purpose. Hand in hand with Alec, I would have gone to the ends of the earth seeking a home!

Our coming into touch with a job on a Montana ranch proved the deciding factor, for to us the opportunity seemed providential. Just a little apprehensive, perhaps, but prepared for the worst and highly resolved to meet unflinchingly whatever befell, we came in March, 1910, two tenderfoot strangers from the East and three babies, to the new little town of Hobson, Montana, which had sprung into being a year or two before when the railroad had been built through the Judith Basin. Any subconscious dread I might have had of lurking danger was quickly and completely dispelled when we were met at the station by our employer and his four-year-old daughter. It was all so different from what I was expecting! Everything about the little town was clean and new; over it and the grassy benchlands stretching away to the foot of the mountains on every side lay the warm spring sunshine, and round about us rose the mountains, dark and blue, like a great barricade shutting us in from the outside world. How near the mountains looked, to my wondering eyes, as if I could walk out and lay my hand upon them! And yet I was told they were fifteen to twenty miles away. We were so thrilled with our new environment, so charmed with the frank, openhearted friendliness of the Western people!

The town and vicinity were in the throes of a real estate boom; wheat farming on the benchlands had been a huge success; everyone seemed optimistic, prosperous, happy. We found everywhere bustle and activity, a growing and prosperous community, peopled by a progressive citizenship. Yet there was so much which to us was new and unusual that we were like two eager children faring forth for adventure, delighted with everything we saw.

We went to work on the Philbrook Ranch, where the old deserted town of Philbrook stood on the banks of the Judith River. Straggling along either side of the one street, in varying stages of dilapidation, were the buildings of the old ghost town; the yards were choked with dry weeds and littered with rusty cans, discarded bedsprings and broken bits of furniture; in the corner, where the road turned sharply and became the street, stood the old hotel, containing fifteen rooms. This building served us for a dwelling. Across the spring run was the old livery stable, which became the ranch barn. Close on the bank of the crystal Judith stood the Clegg building, once a saloon and roadhouse. Across the river a community hall built of logs, where school was held, and opposite it a little frame church where "Brother Van," noted pioneer preacher, held services twice each month.

Very pleasant were the days we spent in this place. The owner of the ranch kept open house, buyers and traders came and went every day, and the personnel of the ranch hands changed every few weeks, so that we were constantly meeting new people. Delightful to me was the innate politeness of the ranch hands; crude and uncultured though many of them were, their courtesy and deference to me, the only woman on the ranch, could not have been exceeded anywhere. Delightful, too, were the stories of life and adventure, sometimes highly embellished, I suspect, for my especial benefit, when the men "swapped lies" around the table, or when we sat around the fire in the big kitchen in the evenings.

In a few weeks Alec went in search of a homestead. I could scarcely wait for his return, so eager was I. Pride of possession and joy of ownership seized me when I learned that we had claim to 320 acres on Lonesome Prairie in northern Chouteau County, to us the first step in the accomplishment of our cherished dream. Long we sat by the fire that night of Alec's return, as he related to me the details of his trip and described the grassy prairie stretching westward twenty-five miles or more from Big Sandy to the Marias River; how three weeks after the land opening every foot of the land had been taken for twenty miles out; how the land locator had taken him out with a party of others who would be our neighbors; of the young Norwegian and his sweetheart but lately arrived from Norway who could not speak a word of English; of the genial old German who, when he found this broad stretch of fertile soil so much to his liking, and a whole section to be had for the taking, hurried back to the telegraph office and sent this telling message to two grown-up sons and a daughter: "Come Henry; come Johnnie; come Mary; come quick!" Then Alec made the disconcerting disclosure that there were rattlesnakes on that prairie! Rattlesnakes? Dear me, wouldn't there have to be a catch in the thing somewhere? I shuddered. Oh well, there was a serpent in the Garden of Eden!

Maybe we could just disregard the rattlesnakes, at least until we got there.

Joyfully we planned every detail of our little shack and figured the cost; eagerly I longed to begin work on my beautiful garden, and spent happy hours poring over nurserymen's catalogues selecting trees and shrubs and drawing plans. Because of our limited amount of cash there could be but a few cherished plants at first, so I felt the selection of these required much thought. We planned to have a well put down on our farm at once to furnish water for our trees and plants. We had been accustomed all our lives to an abundance of water for every purpose and I had no conception of a locality where there was none.

In the spring of 1911 we prepared to move to our new home. Our household goods we shipped by local freight to Big Sandy, while the family made ready to drive overland in the wagon, taking the horses and chickens. As a protection against the weather Alec built up the back part of the wagon box and roofed it over with a little peaked roof like the gables of a house. Then to make it waterproof I brought out a strip of white oilcloth taken from the kitchen table and this he nailed in place over the roof. As neither the boards nor the oilcloth were long enough to cover the space over the driver's seat in front, it had to be left open and exposed. We felt that the whole arrangement would answer our purpose well enough, so why should we care how it looked? Like two happy children we stowed blankets, cooking utensils, and food supplies inside; two coops filled with chickens were wired to the back; a cart used as a trailer was piled with hay for the horses, and Cap, the young stallion, was tied to the rear of the trailer. As last minute touches, various pails, bags, and boxes were fastened on the outside because there was no room within.

On a cold gray morning we started out from the Philbrook Ranch and followed the rocky winding trail past the old S. S. Hobson Ranch toward Utica. The children—Willie, aged four and but recently shorn of his long golden curls, carrying his little spool wagon; Julia, scarcely three, with a cherished rag doll, and Hazel, a scant year and a half—were tucked cozily into a nest of blankets in the sheltered part of the wagon box, and I rode on the seat beside Alec. We started out gaily enough, even in the threatening weather, but the wind was so raw and cold and the jolting wagon so uncomfortable that traveling gypsy-fashion soon lost its novelty.

We had nearly reached the little inland town of Utica when the wagon struck a rock heavily, a tire flew off, and the wheel smashed. Alec groaned despairingly as he climbed down to investigate. "Now, if that isn't hell," he said when he saw the extent of the damage. "Oh, Alec, we're in luck," I cried, trying to pass over the incident lightly, "to have it happen here so close to Utica—maybe we can find a blacksmith there!" We did find one, but he was in no particular hurry to help us. We had to wait patiently. Nightfall found us still waiting, and we spent the night in our wagon, which stood in the middle of the road, exactly where the accident had occurred. But all night I lay wide-eyed listening to the chickens as they chattered discontentedly in their coops, the horses while they munched their hay and pawed restlessly, and occasionally a passing vehicle.

By noon the next day the wheel was ready. We started out once more, following the road northward toward Windham and Stanford. But repairing the broken wheel had taken eight dollars from our scanty savings and delayed us a whole day in our journey. The weather was still threatening and the wind so raw and cold that, although it was May, I suffered intensely, my hands numb and blue, my teeth chattering. When I could no longer endure the cold I crept miserably from my seat and snuggled among the blankets with the children. The mist had now thickened into a driving rain; Alec, alone on the wagon seat, drove stoically through the falling rain, occasionally whistling forlornly, or humming a bit of song to break the dreary silence, while I, crouched down in the crowded space beneath the little roof, became deathly sick from the swaying and jolting of the wagon, and for relief would climb out, white and spent, upon the wagon seat beside Alec until the rain and cold drove me once more to the sheltered wagon box. All the pleasure I had anticipated from the journey faded away beneath the strain of physical weakness and discomfort. When night overtook us in the vicinity of Stanford, it was a forlorn little party of travelers who drew the wagon up beside the walls of an unfinished building which sheltered us from the wind. There we spent the night. All through it the rain pattered down. As I lay cramped and miserable, listening to the raindrops above us, I thanked our lucky fate for the table oilcloth nailed over our little roof—we had come so near to starting out without a shelter of any kind!

Next morning the rain had ceased and by noon the sky had cleared. Our spirits rose accordingly. I felt cheerful, even gay, as I rode again on the seat with Alec and we talked happily together. Both he and I had been reared in the level plains country of the Mississippi Valley and were all unprepared for the rough character of some of the country through which we were to travel. Going northward from Stanford, I noticed during the afternoon a long, low line of what appeared to be the tops of chalky white bluffs coming into view in front of us. Wondering, I asked, "What can that be, Alec?"

Puzzled, he answered, "I, too, am wondering what it can be. Whatever it is, we will have to drive either through it or over it; it is quite evident we cannot drive around it."

"See that moving covered wagon?" I asked, pointing eastward, "I have been watching it for some time. It is steadily drawing nearer to the road which we are following, and I believe will soon come into this trail."

So it proved. Late in the afternoon the two wagons came together at the point where the trails joined on the brink of the badlands which flank the Arrow River. Never had I seen a natural formation resembling the badlands, so that, coming upon this abruptly and unsuspectingly, I was mutely astonished at the spectacle. Looking down into this great gash in the earth's surface, worn by the erosion of centuries, beyond the weird, fantastic forms of butte, bluff, and canyon, I could see the river far below shining through the cottonwoods. It seemed to me like a picture from an unknown world.

The stranger who drove the other wagon was courteous and friendly, as Alec inquired about the route through the badlands. "Have you a roughlock?" asked the stranger; but Alec, inexperienced, plains-bred man that he was, had not even an ordinary brake on his wagon. The stranger told him that between us and the river below was a two-mile stretch of steep and extremely dangerous road, built and used by freighters, so narrow in places that occasionally a wagon went over the brink. "But," he said to Alec's look of dismay, "we will take my wagon down first and then bring the chains back for yours."

So I, with the babies, waited anxiously at the top while they took the first wagon down. I prayed silently and with bated breath as they took the second wagon containing the children and me over that dangerous trail; but happily for us all, we landed at the bottom without mishap. It was a merry little party which camped that night under the cottonwoods at the water's edge. The bright full moon came up over the bluffs and smiled down at us as we ate our supper from the top of a bale of hay, which, covered with a laundered flour sack, served for a table. The obliging stranger shared our supper and our camp that night, but in the morning he left us and we never saw him again. Always I feel it was the compassionate intervention of an all-wise Providence which delayed us at Utica and so timed our journey as to be coincident with that of the stranger who helped us, all unprepared as we were, over this dangerous bit of the trail.

Our way now lay along the valley, through sagebrush and prairie-dog towns, past the low rambling house of the Milner Ranch, overhung by the shadow of Square Butte and supplied with water from the mountainside above; then out upon the bench again we followed the trail past the spot where the town of Geraldine now stands. A railroad has since been built through this section and towns have sprung up, but at the time of our journey there were on the site which is now Geraldine only a lone ranch house and sheep corrals known to us as the Collins-Brady Ranch. This and the winding trail across the prairie were the only signs of human habitation we saw in all that day's travel—

just sky and earth, the ribbon of road, and our solitary wagon—until in the evening we reached a dilapidated old building, once a pretentious structure, known locally as the Halfway House. Here we camped. The following morning the trail led us over Frenchman's Ridge, down through the rocky Shonkin Canyon, and across the Missouri River bridge into Fort Benton.

It was a Sunday morning and the rain had been steadily falling since daybreak. Because of the rain I rode in the shelter of the wagon box. I was very weak and ill, and painfully aware of my own and the children's untidiness. Alec parked the wagon near the ruins of the historic fort and went up town to make inquiries about the road. I crept out upon the wagon seat and sat there miserably in the falling rain. The cool drops on my face heartened and revived me, but I shivered with the dampness and chill. Willie, my first-born, came and perched on the seat beside me, and tried in his babyish way to cheer me. We must have presented a sorry appearance, but I was too sick to care. A man came out of a house across the way, walked past us twice, looking at us curiously, and then came over to the wagon. Imagine my surprise when a hearty voice said, "Hand down that little fellow and come on over to the house; we have a fire there and a hot dinner. Come on over and have Sunday dinner with us!"

"Oh, no," I protested, "thanks a lot, but we've been traveling all morning through the rain and mud, and really we are too dirty to go into anyone's house!"

"Oh, what's a little mud? Come right on," he insisted, and carried the children to the house, so that I could do little else but follow. When Alec returned to the wagon, he was surprised to find us gone, but he, too, was invited to the house.

"Do I know you?" Alec asked, astonished.

"I don't know if you do or not," was the answer, "but it doesn't make any difference. Come on over and have dinner!"

How much we appreciated the warmth and cheer of that hospitable home, none but a chilled and weary traveler can ever know. Every detail of that dinner will remain in my memory while life shall last.

As we left Fort Benton we followed the valley of the Teton until we reached the point where the Marias empties into the Missouri. Here we camped and again the rain fell in a drenching downpour. All night long and a part of the next day it beat upon us. The next morning our team mired down in the slippery mud of the canyon, and we had to pay a man two dollars from our fast-diminishing supply of cash to bring his team and pull our wagon out. When we reached Big Sandy we found it the scene of much activity as busy settlers came and went, hauling out lumber for new little shacks, posts and wire for fences, and machinery to break the sod.

Facing westward from Big Sandy we drove twenty miles to the quarter-section which was to be our home on the wide wind-swept prairie; and just before sundown we stopped on the spot where our shack was to be. Westward lay the Goosebill, long and low; northward the Sweetgrass Hills on the Canadian border, crowned with snow; behind us the Bear Paws made a jagged line against the sky; far to the south in the blue distance loomed the Highwoods. The sun shone on the grass sparkling with raindrops; the wild sweet peas nodded their yellow heads in friendly greeting. As I looked across the rolling expanse of prairie, fired with the beauty of a Montana sunset, I sent up a little prayer of thanksgiving from my heart for this, our very first home. Only a rectangle of prairie sod, raw and untouched by the hand of man, but to us it was a kingdom.

I loved the prairie, even while I feared it. God's country, the old-timers called it. There is something about it which gets a man—or a woman. I feared its relentlessness, its silence, and its sameness, even as I loved the tawny spread of its sun-drenched ridges, its shimmering waves of desert air, the terrific sweep of the untrammeled wind, burning stars in a midnight sky. Still in my dreams I can feel the force of that wind, and hear its mournful wail around my shack in the lonely hours of the night. . . .

The rollicking wind promptly bowled our tent over, that first night at our new home, so again we slept in our wagon. The only water we had for any purpose was contained in a gallon jug, and we did not know how soon nor where we could get more. Consequently, we drank sparingly and in little sips, and bathed our hands and faces in the dewy grass of the morning. We never could keep the tent up—but what matter? Our neighbor lent us the use of a little shack across the way until our own shack was built. There we camped the first few weeks. We had no stove or firewood that first day—no, I had not learned to burn cow chips yet—that was an innovation which came later.

Alec went back to town to bring out our first load of lumber, and the children and I put on our wraps and, to keep out the chill, huddled beneath our blankets in the shack. It took most of the day and well into the night to make the trip into town and return with a load, so in the evening I hung up a lighted lantern to guide Alec on his return to the shack.

At first we set the kitchen range out of doors, but rain and disagreeable weather made this impractical; then we moved it within and, since there was no hole in the roof, stuck the pipe out through the little hole in the side which served for a window. The stove and the folding bed filled almost the entire space. There was no room for table or chairs, so mostly when mealtime came we stood and ate from the plates which we held in our hands. The walls were of unmatched lumber which let in the wind and rain, but at least over us there was a roof. We were real westerners now, and could not shrink from anything which was to be our portion.

The greatest hardship of all was the scarcity of water. The first settlers had dug wells, which eighty to ninety feet down were still dry as dust. At first we were filled with dismay to find no water anywhere. Sometimes we had none even to drink until Alec bought a barrel which he filled with water each day when in town and brought home on top of his load of lumber. We had to stint ourselves extremely for water for bathing, and as for our clothing I washed it a few pieces at a time in the washbasin, because there was no water to fill the tub! We located some water holes and coulees where occasionally we could get water for our horses, but often we had to go many miles for it. My throat con-

stricted with pain when I thought of the well we had planned
with which I meant to irrigate my lovely dream garden. It now
seemed very remote indeed! Later a shallow well was dug in the
coulee a mile away which yielded us a small amount of water
each day.

Once that spring when we went to the coulee for water the
cattlemen were holding their last big roundup on that prairie
since the homesteaders had taken their range; they had established camp by the water hole and had just butchered a young
steer. Here was a bit of the old West about which I had read—
the branding iron on the smoldering fire, the rope corral, the
chuck wagon, the riders with wide sombreros, hairy "chaps," and
jingling spurs! While we were filling our water barrel one of the
cowboys came over and with a grand sweep of his broad hat
smilingly proffered us a piece of the freshly butchered beef.
Could he have known how much we appreciated his gift, or by
any chance have guessed how lean was the larder in the little
shack at home?

We worked happily at our building during every minute of
our spare time. I held the boards while Alec sawed and nailed
them, and in a few weeks the new shack, fourteen by twenty
feet, with two windows and a door, was ready to move into. Joyfully I worked with rugs, curtains, and other things dear to a
woman's heart, making it pretty and livable.

Alec plowed a small plot for a garden and I attempted the
disheartening task of planting it—disheartening because amid
the hard dry chunks of sod I could find no loose soil for covering
the seeds. Patiently I took up the sods one by one, and with my
hands pounded and shook soil from the matted grass roots and
carefully patted it over my seeds. But disillusionment sat heavy
upon me. As I worked the tears fell, and truly I "watered my fur-
rows with tears." No more rains came, the grass shriveled and
dried up, and shimmering heat waves danced across the landscape. The only seeds in my garden which found moisture
enough to grow were the beans, and then as soon as the seed

leaves appeared above the ground the chickens promptly snapped them off. My first garden on the homestead became only a sad memory.

How much I feared the rattlesnakes, not on my own account alone, but for the sake of my little children! I warned them repeatedly as they played about the dooryard to look out for "ugly creeping things" and to beware of buzzing noises. But we never saw any—*not one.* One day, as Alec and I walked about our so-called garden, we noticed a great black beetle shambling along among the clods and pointed it out to our little son. Imagine how I felt when the little fellow shrank back, his face pale and eyes round with fear as he gasped out, "A rattlesnake!"

Life on the homestead was becoming a serious problem to us now, for our money was all gone and food supplies almost exhausted. There was still a little flour and a bit of lard, I remember. There was no yeast or other leavening; for bread I mixed the flour with water and a little lard and baked it in small cakes. There was rice, but no sugar, so I put in a few raisins for sweetening. There was absolutely nothing else, so far as I can now recall.

Alec was faced with the necessity of leaving his family on the homestead while he went in search of work. I tried to be very brave, but my heart sank at the thought of facing life in that lonely place without Alec. Many of our neighbors, too, went away looking for work, so that I was left very much alone except when some distant settler passed by, sometimes bringing my mail and supplies. At times for days I saw no one; and then the terrifying loneliness and silence of the great prairie appalled me, and I sobbed aloud to shut out the eerie sound of the coyote's wail, or the dreary soughing of the wind beneath the eaves of my shack.

I went to the coulee a mile away each day for water, and occasionally the children and I made the trip afoot to the store and post office; but as these trips always left us all very much exhausted, we did not attempt them often. Alec wrote every week, sometimes oftener, and his letters were always a delight—long, and filled with details of his work and associations. After one of his letters came I could forget my loneliness and sing at my work for hours.

I busied my mind and my hands with homely little tasks, making over garments for the children's wear and preparing a layette for the new baby soon to come. I sighed over the layette, for mostly it was composed of clothes which my other babies had worn, and I found myself longing intensely for at least *one* new little garment for the precious darling. I had a large-sized sugar sack which had been carelessly tossed into Alec's wagon one day at the store; this I carefully ripped open, washed, bleached in the sun, and pressed. I drew threads painstakingly and made a drawn work yoke of exquisite pattern, hemstitched ruffles for the neck and sleeves, and with a deep hem at the bottom it became a dainty little dress which with a sense of deepest satisfaction I laid away in readiness for my baby's coming.

Summer waned, and the frosty mornings and the calm sunshiny days of autumn came on. Alec was to come for us soon, as he was making plans to take us to the Judith Basin where he worked, so that I might have the care of a doctor and a nurse in my hour of need. I wrote to Alec setting the date for his coming in early October, since I expected my baby in November, giving myself, or so I thought, ample time to make the trip and get rested afterward. Twenty-four hours after mailing that letter I was startled by premonitory pains of an alarming nature, and as they constantly recurred at decreasing intervals I became more and more uneasy. Could I have been mistaken in the time? Could this be approaching childbirth? Maybe if I rested quietly for a while . . . maybe, oh, maybe—no, there was no longer any doubt—my baby would arrive before the letter could reach Alec, before competent help could ever reach me! Pains oftener now, and more severe! Heaven help me now, I must think what to do!

Calmly I went about preparations; trying hard to keep a firm grip upon myself, trying hard not to become panicky. I *must* be brave; I *must* keep my head. Babies had been born before like this. Everything was all right. Oh, if I were only sure what to do!

If I only had someone—anyone, to look to for help! I watched for a little boy who occasionally rode past my shack in search of his cows which roamed the prairie, and luckily tonight he came within calling distance. "Johnnie, take this note to your mother!" "What is it, a party?" the boy asked eagerly, as he took the note. "I want your mother, I need her help. Oh, please hurry!" I gasped. The gray pony bounded forward and disappeared into the gathering dusk. As darkness came on I put the children to bed and waited tensely for the help which *must* not fail me! Prayerfully I waited, and walked the floor listening, listening—almost in despair as my need grew greater. Such a wave of relief surged over me as I heard scurrying footsteps in the darkness! My sister-in-law arrived, frightened and tearful, and Mrs. Warren, capable, motherly, master of the situation at once. An hour later my wee new daughter was born!

Call it premonition or otherwise, Alec decided to surprise me by coming home much sooner than I was expecting him, and at the same hour that I was waiting for help to come in my desperate need, he was speeding toward home as fast as a train could take him. The train pulled into Big Sandy a few minutes after midnight and Alec stepped out into the darkness without a moment's pause and set out afoot to walk the twenty miles to the shack on the great brown prairie, which held his loved ones. He arrived home soon after daybreak, to find me in bed, flushed with happiness, a newborn daughter by my side.

The children, wakened from their sleep by Alec's arrival, climbed upon him as he sat on the edge of my bed and began opening the parcels he had brought to them. Suddenly they discovered a tiny sister nestled in mother's arms, whereupon they fell upon Alec with fervent hugs and kisses, calling him "the dearest daddy in the world" for bringing them, besides new shoes and stockings, a brand-new baby sister!

The settlers of our prairie were of many kinds and classes and had hailed from many different states, both east and west, but we were all one great brotherhood. If a man had a homestead alongside the others, he was accepted by all the others without question. We helped one another; what one had, he shared with the next. If one man owned a team, his neighbor some harness, and a third one a plow, they managed a plowed strip for each of the three. Many were the makeshifts and privations which made us all kindred souls. One old man bought a boy's farm wagon in which he used to take his supplies home; another brought his things from town in a wheelbarrow; while I, truth to tell, took my baby carriage and trundled it across the prairie to bring home my sack of flour and other groceries.

Always we were handicapped by the scarcity of water. Alec spent many long hours hauling water for our livestock and for our domestic uses. We lived on the homestead during the spring and summer months; there was never money enough for us to spend a whole year there. The winters we spent in the Judith Basin in various ways and places at whatever work came to hand, but spring always found us returning like homing pigeons to the little shack on the prairie, each year putting in more crops and adding to the improvements on the farm. Many times we made the trip across country in our wagon, but later it had a canvas cover in regulation prairie schooner style, and for bad weather a stove. Once we started out, after a week of balmy weather in March, only to be overtaken by a howling blizzard. For two days we drifted with the wind and flying snow, so that the stove and fuel we had in the wagon saved us from probable freezing.

Two more boys were born to us, and then in rapid succession two more daughters. The family prospered, so that at last we could spend all our time on the homestead. We owned a car and the fourteen-by-twenty shack became a five-room cottage—but never was it the home of our youthful dreams. My lovely garden, so soul-satisfying and enchanting, was never aught but a beautiful dream—the trees we planted pined away and died for lack of water, while my flowers bent their frail heads and the brazen sun turned them into nothingness.

The war had come, bringing with it high prices for the farmer's grain, and copious rainfall had blessed the settlers' efforts with bounteous harvests. The four elevators of the prairie town were

236

kept filled to overflowing with golden grain, and every day the golden flood poured in, hundreds of wagons waiting for freight cars, so that the farmers might take turns unloading their precious cargoes. With wheat at $1.87 a bushel and granaries and bins filled to bursting, the settlers bought more land and high-priced machinery to grow more and bigger crops "to help win the war."

But the bad years came when we staked our *all* on the caprice of the weather and a wheat crop which might never be harvested. As drouth, weeds, cutworms, and hailstorms took their toll from the grain fields, the eager illuminating light of hope died out of the settlers' faces and gave place to a look of morbid apathy and despair. We looked across the broad acres of stunted, shriveled crops, dotted with Russian thistles, and the mortgages mounted higher and the bankers clamored for their interest.

Then came a year when no rains fell and no crops grew, and the bewildered settlers faced a winter with no money, no food, no clothing for their families, no feed of any kind for their livestock, no work. Dumb with despair, the men set about finding some means of providing for their families. Most of them went away to work while the women and little children stayed on in the homes, carrying on as best they might. Alec found a job on a ranch near Billings. When he went away I was left on the homestead once more without him, but this time with nine children instead of three, the youngest a baby three weeks old.

Alec sent every dollar of his wages home as fast as it was earned, yet with me the winter was one long struggle with circumstances to keep my family warmed and fed and to save our horses from starvation. Upon the horses depended our ability to put in one more crop. With the help of my twelve-year-old boy I braved the storms, waded snowdrifts to keep the horses fed, and stood upon an icy platform in below-zero weather drawing water while the horses crowded and pushed about the watering trough. Topsy, the black mare, had a young colt running with her and we decided it was best to wean the colt, so we shut him in the barn, leaving the mare outside. But the faithful mother refused to desert her offspring and took up her post just outside the barn door, calling to him in anxious whinnies or soft nickers of love. All night long she kept the vigil. Refusing to seek shelter for herself, she stood where the keen blasts of an icy wind struck with fullest force. When morning came Willie and I found her crumpled form in the snow by the barn door, frozen dead! Mother and son, we wept together over the loss of a faithful friend, while the wind ruffled the icy mane and sent little eddies of drifting snow across the frozen body. Two other horses we lost that winter and each time I felt the loss keenly, as that of a valued friend; but when spring came we still had nine left of our twelve —gaunt, shaggy creatures, covered with vermin.

The feed for my pigs gave out. When a week had gone by I thought desperately of trying to butcher the sorry little creatures. I wept over their plight, and my woman's nature quailed at the thought of undertaking the butchering alone with no help but Willie's. At last my brother-in-law and two neighbor lads came to help, but the day we set for the butchering was bitter cold with freezing blasts of snow-laden wind sweeping out of the north. Scalding and scraping the pigs was a painful task as the water cooled and changed to ice rapidly; but at last the eight of them were cleaned and scraped after a fashion and left hanging in the shed while we ate our dinner. We ate hurriedly, so as to return to our task before freezing interfered with cutting the meat into pieces for curing. But when one of the lads hurried out ahead to examine the pigs he called back, "They're frozer'n hell right now!" Stiffly swinging from the rafters, they hung like graven images carved of stone; no knife could penetrate the frozen forms. To save fuel we moved the kitchen range into the large living room—here, too, had been placed our beds—and here we carried the frozen pigs and placed them in formidable array across the dining table. They stood at various rakish angles, each firmly upon his feet, ears outspread and tails extending stiffly straight out behind, to be left until they thawed out.

I sat up late that night keeping a brisk fire burning and writing a letter to Alec. It was so cold the timbers of the house popped and the frost crept higher and ever higher up the door. The hands of the clock pointed almost to midnight. Suddenly I was startled by footsteps in the frozen snow and my name called in a familiar voice, "Open the door quick! We've a girl out here who's nearly frozen!" Hastily I opened the door and recognized Dan, a friend of the family, and another man supporting between them a slender young girl. We carried her inside, where I removed her thin shoes and rubbed her aching hands and feet. When she was warmed and resting comfortably Dan turned about, glanced at my sleeping children in the cots, and then at the frozen pigs upon the table. "My God!" he said.

The girl—a homesick child—had been attending school in Big Sandy, and longing to spend the Thanksgiving vacation with home folks, had attempted a twenty-five-mile ride atop a load of coal, when the thermometer stood at thirty degrees below zero. I took her into bed with me for the rest of the night and the men went to a neighbor's.

Thanksgiving morning dawned clear and cold; the morning sun shone across a white and frozen world lying crisp and still in the crinkling frosty air. The Russian thistles had caught the drifts and each was a hummock of glittering snow—no sign of life in the white expanse except for the smoke which curled lazily upward from the housetops dotting the prairie. My little guest of the night before continued her journey that day and reached home in time to partake of Thanksgiving dinner with home folks.

One of my greatest problems was bringing supplies from town, especially hay and fuel. Never having money enough at a time to buy any great quantity, I lived in abject terror of exhausting my supply before I could get more. Alec wrote: "If your fuel gives out, burn the fence posts, tear boards from the barn and burn them, burn *anything* about the place—don't take any chances of freezing!" Sometimes when food supplies ran low I was driven to parceling out our meals in bits, and at times the pinched, ill-nourished look on the faces of my children made me sick with apprehension.

Once in the coldest weather it was imperative that we get

supplies from town. I hesitated to send my boy, small and frail as he was, but there seemed no other way. Pridefully, manfully, he set out with the team and sled, in company with his uncle, to bring hay, coal, potatoes, flour, and sugar—there was little else we could afford to buy. The roads were piled with frozen drifts so that bringing out a loaded sled was a slow and tedious matter, and the boy, inadequately clothed and with ragged overshoes many sizes too large, walked stumblingly through the snow-drifts all the long way from town behind the slow-moving sled. It was hours after dark before I heard the jingling of the harness and the creaking runners of the returning sleds. The boy reached home shaking with cold and reeling with exhaustion.

As I worked over the worn-out child, rubbing with snow his numbed hands and frostbitten feet, my mother's heart swelled with fierce, hot rebellion over the fate which imposed such hardship upon so young a child. I made a swift, determined resolve not to let my children be crushed by the sordidness of circumstances, to secure for them their just measure of the beauty and brightness of life, and to make up to them by every means at my command for the privations they now endured.

December brought a chinook and the snow disappeared with the warm southwest wind like ice beneath a July sun. Water filled the puddles, overflowed the ponds, and rushed in torrents down the coulees. No longer need I worry about hauling water, for the rest of that season at least!

Christmas Day the neighbors gathered at my home for a community Christmas dinner. None had much, but all brought something, and assembled, it seemed an abundance. Jollity, friendship, and goodwill radiated from the fun-loving crowd, the day being shadowed for me only by the lack of Alec's presence. It was but one of many good times the community shared together.

Alec returned with the coming of spring and together we planned the planting of one more crop. During the long winter months another plan had been slowly forming in my mind, a plan to which I gained Alec's reluctant consent. Leaving my nine-months-old baby in the care of a neighbor, I washed and pressed my one dress, mended the only shoes I possessed, and in a shabby black coat and khaki hat I went to town to write the examinations for a Montana teacher's certificate. Timidly at first, then glowingly as I warmed to my subjects, I wrote and wrote, and then feverishly awaited the returns from Helena. When I was once more the happy possessor of a teacher's certificate I went to my local board of trustees and asked for a position, and they were too surprised to say "No." Three years I taught my own and my neighbors' children and some of the happiest hours of my life were spent in that tiny prairie schoolhouse where zealously I tried, out of my own knowledge and experience, to bring beauty and joy into the lives of the thirty-three children whose only experiences had been those of the drab life on the bleak prairie. All the love I put into my work there has been returned to me a thousandfold. The money I earned helped to feed and clothe my family and started my boy to high school.

Courageously but hopelessly the settlers struggled on, trying vainly with borrowed money to battle the elements, to tame the desert, and to carve home and fortune out of the raw land. Then came the grasshoppers, newly hatched, swarming out of the unplowed fields and covering the growing crops with a gray, slimy, creeping cloud which hour by hour steadily advanced, wiping out the greenness of the land, leaving only dry, bare clods in the fields. Despair over the ravaged crops filled the farmer's hearts.

On the billowing, russet prairie stands an empty farmhouse, its windows gone and doors sagging; beneath its eaves the wind soughs mournfully, the desert sand drifts around its doorstep, and the Russian thistle tumbles past. Desolate, silent it stands, grim witness to the frustration of a man's hopes and a woman's dreams.

We have no regrets; life is fuller and sweeter through lessons learned in privation, and around our homestead days some of life's fondest memories still cling. We are of Montana, now and always, boosters still—and in a fair valley of western Montana where the melting snows of the Mission Range trickle out in clear streams across the thirsty land, our dreams of the long ago are slowly taking on life. The grass grows green about my door-step, the vines clamber about my porch, the flowers bloom, the birds sing, and Alec's much-loved Brown Swiss cattle graze in lush fields. . . .

Tonight, as I write, the mellow glow of our electric lights shines over our happy home circle, the rooms vibrant from the tinkle of a piano, the melodious wail of a violin, and the lilt of happy youthful voices. I feel that creating a home and rearing a family in Montana has been a grand success, and my cup seems filled to overflowing with the sweetness and joy of living.

—•◦◾{ RANCHERS }◾◦•—

# Plains[1]

## ROBERT NELSON

Black, falling rain.
Drip from the sombrero brim.
Head down, cattle bunched.
Move along, cayuse,
Move on.

White clouds, dirty gray,
Stinging hail, driven down.
Slicker on, cattle bunched.
Move along, cayuse,
Move on.

Scudding clouds, blizzard on.
Cutting, knife-like snow.
Biting wind, cattle bunched.
Move along, cayuse,
Move on.

Summer sky, beating sun.
Alkali bitten men.
Neckerchief tight, cattle bunched.
Move along, cayuse,
Move on.

[1] *Frontier*, Vol. IX, No. 1, p. 51.

# Blue Blood, Horse and Man, on the Mizpah, 1887

## H. C. B. COLVILL

ESPECIALLY DURING THE LAST TWO DECADES of the nineteenth century, Englishmen, often remittance men, came to Wyoming and Montana to raise cattle and horses. With foreign capital they often set up large spreads. Stories have been written about the second sons of Britishers, the blue bloods of Colvill's account, which first appeared in *Frontier*, Vol. X, No. 4, p. 332.

Earlier the British, Scotsmen in particular, helped explore the West, principally through the search for furs with the Hudson's Bay Company and the North West Fur Company. Later much British money was invested in western mines.

The Englishman took England with him into any new country, as Colvill took his "little rubber bathtub," and was seldom mistaken for a native. Therein lay some of his success as a colonizer.

The Mizpah River runs between the Tongue and the Powder rivers in southeastern Montana, joining the latter about ten miles southeast of Miles City. It was prime cattle and horse country.

I JOINED THE ENGLISH COLONY in eastern Montana late in 1886. Horse ranching, blooded stock, and blooded man, was the combination, and it worked well at that time.

The following quotation from an English paper shows how well it worked:

> Import of American Horses—On Saturday General Ravenhill, head of the Army Remount Department with Mr. S. Tattersall, head of the great Tattersall horse auction establishment, "Tattersalls," Mr. R. Morley, and Mr. M. Walton, accompanied Captain Pennell Elmhirst to Kings Curry to inspect three young horses recently brought to this country from his breeding establishment in Montana, Western America, the precursors it is understood of many large shipments in the future. The horses called forth strong ex-

pressions of approval as to their shape, strength, and quality. Two of them had been already sold, and General Ravenhill bespoke the third for army use.

Here is another paragraph from the Miles City paper, dated 1886, which announces the arrival of the writer:

H. C. B. Colvill and H. O. Boyes, both of London, England, were at the MacQueen House on Monday. They have crossed the deep blue sea to visit their friend, Mr. Lindsey, who is associated with Capt. Elmhirst in the horse business. They departed for the ranch on Tuesday, where they will spend some months.

The sixty miles to the ranch in an open buggy through three feet of snow badly drifted today I would call a hard trip. Lindsey had the usual winter clothing on, but Boyes and myself were dressed as we had been on board ship, and had not even rubber overshoes. At that time, however, I don't believe we even felt cold. Some drifts we had to dig through, shove through, and tramp through—1886 and 1887 was a notable winter. Ninety per cent of the cattle on the Mizpah Range froze to death, and one of my first jobs when it broke in the spring was to haul carcasses away from the ranch, so that the smell of their rotting bodies would not offend our aristocratic noses. The smaller cattlemen were cleaning out; but on rounding up our horse stock in the spring it was found that only one old mare had died.

Hope therefore ran high and it was decided that the Mizpah and Powder River badlands was a natural horse country, and that there never again would be enough cattle there to spoil the range. L. O. Holt, at the Mizpah crossing eight miles above us, however, changed our notions, for he began trailing in cattle herds from Texas as soon as he found out what was up. Riding up to the crossing for the mail one day I got my first cussing from a Montana cowman and from old L. O. in person. Having become tired of waiting for his confounded herd to pass by, I forced my horse through the center of it. He told me what he thought of Englishmen riding pad saddles, wearing tight breeches, a sun helmet, and carrying a broken umbrella handle, and how such alien and strange animals were not wanted in Montana and never would be. Principally on account of this unreasonable dislike to that style of dress, when I left that country I left on the ranch about five hundred dollars worth of clothing, and never sent after it.

Hauling hay for the blooded stallions was our hardest job that winter—twenty-five miles straight across country, and across Powder River, with a wagon and four horses. Three feet of snow, and drifted; but we made it, and did not even freeze a finger. Early breakfasts in the dark, and long hours in the saddle, getting back to the ranch long after dark, constituted the main work up to July 4 of each year.

Gathering up wild stock in the badlands is no dude's job. In the hunting field the water jump is considered the hardest and most risky jump. Not that a horse cannot jump a long jump easier than a fence, but because he seems to have a natural prejudice against the water jump and will very often stop at the edge and spill both his rider and himself head over heels into the water. After wild horses, however, a horse forgets all his natural fears. I remember once jumping six washouts one after the other, that when I started I had no idea were there, one or two of them more than twenty feet across, to head off a bunch. There was a cut bank close to the home ranch that I once saw the foreman put his horse to, heading off a wild bunch of mares. This horse barely got his front legs on top and I expected him to fall backwards, but with a yell and a lunge, they were up and away. If my memory is correct, two of us measured a jump made across Mizpah Creek by our finest full-blooded stallion, when he got away one day after some mares; the jump measured thirty-five feet from take off to landing, and the horse could have carried a man just as well as not. A stallion used to come over from the C Dot Ranch, and cut out mares from the herd I was holding up for breeding. Two of us tried to stop him one day; shot all around him with a rifle; ran him miles to the C Dot Ranch; but he beat us both and took the mares away. We had to corral him over there with his own bunch, and with the help of the C Dot outfit,

to get our mares back. We did not give him time enough, however, to do any harm, so there were no mixed strains the next year.

There were other stallions on the range that would fight a
rider, and put up quite a fight, too. "Cannot kill valuable stallions," said the boss. "It simply is not done, don't you know.
Better lose a rider or two; don't cost so much money."

Haying time always started on July the fifth. There was a
legend that the E. P. E. had once hoisted the British flag over the
home ranch on July 4 and that a delegation of punchers had arrived and shot it all to pieces. That was never done in my time.
Haying consisted in racing the L. O. people for the wild hay up
and down the Mizpah. The first mowing machine to cut a swath
around a patch of grass held that patch against all comers.

Two humorous incidents are the high spots that I remember
best. Three of us had almost finished a large stack in a draw, and
we had enough hay down to top it off. That night there was a
cloudburst which flooded our camp, and we rescued our
blankets by wading knee-deep to higher ground. Early next
morning the "Captain" rode up to see if we were doing all right.
We told him we were, but when we took him to see our stack, it
was not there, and we never saw it again.

The second incident got me fired, and this is how it came about.
I, like all the other Englishmen who ever joined the colony,
brought along a little rubber bathtub and a sponge a foot across.
Sunday was the day we washed ourselves and our clothes. This
particular Sunday we had a lot of hay down that needed raking.
I volunteered to rake it, on the understanding that I should have
Monday to wash up. The other boys were haying busily on Monday when up comes E. P. E. "Where is Colvill?" asks the boss.
"Oh," said the boys, "he is probably in camp sitting in his rubber
bathtub, and sponging the top of his head with that big sponge
of his." Nothing said about my Sunday work. E. P. E. set spurs
to his horse, mad as a wet hen. He drew rein close enough to
where I was sitting in my rubber bathtub, sponging the top of
my head, to scatter dirt all over me. "When you get through,"
says he, "come up to the shack and I'll give you your time." "All

right," says I, and that was all the conversation we had. Next day I rode down to Powder River, and put in the rest of the summer helping a cowman who had lost nearly all his herd in the bad winter of '86–'87 put up some hay for his saddle string. He was a fine rider, and being an educated man had the science of riding the western saddle down fine, theory and practice. We had to keep his string gentled down, and so I spoiled my English seat on horseback, something the English colony was very particular about, for they all went home in the winter for the hunting. Then anyone without, or who had lost, a perfect hunting seat would be an object of disdain—offensive, in fact, to his companions.

While on Powder River I was told lots of funny stories about the English colony that I should not have learned otherwise. There was the gag on Whallop (or Wachoup, as it should be), recalled a year or so ago to be a member of the House of Lords. Whenever he was in an awkward situation, and some were racy, he would say, "I wonder what my mother, the Duchess, would say if she could see me now." All the cowboys in the country would get that gag off every once in a while. Sidney Padget was asked one time by a curious puncher called Billy, "Say, Sid, is it true that in the old country you are the son of a lord?" "Billy," says Sid, "in the old country they call me a son of a lord, and in this country they call me a son of a bitch, but it's the same old Sid all the time." Then there was the horseman whose ranch was on Pumpkin Creek—I forget his name—but his brother, the Major, came out one summer with his valet. The valet got sick one day, or something happened to him, and the Major called on one of the boys to shine up his riding boots. "Sure," said the puncher, "I'll do 'em," and he did a good job. Then the puncher told the Major to do just as good a job on his (the puncher's) boots. The Major put up something of a kick, and tried to work the single eyeglass trick, but cowboy would not stand for it—was not quite satisfied, even after the Major *had* shined his shoes, that it was as good a job.

I finished the year out, and nearly finished myself, at another horse outfit on the lower Powder. I was to furnish meat for the

249

ranch and run the outfit if everyone went to town. In return I was to have the use of two horses to work a poison line for wolves, the hides to be mine; but no poison was to be put out within three miles of the ranch house, because the foreman, Al Smith, had a favorite dog. One of the horses in my string was branded Rattle Snake Jack the full length of one side. One of the rules of the range is to throw the lines, by a twist of the wrist over the horse's head as one dismounts. Rattle Snake Jack remembered that rule one day, and I forgot it. I never forgot again after walking fifteen miles home. If the lines hang down from the bridle on a cow horse, he stands still, for he has learned that stepping on them hurts his mouth.

One day—five feet of snow on the level and blowing hard— the foreman's dog came up poisoned, and Mr. Foreman and myself spent the night, each with a pistol in his hand. I got tired of the strain on my nerves, and pulled out before breakfast for the E. P. E. Ranch across the Powder River divide on foot. On the way I noticed footsteps and looked out for some other fool pedestrian. Investigation revealed the fact that I had made a complete circle about a quarter of a mile in diameter. Night found me on the divide about five miles from the E. P. E. horse camp, deserted in winter, but the only available shelter. I was getting weary, not being used to walking. The snow also filled the gullies from five to six feet deep. Just as I felt like crawling into a snow bank I struck a wonderful beaten track as hard as a rock. I had no idea where it would lead me, but it turned out that my old crowd had put up a small haystack at the horse camp, and the track took me straight to that stack, two hundred yards from the shack, where wood and food had been left handy for anyone coming that way. Cattle had tramped a path smooth to look at the hay. The next day I made the home ranch. The bloods having gone home for the hunting, and the foreman, having heard the right story from the repentant haymakers, hired me again.

This led to another ludicrous incident when E. P. E. came back in the spring. By that time I had entire charge of a large bunch of mares and five blooded stallions at another horse camp eighteen miles up the Mizpah. I had a string of eight horses that had belonged to my predecessor known as the Black Eyed Kid. To prevent the bloods from grabbing any of his string, the Kid had taught each of them to pitch (or buck jump) at different signals. I experimented and finally found out most of these signals, but with one, a big blooded gray, I never did find out. He would hunch his back when I first got on, but he never did let himself out on me. The first time I saw the boss in the spring and also the first I had seen him since he had fired me, he came up with a man called Benson to look over my herd. He asked me if I had a gentle horse he could use, as his was tired. I told him I had a big gray on the picket that had never pitched with me. So I got him up and the boss mounted. If you had never seen a horse pitch you would have seen one that day. Benson finally ran in and grabbed his head and the two of us brought him to a stop. The old man had ridden him all right, but had got it in his head that I had played that trick on him to get even for having been fired. He told me he could ride the worst of them, but that he was getting old and did not like it any more, and that he did not have to ride the pitcher if I had told him the truth. He came pretty near firing me again.

That summer I reaped the benefit of my friendship with the C Dot punchers, for it was the wettest summer that had ever been known, and colts dropped by mares held in the herd at the home ranch were dying like flies. The C Dot men told me, "Never mind what the boss told you to do, just let the herd go. Then as soon as the storm lets up for good hustle around and gather them up. You will find that they have not gone far." If E. P. E. had come up while I was toasting my shins by the stove, he would have fired me for sure. When he finally did come, accompanied by the foreman, I had the herd together and had not lost a colt. I never told E. P. E. but the foreman took me on one side and asked me how I did it. I told him, and he said it was what he had been trying to get the boss to agree to all the time.

That summer they gave me an army mule and a wild unbroken colt to drive on the mower. My first swath was five and a half miles long straight up and down the creek, and the pitchers raked up three and a half big loads of hay before I made a turn. Some skill was required dodging the sagebrush when driving horses on the dead run, but the machine was not broken. I had three teams and two mowers that year. When a team got tired, or a mower dull, my assistants promptly brought me another team hitched to a new sharp mower. We had an old country hay stacker who started his stacks on a handkerchief, brought them out as wide as a house, then drew them in; ranchers came from all round to look at these agricultural curiosities.

This year there was a strike amongst the boys, who insisted on potatoes as well as beans with their sowbelly. E. P. E. explained that beans were a sure antidote for the alkali water, but finally had to have a few potatoes freighted out from Miles City. I got some of these and planted them. The resultant crop was, as far as I know, the first, and maybe the last, ever raised on Mizpah Creek. I found also that I could not work with the drags and eat with the bloods, so resigned from the first table.

That fall I bought a perfectly trained hunting pony and kept the ranch supplied with meat. Three incidents stand out in my mind as hunting episodes. The first was coming on antelope, feeding in a hollow, with a strange wind blowing. By riding on the lee side I got within a few feet of the top of the hollow. By crawling a few feet I was able to push my rifle and actually touch the side of a buck before I pulled the trigger. Crawling back, I mounted my horse and rode up to find the rest of the herd had not realized that anything out of the ordinary had occurred. The second was meeting a big blacktail, head on, when riding a narrow trail, then slipping off my pony and shooting between his legs at a mark hardly a yard away. The third was packing three blacktail on that pony a short distance to the ranch house late at night, then climbing on top of the load and calling the crowd to the door, to their great amazement. Another that did not come off was getting my rope on a mountain lion, which luckily worked himself loose before anything much happened.

Chickens tree in the fall along the Mizpah. It took just twenty-five chickens to make a good curry (an aristocratic dish). I made a deal with the girl cook. There were two girls (a cook and a ladies' maid) on the home ranch. The cook stayed the year around and finally married the foreman. The deal was for curry every Sunday. By shooting the lowest bird on a tree first, every bird there could be killed with a rifle, but they would fly if a shotgun was used. A treeful often made the curry.

The two girls had a great time. Every male on the ranch of the two-legged species must have made love to them sooner or later. They thought the life very rough, but their *bête noire* was the skunk. There must have been hundreds of skunks up and down the Mizpah. About every day or so the girls would be heard screaming and every man within earshot would rush to their assistance. The girls invariably would be found standing on the table holding to each other with one hand while the other hand held their skirts closely about their legs. The proper system then (invented, I believe, by the foreman) was to seize a dipperful of water and gently sprinkle the water on the ground behind the skunk, heading him towards the door and finally through it. No shooting or noise was allowed until the skunk was a hundred yards or more from the premises. In that way skunk odor never, to my knowledge, scented kitchen or premises. At the horse camp at the head of the Mizpah, however, a skunk got into the oven of a perfectly good stove. Someone slammed the oven door shut and no one present was found with the courage to open it. When the fire died down and the stove got cool it was removed, skunk and all, and buried under three feet of dirt. All the rest of the year cooking was done out of doors, for the stove was never replaced.

Just before Christmas I got an idea to ride up to Canada. To complete my outfit I had to purchase a pack horse. Ben Mason, at Powderville, who had just shot a man, not his first by any means, had a horse that he had used packing elk to the troops at Fort Keogh. I spent the night with Ben popping popcorn and talking about the shooting. According to Ben it was getting so expensive to kill a man that it was going to take his whole ranch this time to get clear. At that Ben said he would just as soon kill a man as a coyote. I was careful to agree with Ben on nearly every subject. So we got along fine and I bought old Baldy from him for thirty dollars. Ben said, "If you get into a pinch just leave it to Baldy, for he knows more than any tenderfoot can ever learn." Ben was perfectly correct on this statement, as you will see later.

Crossing the Crow Reservation I fell in with Jim Hucy from the N Bar. We then picked up a bunch of Crows going our way from a food distribution at the Agency. Camping in their tepees on snow-covered ground we found luxurious, and tepees fine warm shelters. One bunch forked off to Pryor Creek. They told me there was a good ford at the mouth that would save me many miles. When I reached it I was alone, and I expect I never struck the ford at all, for I was carried downstream a long way amongst great ice blocks before I got across. I ran into a ranch house still dripping wet. The caretaker asked me where I had come from. I said, "Out of the Yellowstone River." He replied, "You look like it. Go on in and get your clothes off; I will take care of your horses."

The next high spot of the trip was crossing the Marias River near Fort Benton. I got halfway over, then the ice broke and let us all into water up to our shoulders. This time I remembered what Ben Mason had said. So I worked Baldy up on the lead and told him to get us out of it, for I did not know what to do. Baldy seemed to know what I meant and stood up on his hind legs, pack and all, then came down on the ice hard as he could. He kept breaking a trail that way, until the river got shallower. Then we were all able to scramble out.

The next highlight was starting that eighty miles from the American to the Canadian side north of Assiniboine. I traded a cowpuncher a pair of sleeping socks to put me on the right road. He did this, and pointed out some landmarks in the snow-covered waste. He had not been gone more than three or four hours before I found out I was lost and the back trail was well drifted up. Upon serious reflection I came to the conclusion that if there was

254

not, then there should be, a telegraph line between Fort Assiniboine and the Canadian Mounted Police station at Maple Creek.
Further reflection convinced me that I might as well advance in
that direction as stand still and freeze in one of the coldest bliz-
zards that ever came out of Medicine Hat, a short distance north.
So I struck out to cross that telegraph line, if there was one. As
luck would have it, there was one; for I bumped into a post in the
dark. After that no one could have dragged me away from that
telegraph line. I unpacked my bedroll in the night, but found it
too cold to sleep, so saddled up after an hour and rode till the
line ended at a Mounted Police post. The troopers repeated that
old question, "Where did you spring from?" "Montana, U.S.A.,"
was the answer. Then they remarked that two fools, just like me,
had frozen to death crossing on the wagon road a few days before.

Near the end of the line I found another blooded man with
blooded horses. He knew all the Powder River aristocrats. In the
spring on my way back I helped him with 150 of the finest horses
anyone could ask for, which he was breaking to the saddle for
the great Canadian Mounted Police. Those police, at that, would
have to ride some, for three rides was all the breaking considered
necessary before a policeman got a horse.

That was the end of my connection with blooded men and
blooded horses. I don't believe that I have seen a specimen of
either since. Altogether, I rode over eight hundred miles that
winter, or a thousand counting the trip out in the spring, averag-
ing twenty-five miles a day.

# Journal of a Ranch Wife, 1932–1935

HELEN CROSBY GLENN

*Note by Helen Glenn:* This journal is an excerpt from the life of a young ranch wife. It recounts the day-by-day happenings in the lives of two young westerners who married during the Great American Depression. In those bleak, terror-stricken days one found people becoming hopeless, stolid, plodding. But the young wife was luckily married to a man who taught her, unconsciously, the secret of happiness which was known to many of our pioneer forefathers—a sense of humor nourished by an abiding interest in and appreciation of the homely, inconsequential events in daily life. This creed has allowed the western rancher to go on in the face of the economic ups and downs of our times. These young people also faced hardship, and finally an illness which brought this journal to an end.

Jeff's father, the first Jeff Tiernan, came to Montana from Texas in the late '80's or early '90's. He later was one of the best-loved roundup bosses in southeastern Montana. He was a well-educated, generous man who ruled his home, his cowpunchers, and his blooded horses with a firm, kind hand. He died when the young Jeff was eight years old. Even in the space of eight years he had managed to pass on to his son much of the knowledge which makes an all-round man. Young Jeff went to work at the age of thirteen and by the time he was twenty-two, when this story opens, he had accumulated a small bunch of cattle, some blooded horses, and a great deal of knowledge of the working of a ranch. He was an industrious, sensitive, hot-tempered young man with an abiding love of horses and of ranch tradition when he married Lynne Carson.

Tod Carson, Lynne's father, lived on a ranch in South Dakota, until, in 1890, when he was twelve years old, his father moved to Montana. A few years later, being a top hand, he rode rough-string for outfits on the Powder River. After his marriage to a little Irish schoolteacher, he established a ranch on the Mizpah; also, he freighted wool from the north side of the Yellowstone River to Miles City. Generous to a fault, although a successful rancher, he lost much of his profits by lending money to his friends. Lynne, being the youngest of three daughters, was favored by her mother, who sent her to college for three years. An introspective child with a love of beauty, we find her at twenty-one marrying Jeff.

The events here recorded take place in the country which lies south of Miles City in southeastern Montana. It is a country of valleys, rolling hills, badlands. Here are pine-covered hills, cottonwood, ash, and willows along the muddy streams. Here there is bluejoint, reminiscent of unfenced range, Russian thistle, grim souvenir of the dry-land farmer. Queer rock formations, black and yellow gumbo, little caverns honeycombed throughout, and the sparse foliage—sagebrush, cactus, greasewood, and Spanish bayonet—form the fantastic-appearing country known as the badlands. Farther south, near the Cheyenne Reservation, lie fertile valleys, flanked on either side by high hills, and in the distance the misty form of mountains. The journal appeared in *Frontier and Midland*, Vol. XIX, No. 4, p. 258.

*May 28, 1932*

My wedding day. I am now a cowpuncher's wife, as was my mother before me. My wedding, in the midst of all the ceremony and convention attendant upon such affairs, held its touch of the West. Uncle Cary happened to be in town (Miles City) from the CBC horse roundup and was one of our witnesses. He was wearing a torn shirt, dirty California trousers, his boots, and a dusty black Stetson. Should the bride be writing of her own attire? It was very ordinary. Cary's clothes interest me more. They are typical of my life from now on and the background of my childhood. They comfort me in the strangeness of this new experience. Jeff was *so* brushed and shining in his dark suit and white shirt. The only familiar things about him were his boots, and even they were shined until they looked like square-toed mirrors.

*June 1*

Jeff left for the Swinging-H this morning to break the news to his boss of our marriage, and to see if arrangements could be made for us to be placed in a cow camp for the summer.

*July 1*

I am still in town and am terribly lonely. I feel like a broomtail filly that has been separated from the rest of her bunch and thrown into a pasture with a bunch of gentle old work horses— I keep running up and down the fence, trying to find a way back to the open country and freedom. Jeff is in camp at the old Diamond-L Ranch on Soda Biscuit Creek, with the foreman and his wife. Mr. Kent, the boss, doesn't believe in putting two women in the same camp, so it doesn't give me much hope of being with Jeff before fall. He comes in to see me every chance he gets, but they have been busy with the spring roundup and calf branding.

*July 16*

A faint ray of hope has appeared. Sam Green, the foreman, is in the hospital and may have to have an operation. Annie, his wife, is in town with him; which leaves Jeff alone at the camp.

*July 21*

At home at last. The hay crew is here from the main ranch putting up bluejoint and alfalfa hay. They decided to charivari us, so took us for a ride in the ice cart. It is a disreputable vehicle mounted on two old buggy wheels and has handles like a wheel-barrow. They tied it to the rear end of the Ford pickup, all piled in, and took us, seated in state in the cart, down across the hay meadow, driving over all the bumpy places they could find. They brought us back to the horse tank, and after threatening us with baptism by immersion, let us go because we didn't protest.

The crew all filed up to the horse tank and wasted several bars of hand soap during their daily bath after sundown. The horses won't drink out of the tin tank during this hot weather as the wooden one beside it keeps the water much cooler. The tin one makes a wonderful bathtub for the men. . . .

Jeff presented me with a pair of spurs today. They are about thirty-five years old and were the property of his father. They are very precious to Jeff for that reason; and that in turn makes them doubly precious to me. They are the final seal set upon my new title of Mrs. Jeff Tiernan. They were quite rusty, so I scoured them and the silver mountings now gleam bravely when the sun hits them.

*3 days later*

The hay crew is gone, cook and all, and I am learning to cook. Hot biscuits and steak and gravy is Jeff's favorite breakfast. *Biscuits!* Jeff is struggling to teach me and I am struggling, even harder, to learn. Oh, for some toast made in an electric toaster, and halved grapefruit with powdered sugar! I wept bitter tears over the ruins of my biscuits this morning, but managed to greet Jeff with a smile when he came in from his morning chores. It humiliates me no end that he is an A-1 cook and all I can manage to do, so far, is to make coffee; although that is really a redeeming feature. A rancher's wife who makes poor coffee is a total flop, regardless of how good a cook she may be in other respects. Another thing she must be able to do is to cook meat well. I am receiving my first lessons in frying T-bone steaks. It is easier than making fluffy biscuits. My next hard task will be learning to make light bread.

*August*

The biscuits are better but the bread is terrible. If it rises nicely in the pans, I burn it in the oven or my fire goes out and it remains soggy in the center. However, don't you know (as Keith Gray, the old Scotch cowman says), I'll learn.

That's a queer thing, which I never realized until I wrote it down; most Scotchmen in this country are sheepmen, but Keith is a dyed-in-the-wool cowman and hates the smell of sheep as all cowmen do. . . .

Jeff has told me a lot of the history of this creek and this particular ranch. He was raised about seven miles up the creek from here. He and his brother, two sisters, and mother still own the old ranch, but it is leased to Mel Willcox. Jeff has promised me that we will ride up there soon, as I have not yet seen the place.

The Diamond-L, where we are in camp, belonged to old Frank Hitchinson, whom Jeff knew very well. Frank was a fascinating person to talk to. He had been a close friend of Jeff's father, so enjoyed talking to the youngster, and poured plenty of tales of the old days into his eager ears.

Frank first came to this country with a trail herd for the Jingle-Bob outfit from the Nebraska sand hills, in the early '8o's, and for a long time was known as Jingle-Bob Frank. The Jingle-Bob derived its name from the earmark they used on their cattle. It does away with having to look a critter all over for its brand, as the earmark can be seen when facing the animal, or when behind it, so it is not necessary to see the animal side-view to read its brand on the hip, side, or shoulder. One or both ears are partly or wholly cut away in various shapes. The Jingle-Bob outfit split the ear just above the center, leaving the lower half dangling. This piece of skin bobbed around when the animal moved its head, thus earning its name, the Jingle-Bob.

A few years after their arrival here, in the spring following the hard winter of '86, the herd being sadly depleted, the remnants were sold to Pierre Wibaux, who shipped them out of the country the next fall. That is why you never hear of the Jingle-Bob outfit nowadays.

In the evening, when the supper dishes are washed and put away, we sit on the long low porch on the south side of the house and watch the cattle leave the water hole up the creek and trail out to graze until morning. They hang around the water during the heat of the day and eat when it is cooler. Along in the evening the air cools and freshens. Then it is a comfort to escape from the heat of the kitchen range and listen to all the small sounds of the sunset hour—the frogs make little blurping noises in the creek, a meadowlark sings a sleepy note of farewell to the last rosy light of the sun. As the warm hue fades, the sage shadows become tinged with purple; in the big cottonwood below the corrals, there is an owl hooting mournfully. Off to the right, up Ranch Creek, a cow is bawling for her calf, while a coyote yaps in derision. Jeff and I turn to our slumbers in the rambling old T-shaped log house. The range land is at peace with the world. In a few hours the full moon will shed its chilly radiance over the creek bottom and surrounding hills; and perhaps the ghost of Jingle-Bob Frank will roll a cigarette and light it—the flame flickers for an instant in the shadow of the corral. Has Jeff's wrangle horse seen it? He snorts, or is he just clearing his nostrils of dust so that he can sniff the clean air of the night?

*A week later*

Jeff is the proud possessor of a small bunch of cattle, and some half-bred (part-thoroughbred) horses. His uncle runs the cattle for him on Lister Creek; the horses run on the Hat Creek range.

A bunch of officious honyocks [homesteaders] are incessantly chasing the horses, as there are a few slicks [unbranded animals] running in that country and the "honnies" live in the hope that they may some day be able to corral them. Our horses are, at first sight, hard to tell from the slicks, as they wear a neat little brand on the jaw. The honyocks evidently grew tired of being fooled, so they shoved them into one of the Diamond-L pastures, in order that they might not again pick them up. Jeff discovered them the other day so he took me along to help put them back out on the range. He would have moved them alone, but they have been chased so much that they are wild as deer and as apt to go through a fence as a gate, if excited.

We were lucky to find them near the gate which leads out to the range. Cautiously, we eased towards them and were able to get quite close. Jeff pointed out each one in turn and gave me its history. The mares are half-bred and the younger horses' grandsire was a race horse, bred on the Mizpah, where blooded horses were introduced by some Englishmen in the '80's.

A buckskin two-year-old caught my eye. He stood with his head above the rest, ears twitching as he watched our every move. Long-legged, high-withered, with a deep chest and a fine intelligent head, dark mane and tail waving whenever he moved, the sun reflecting from his glossy fair hide.

Jeff circled around and opened the gate while I sat on my horse and whistled. The buckskin never took his eyes from me and his ears were never at rest, first one cocked toward me and then the other.

As Jeff rode slowly toward them, I fell back farther into the pasture until they were started through the gate and I knew that they wouldn't attempt to dodge past me. We followed them for a short distance into the badlands. The buckskin stopped on a gumbo butte and faced us; then, with a rush, he was gone down the draw, trailing behind the others to the water-hole. . . .

*Mid-August*

We reached home [from a dance] just as the sun was making its appearance above the pine-covered hills to the east of us. Cliff [Jeff's younger brother] was still rolled in his sougans, in the shadow of the old bunkhouse, at dinner time, and it took a bit of physical force on the part of Jeff and Sandy [the boss's nephew] to rouse him. . . .

Jeff and Cliff, being thoroughly awake by the time the heat of the day began to subside, put on a roping exhibition for my benefit; using the two milk cows' calves to practice on—running them up the little lane from the corrals to the horse tank and back again, until calves, horses, and riders were exhausted and it was no longer light enough to see.

Jeff then decided it was time to milk the cows and gave Cliff the gentlest cow, "who never kicks." He no sooner got the words out of his mouth than the pail went one way, Cliff went another, and milk flew everywhere.

Art's mother stopped on her way to town last week and brought me two little black-and-white kittens. Jeff has named one Lynne and the other Carson. Lynne has a black spot on her nose, which gives her the appearance of having a very dirty and impudent face. Carson's face is all white and bears an angelic expression, but she is really much the more venturesome and curious of the two. She insists on smelling of the pegs when Jeff and I are play-

262

ing horseshoes in the evening, and scampers forward to investigate the position of every horseshoe thrown.

We took the kittens to help us get rid of our mice tenants, but they are such babies they aren't much help to us yet. This house is lined with cloth, whitewashed over, as so many old log houses are. The space between the lining and the roof is an ideal place for mice nests, so the house is full of the creatures. All night long they "buck and play" (quoting Jeff) above our heads. What's more, they get into everything, not only food, but into the bureau drawers. . . .

We have, also, pack rats on the premises. I had a pair of old net stockings, and left them, with my pumps, on the floor the other night. . . . Next morning my stockings were missing, and although I hunted high and low, I could find them nowhere. . . .

*Late August*

Jeff and I rode up to the old ranch last Sunday. It is on the head of the creek in the pine hills. We rode through the chokecherry bushes in the lower hay meadows and ate so many berries that we were unable to get our mouths unpuckered for several hours.

The house has about seven rooms and is fitted with carbide lights and running water. It is one of the handiest ranch houses I have seen. I doubt if we will ever take the ranch and try to run it ourselves, as there are only four sections of land included in the ranch proper. All the land around it that used to be open range is homesteaded and fenced; and anyone trying to run cattle would never be able to manage on those four sections.

Mel has sheep and leases summer pasture away from home. It is an ideal place for him as it produces quite a bit of hay. It is possible to flood-irrigate the meadows from the creek, and they are seeded with alfalfa.

Early in the summer, Jeff began working with a bronc, but was unable to stay with him consistently during the intense heat for fear of overdoing him. This last week has been a little cooler so he has been busy trying to get him acquainted with the rudiments of roping. The little booger seems to take to it. He is, ordinarily speaking, a chestnut sorrel, but during the hot weather his hair has bleached until he is a cross between mouse-gray and mustard-yellow. We decided to call him Booger because he is a "smart little booger" and is constantly getting himself all "boogered up" by getting tangled in wire and performing other such antics.

*September 1*

Mr. Kent sent George over, night before last, to gather the cavvy and take them to the main ranch; also to tell Jeff to close up the camp and move to the ranch himself. They are starting the fall roundup.

Jeff and George left with the cavvy yesterday morning. When they had gone, I busied myself with the task of packing our clothes. Each hour seemed twice as long as usual, as I waited for Jeff's return. George had said nothing of my going to the main ranch too. Did Kent mean that there was no room for me there? Was I once more to be exiled in town, away from Jeff?

At last Jeff appeared in the jitney and quickly dispelled my fears by announcing that I was going with him. They have a cook, Maude, and I am to be her helper, so here we are at the Swinging-H. Mrs. Kent welcomed me with open arms; she is the sweetest little old lady I know.

The boys have been rounding up cattle, cutting out the beef, branding the late calves and a few that were missed in the spring roundup. . . .

The other morning George decided to ride Dixie. Dixie has not been ridden all summer and is full of life. George knows it, so he was trying to be very careful. He tried for at least five minutes to get Dixie to stand still long enough for him to get safely on. Finally the others, who were all mounted and were getting impatient, shouted, "Oh, hurry up and get on, George!" George made one last desperate effort and landed behind the saddle. Dixie went straight up and so did George, coming back to earth head first. When he picked himself up, his pipe, which was still firmly clenched between his teeth, was brimful of mud. George has been going around with his face "all rolled up like a bed" ever since. Anyone who speaks to him gets only a grunt.

Ole got piled the other day, too. Ole is not rightly a cowboy. Last year he herded Kent's sheep, and he has been on the hay crew all this summer; but he is pathetically eager to show his worth as a rider. Don, being short of punchers, decided to let him ride; and in his string put a little horse called Satan. Satan has, in his younger days, lived up to his name; now he is just an ordinary cow pony that will buck occasionally if something touches him off.

Ole has always been a little leery of him, because of his past record. Satan, having good horse sense, of course knows it. A piece of sagebrush happened to tickle him; Satan thought, "Now's my chance to have some fun with this fellow, since he's so scared of me," and away he went. He wasn't bucking hard and Ole was doing a fine job of sticking on until someone hollered, "Stay with him, Ole!" Ole very foolishly turned his head, said "Huh?" and found himself rolling in the sagebrush.

Maude, Ole's wife, and I have our troubles too; but they are mainly with old Tim Shea, the choreboy. He invariably comes in with muddy feet just after we have scrubbed the floor or brings up a scuttle of coal so full that he leaves a trail of coal behind him. He also has difficulty in hoisting the cakes of ice up into the ice compartment of the huge refrigerator, and wants us to help him. He had a bad habit of bringing the smelly hog pail into the kitchen to scrub it, but I think I have put an end to that practice.

Tim, along with his other varied duties, has charge of the chickens. A coyote has been grabbing off a few of them lately, so Kent told Tim to set a trap where it had been crawling under the chicken-yard fence. Tim accordingly set the trap and awaited results. It happens that Kent has three collies and is very fond of them. Two of them, Missy and her son Tex, are white collies. Tim started out at dawn to inspect his trap, taking Missy and Tex with him. Tex ran ahead, started sniffing around the trap and got his paw caught. Tim tried to extricate him, but while he was doing so, Missy ran up anxious because Tex was yelping, and got a front leg caught. When Tim tried to get her out, she snapped at him. He was terribly excited by this time and hurried for the bunkhouse to get help. Jeff was just coming from the big house, as he had risen early to wrangle the horses. In the gray light he could see Tim hurrying toward the bunkhouse and could hear Missy and Tex yelping, so he hollered out, "Did you get your coyote, Tim?"

"Both of 'em, the two white ones; help me."

Jeff drawled, "White ones—h-m-m—I never saw a white coyote."

"No! No!" shrieked the old Irishman. "The dogs, the white dogs; help me, Jeff!"

Between the two of them, they freed the collies. Missy's leg swelled, causing her to limp a bit, although Tex was hardly scratched. Kent noticed Missy, but said nothing until that noon, when he inquired, "What's the matter with your hand, Tim?"

Poor old Tim, he had smeared iodine all over the back of his hand where Missy had bitten him, and now was quivering with the fear that he was going to be bawled out for taking the dogs with him when he went to the trap. He made a great effort to be casual, "Oh, I scratched it on the fence this morning." Kent smiled, "Well, after this, try to catch the gray coyotes, Tim. I'm not so fancy that I have to have white ones."

Kent is vice-president and general manager of the Swinging-H Ranch and John McCrea of Chicago is the president and largest shareholder. He makes annual visits to the ranch, although he is getting old and feeble.

He brought a young fellow, from the Chicago office, as chauffeur on his recent visit. Ed is twenty-nine and although he has worked for the commission company for several years and knows a lot about that end of the cattle business, he has never before visited a ranch. Mrs. Kent decided that he should see everything that was to be seen. Accordingly, she outfitted him with hat,

266

woolly chaps, and muffler, and had a horse saddled for him. He was then escorted across the river to the big corrals.

After he had sat stiffly for some moments, watching the calf branding, his hat blew off. Gazing at it, and contemplating his horse's twitching ears, he carefully climbed off, on the wrong side. He ventured blithely into the midst of the milling herd of cattle, the cowboys watching aghast, retrieved his hat, and returning to his horse, climbed stiffly on, again on the wrong side.

Every horse is broken to be mounted and dismounted on the left side; only some of the Indians made an exception to this rule and their horses are used to it. But anyone who attempts to mount the ordinary pony from the right side is in for a lot of trouble. It just happened that Ed had been given the oldest, gentlest horse on the place. Another thing that is never done is to walk into the middle of a herd of range cattle (especially cows with calves) on foot. Why that herd didn't scatter will always be a mystery.

## Late-October

The boys left early last Sunday for the railroad with the beef. The day they left was a perfect Indian summer day; so Hallie, Don's wife, and I went over to the chuck wagon for dinner. They were camped at the old 71 corrals on Soda Biscuit Creek. It was like stepping back forty years to see the noon camp. Lebler, the cook, had everything spread out on the table board of the chuck box, and smoke drifted lazily from the pipe of the little stove, which stood a few feet from the wagon. The cattle were grazing quietly in the creek bottom; farther off the boys were throwing the cavvy into the corral to catch their fresh horses. Two of the boys came in to eat, then rode out to relieve two more who had been day-herding the cattle. Lebler had a dinner of beef stew with dumplings. He has done a lot of cooking on roundups and at one time had an outfit of his own in Dakota. He talks in a peculiar falsetto most of the time and then suddenly booms forth a few words in a deep bass. When he gets excited about something, his voice gets higher and higher until it ends in a squeak....

Hallie, little Don, and baby Virginia and I watched them

break up camp and start on their way; then we headed for the ranch. When we reached there, the wind was blowing and the sun was hidden by big gray clouds. I went on up to the hay camp with them, as Hallie planned to take advantage of Don's absence to do some calcimining and varnishing.

Before we finished supper it was raining, and when we woke the next morning, a blizzard was in full progress. We knew the men would never be able to make it to town by Thursday, to load out, as they had a lot of calves newly weaned from their mothers. They had made the nights musical for a week before leaving for the road. Now that I was in a strange bed I woke several times during the night and wondered at the stillness. I was lonely for the bawling of the calves and cows, and for our own room at the ranch.

In spite of the blizzard, Hallie and I got busy with brushes. She calcimined while I varnished the woodwork. We had planned to go to town to meet the boys and, incidentally, paint the town red, but the storm raged on; and as the wet blanket grew deeper the highway grew muddier and muckier.

We had expected the boys back Saturday, but they didn't put in an appearance until Monday morning. They had reached the main ranch late Sunday night, with the cavvy, so dead-tired from riding fifty miles in the mud that they tumbled into bed. Now they were preparing to comb the pastures for strays.

After supper I started home with them, mounted on Dumb-bell, Jeff's horse, while he and Art rode double. I had ridden Dumbbell only once before as Jeff doesn't consider him suitable for a lady's horse. He is part Arabian, a little bay with big eyes and large nostrils. He is a perky little thing and travels along with tail crooked into a perpetual question mark. He is smart and ornery. But there I was, riding him on a night so black that I could barely make out the outlines of Jeff and Art as they rode beside me. George was pooched as usual and rode far enough ahead that we couldn't see him, but close enough that he could snarl in reply to the teasing remarks Jeff and Art directed at him, concerning his adventures as a Lothario in Miles City.

268

*November*

I celebrated my twenty-second birthday the other day, and as a present received my first pair of made-to-order boots. They are square-toed and high-heeled. I am just as pleased as a kid. Even George shows an interest in them and asked Hallie if she had seen "the cute little boots down at the ranch." I initiated them by wearing them when Jeff and I rode down to the Garland school, to cast our first votes in a presidential election. I'm afraid it didn't do us much good to vote, as we canceled each other's vote.

Jeff mounted me on Dumbbell and he rode Scarfoot, who was spoiled when he was broke and is apt to blow up and buck at any moment. We stopped down the river and spent the evening drinking homemade wine with some friends. The night was ebon-black and softly moist and warm when we started home. We were having a lovely time, riding along in the darkness, singing, until we reached the lower pasture. Scarfoot stepped into some barbwire. It so happens that Scarfoot got his name from a scar on his foot as the result of a wire cut, and once a horse gets tangled up and cut in wire he is deathly afraid of it. I was afraid to try to help Jeff unravel it for fear Dumbbell would get wound up in it too. That would mean more trouble, so I sat pat while Jeff stepped off and began to unwind the wire. I held my breath and prayed that Scarfoot wouldn't get scared and start bucking and running. I had horrible visions of Jeff being dragged and cut to pieces. My prayers were answered, for luckily we were in some tall dry weeds that rattled and cracked in the breeze, and Scarfoot remained blissfully unconscious of the fact that he was in wire.

Last spring when the LO outfit was trailing their cattle home after wintering up the river, one of their horses, Goldie, went lame. They left him at Don's, telling him that when Goldie recovered, he might have the use of him. Little Don had been riding him to school all fall until one of the punchers came over from the LO the other day after him. He and Jeff made a trade, the LO puncher taking Dumbbell while Jeff got Goldie for me.

I am heartsick over it. I loved Dumbbell, and somehow I can't feel attached to Goldie, although he is a good-looking horse, well gaited. He is a tall sorrel with three white feet and a white stripe in his face.

## Thanksgiving

Our first Thanksgiving together and we have much to be thankful for. Jeff has a job and we are together. Wages are lower than they have been for years and jobs are scarce. Jeff is a top hand, thus being able to keep his job. The boss has thinned his crew to winter proportions. There are only Don, George, and Jeff doing the riding. Tim Shea is gone and Ole has been demoted to the position of choreboy. All of the hay crew have been gone since early October. Stafford, who is the farmer of the ranch, is still here; but he does nothing but bustle around like a wet hen when Kent is here, and otherwise nothing at all. Sandy is here when he is not at the sheep camps.

Jeff and I spent the morning shoeing Goldie. He is mean about standing still, so I held him while Jeff put the shoes on.

After dinner, we decided we wanted our pictures taken on our horses. Accordingly Jeff and I headed for the corrals, with Stafford trailing along as photographer. I was showing Stafford how to manipulate the camera while Jeff topped off Blue Rocket in the corral. Goldie was tied to the outside of the corral and the big gate was left open, so that Jeff wouldn't have to bother opening it when he came out with Rocket. I started to untie Goldie, as he trotted Rocket around the corral and remarked, "Well, I guess he's going to be all right. I thought he might decide to put on a show for us; I haven't ridden him since we took the beef to the road." Blue Rocket just then reached the open gate and came out like a bucker out of a rodeo chute, almost knocking down Stafford, who was still peering interestedly at the camera. He bucked straight for the river, turning his belly up to the sun at every jump, while Jeff waved his hat and shouted, "Take my picture." But Stafford was so startled it was all he could do to hold the camera, much less take a picture. When he did finally

270

take a picture of us, Rocket was looking very pious and gave no indication of the mischievous nature he had just revealed.

## December 1

There has been some talk of Kent buying the hay at the Houston Ranch, about twenty-five miles up the river. If he does, Jeff and I will be in camp there this winter, with about eight hundred calves and a small bunch of cows to feed.

## December 13

It would certainly seem that the thirteenth is an unlucky day, although it isn't Friday. I was upstairs cleaning our room this morning and, as usual, glancing out of the window at intervals to see what was going on. It has been cold lately and there are many icy patches of ground. One of them is on the road, directly in front of the house.

Don, Jeff, and George have been bringing in a few cattle. One big yearling broke away each time they got him to the corral gate. Jeff and Don went after him and Jeff roped him; he was riding Bedwagon, a rangy, nervous black horse with a look of power but very little real strength on the end of a rope. When the yearling jumped up and ran off to one side, it jerked him down on the icy road. Jeff had his overshoes on so was unable to kick free of the stirrup and Bedwagon fell full force on his leg. I saw Bedwagon scramble to his feet; Jeff stepped off, tightened up the saddle cinch, got back on, and they dragged the yearling into the corral. I breathed a sigh of relief.

Half an hour later, Jeff came limping to the house and said his foot felt numb. I helped him off with his boot; his foot didn't seem to be swollen any. He hobbled down to dinner. Hobbling down those stairs proved to be the undoing of him as his foot began to pain in earnest. He had to leave his dinner untouched and I helped him back upstairs. By mid-afternoon there was no doubt that he had a broken bone, so Kent sent Stafford to town with us. I propped a pillow under Jeff's foot, but Stafford was afraid of driving too fast, and, in trying to ease the old Ford over the bumps, made poor Jeff suffer untold agonies.

271

By suppertime Jeff's foot was in a cast and the doctor had told him he could return to the ranch. He will be on crutches for at least three weeks. They will probably send someone else to the Houston Ranch, now. Kent and Don are going up tomorrow to measure the hay. Jeff had finally gone to sleep with his foot propped on a pilow, and I am thankful it wasn't his leg that was broken. It is a small bone and should mend easily.

*December 14*

Kent and Don returned from the Houston Ranch this evening with good news for us. We are to go, as originally planned; Kent is hiring Ted, a puncher from the Crow Reservation, to go with us and take Jeff's place until he is able to work again. We leave next Sunday morning. Babe Lee, who hauls freight up and down the river, will move us.

*December 17*

Our last day at the Swinging-H. This afternoon we hauled our grub and personal belongings across the river on the bobsled; and unloaded it in the garage for Babe to load in the morning. It is awkward for Jeff to work with his crutches, so I unloaded all of the smaller boxes and helped as best I could with the flour and other large items. Jeff let me drive the big sorrel team. Are there any joys equal to that of skimming along through the snow in a bobsled behind a well-matched, lively team of horses? I believe I was born thirty years too late.

Terry Brown and Louise Anderson, the Lister Creek schoolteacher, rode down from Ty Green's to spend the night. Terry worked here last year and is Jeff's best friend. He ran away from his home in Michigan when just a kid and joined a wild west show with a circus. Since then he has worked all over the West; his last stop before coming to this country was Nevada. He has been training polo horses for Ty, who raises thoroughbreds, all summer and fall. A couple of weeks ago, he cut his foot while chopping wood and has been on crutches ever since. I have known Louise since we were in grade school. She and Terry are going to be married soon.

*December 18*

After the four of us ate our breakfast this morning Louise and I took across to the garage the few remaining suitcases and the things that Jeff and I didn't load yesterday for fear of freezing; while Jeff and Terry nursed their crippled feet by the dining-room heater. They laughed at us and called us their squaws. It is a very timely name for me now. At the end of our journey, here in camp on the Houston Ranch, we are just a mile from the Cheyenne Indian Reservation. We are eight miles below the little town of Ashland, where the St. Labre Mission is located. I feel at home, as I have heard my mother speak of this country often. When she first came here as a child, she worked for Mrs. Brown, on the old Three-Circle Ranch several miles above here, and attended the Mission school with the Indian children, as there were no public schools at that time. . . .

*Christmas, 1932*

We spent a very quiet Christmas alone and ate a very simple dinner. They sent us up half a hog from the ranch, the other day, and it turned out to be practically a whole hog, minus only the hindquarters. It was frozen, of course, and Jeff and I have had a struggle trying to cut it up. If anyone can imagine a man on crutches and a ninety-five-pound woman wrestling with a huge frozen hog, they might get some idea of the ludicrous picture we must have presented. We finally managed to get a nice roast for our Christmas dinner, so dined on roast pork, browned potatoes, hot biscuits, applesauce, molasses pudding, and coffee.

We haven't seen much of our neighbors, in whose back yard we live, as Mrs. Houston has been ill with the flu since some days before we came, although we do see Mr. Houston occasionally. Their hired man, Walter, a big raw-boned, hill-billy kid, is a constant visitor and in between trips with kindling wood for me, toasts his feet at our fire and brags of his prowess as a bronc stomper.

*New Year, 1933*

Don, George, and Ted brought the cattle up, the early part of the week. Ted is now settled in the living and dining room, which also serves as a bunkhouse.

Yesterday Jeff removed his cast and donned an Oxford, as he is unable to wear a boot owing to the tenderness of his foot. He insists, however, on wearing a boot on his other foot. He has the appearance of having one leg shorter than the other.

Today, we went down to Hallie and Don's to a New Year party. Terry and Louise were there and were the objects of much good-natured chaffing, as they were married in Miles City a little more than a week ago.

This afternoon, little Don and George went skating on the river. Hallie with baby Virginia, Terry and Louise, and Jeff and I trailed along to watch them. Terry and Jeff got the idea they wanted to skate, as they feel very cocky at being off their crutches. As Louise and I vigorously vetoed the idea, they amused themselves by laughing at George, as we all did. On skates George is as awkward as a day-old calf. He fell down periodically every few minutes and spent the rest of the time trying to save himself from falling. We laughed at him so much he finally started up the bank to take his skates off; he was so blinded with anger at us, that he fell back down the bank, popping his head on the ice.

The skating exhibition being over, we went back to the house to see how the poker game was progressing. The men played until near midnight and when we started home Ted's pockets were full, while the others couldn't bring forth even one forlorn jingle from theirs.

*Mid-January*

Ted went to the ranch last week to help Don and George gather some cattle. He hadn't as yet returned, when the river started to break up and Jeff found it necessary to bring the cows across the river to the feeding ground. I bundled up to help him.

We first rode down to Jim Holton's for dinner, as Jeff wanted to see him about a horse he lost last spring. Jim is a husky, fine-looking old fellow with a gray mustache and kindly blue eyes.

274

While his wife was preparing dinner, Jeff and I sat near the heater in the living room and talked to him. Every few minutes Jim dropped off to sleep. His foot, which was propped on the heater, would start to slide and would finally hit the floor with a thud which awakened him. He would then resume the conversation until sleep again overcame him.

After a dinner topped with Mrs. Holton's golden biscuits, we started for home, picking up the cows en route. We got them to the river and there the fun began. For an hour and a half we struggled to get them out on the river. There were about three inches of water running on top of the ice. Although we got the cows started nicely, the calves refused to follow. They stood on the bank and bawled; the cows of course came back to them. Finally Jeff roped a calf and dragged it across, hoping that its mother would follow and that the rest would follow her. The calf lost its footing and I was afraid it would drown, being dragged through the icy water; but it wobbled to its feet and bawled piteously when Jeff reached the opposite bank with it. He then tied it to a willow and came back across. The mother ran out into midstream, then, like all she-creatures, changed her mind and came back.

For another hour we struggled in the cold while the sun sank lower. Along about five o'clock of a January afternoon it gets plenty cold. My feet felt like pieces of wood.

Two or three times the cows got back up on the bank and ran off amongst the bushes. Each time we brought them back and crowded them onto the edge of the ice. Finally, one poor weak heifer was crowded into midstream by the others, and, following the line of least resistance, went on across. We closed in behind the others and waited, almost not daring to breathe, while they trailed after her; the calves close beside their mothers, trembling as their little legs moved gingerly through the icy water. At last, they were across; Jeff untied the shivering calf from the willow and we rode swiftly home in the cold dusk.

"Punching cows" is fun when the weather is nice; but it takes a real love for the cow business to make one forget stiff limbs and cold feet. Jeff's bum foot throbbed painfully when it started to warm up; my numbness was swiftly forgotten as I began preparations for our supper.

Our kitchen range is one of those temperamental stoves which has to be coaxed and, with green cottonwood, doesn't coax well. Jeff is the only one who can get it to burn; after he has fixed it, the heat becomes so intense one can hardly stay in the kitchen.

Some of the punchers from the Rosebud happened along the other night just as I was getting supper. I had enough pinto cake (molasses marble cake) for my own family of cowhands (including Don, George, and Ted besides Jeff) but not sufficient for three more hungry waddies, so I made apple pies. The stove was in a sulking mood, but Jeff came to the rescue with a couple of pine knots. Where he unearthed them is a mystery, as I didn't know there was even as much as a twig of pine in the entire woodpile. The stove became a roaring inferno as the knots blazed. Fearfully I gazed in the oven, the piecrust was already more than golden brown but the apples were still not cooked through. In a panic, I summoned Jeff. "What shall I do?" I wailed. "The pie is ruined and I haven't any dessert for the men!" Jeff hugged me and whispered reassuringly, "Leave the oven door open, Honey, and let 'er cook." "But the crust will burn," I protested. Jeff shook his head. "No, it won't. The boys will like it anyway, just because it's apple pie."

Altogether it didn't take more than fifteen minutes for the pie to get thoroughly done, the crust miraculously didn't burn, and the pie received high praise. As I washed dishes, Jeff entered the kitchen his eyes twinkling. "Well, honey, you certainly know how to manufacture the pies, but from now on you'd better let your old man fix the fire to bake them."

Ted had little or nothing to do, Jeff getting along fine and able to do all the necessary riding, so Don has paid him off. He headed for the Crow Reservation, which is home to him. We hated to see him leave, as he's good company. But it probably won't be long until we shall have to start feeding. Then Don will hire someone to help Jeff again, as he will hardly be able to feed nine hundred head of cattle by himself. I'm afraid the next one may not be as nice to have around as Ted was.

### February 1

We had a big blizzard about ten days ago and have nearly frozen to death in our shack. The bread, which I put in the warming oven at night, is frozen in the morning; the work table in the kitchen gets a thin film of ice on it when I wipe it off with the dishcloth, and I haven't dared mop the kitchen floor for fear of getting pneumonia, as I know it wouldn't dry.

Ray Hedges was helping feed the cattle, but is no longer with us. He and Walter visited a moonshiner last week and Ray became very ill from imbibing too much raw whisky. His father, Lyman Hedges, has taken his place. I am actually afraid to sit next to him at the table as he insists on telling stories while he eats. That sounds harmless, but telling stories is a very active business with Lyman. He smacks his lips, shuffles his feet, and waves his knife and fork around; I am constantly dodging.

### Mid-February

It was cold before; now it is colder. We have had thirty-five and forty degrees below zero for three days. Jeff pitched hay and fed his stock, regardless of the cold; and froze a spot on his chin the size of a dollar, which has a beautiful blister on it. He very foolishly got down and drank out of the hole in the ice, where the cattle drink. When he arose, the water froze on his chin before he could wipe it off. Lyman had a very opportune breakdown with his sled and has been working on it in the shelter of the blacksmith shop.

Jeff gets up and prepares breakfast for the men, wearing his sheepskin vest and his overshoes, while the house is getting warm enough for me to get up and dress; although it doesn't get above the freezing point, I know. I have been wearing the first woolen underwear since my childhood, wool trousers, a jersey turtleneck sweater, and woolen socks under my boots. Still I shiver as I prepare dinner over the red-hot range. If I roll up my sleeves, my arms get cold. When my feet get cold, I go prop them up on the little heater in our bedroom, which has proved to be the warmest room in the house. We gather around the big heater in the dining room and can see the vapor from our breath as plainly as though we were outside.

Yet all things must come to an end; at night, under wool blankets, sougans, and a feather quilt, I am able to forget that it is forty below zero. The cattle, however, have nothing to look forward to save the remote promise of spring. They are doing very well, though, and we have lost but one cow and one calf. A couple of calves have frozen feet.

*March*

We had Indian visitors the other day. Chief Little Eagle and his grandson were here looking for dead calves. (The Indians will eat anything. They seem to be able to smell it in the air when one is butchering. They always show up and make off with the entrails and stomach.)

Jeff decided to bargain with them and told them that if they would help him pitch a rackload of hay (a regular afternoon procedure, in preparation for the next morning's feeding) he would show them a dead calf. Little Eagle said, "No—work—get two dollars," holding out two fingers. "All right," said Jeff, "then I won't give you the calf." At this moment the grandson, Jim, whose mouth was evidently watering for veal, began to jabber earnestly in Cheyenne. Finally, Little Eagle nodded, "All right—work—get calf."

Jeff, meantime, sensing a chance for more trading, showed the Indians a rawhide noseband for a hackamore, which he had just completed with some very fancy braiding in two shades of soft leather over the nose. Jim wanted it badly. Jeff said, "Two dollars." "No!" said Little Eagle, and, reaching for Jim, he unbuttoned his coat and shirt and fingered his underwear. "Government just give 'em—new—wool—trade for noseband." Jeff suppressed a desire to laugh. "No, Little Eagle, two dollars. I don't need underwear; I have some. Two dollars for the noseband."

Little Eagle shrugged and Jim gazed longingly at the bright

leatherwork. Little Eagle gazed at Jim, asked a question in Cheyenne, and at Jim's reply turned to Jeff once more. "All right—two dollars—get government pension check first of month —get noseband then. Save 'em for me."

So saying, they headed for the meadow. After the hay was loaded, Jeff led the way to the dead calf. Little Eagle poked it with a finger and turned to Jeff in disgust, "No good! Frozen!" Then waving his hands toward the sun, "Sun get hot, make calf soft. I come back, get 'em."

We have new neighbors. Ty Green has bought the old Herbert place, to the south of us. He and his hired man were here for their meals while moving their household goods. Now that his wife and nine children have moved in, they are no longer boarders.

Ty has a black mare called Chita. He asked Jeff to take her and "knock the rough off her," as she is a bit too much of a handful for Ty to manage. Thus far, the mare has "knocked the rough off" Jeff. He rode her, the first time, in Ty's corral. Ty hasn't as yet had time to do much repairing and, like everything else on the place, the corral is in bad shape. Ty stationed a boy in each gap. The barn has big half-and-half doors, enabling one to close the lower half and leave the upper half open for ventilation. Inside the big barn, about halfway back, is a gate. Jeff mounted Chita and she "turned 'er on." Being wild as a coyote, or wilder, she steered clear of the fence where the small boys were stationed and headed for the barn, in through the open upper half of the door she went and stopped just short of the inner gate. Jeff was still safely in the saddle, which was rather a surprise to himself as well as to Ty. As he gazed around, voices came from above: "My gosh, he's still on her!" Leaning out of a trap door in the haymow were three tousled little heads, three pairs of round eyes, and three gaping astonished little mouths.

After riding her at Ty's, Jeff brought Chita home. Next day he started out of the east gate of the corral on her. Because of an April snow, he was wearing overshoes. He was halfway into the saddle when she started bucking. He had his left foot in the stirrup but couldn't manage to get the right one in. She bucked straight for a pile of machinery by the blacksmith shop; she stopped just short of it, wheeled sharply, heading out through the yard gate, barely missing the gatepost. Jeff had to kick loose of the stirrup in order to save his foot from being crushed. From then on, having neither stirrup, he had to do some fancy riding. Chita bucked and ran all the way from the yard gate to the mailbox, a quarter of a mile. Then she decided to behave herself and has been a perfect lady ever since.

We had to leave Booger at the ranch when we came up here, as he was badly wire-cut and we were afraid for a while that we might have to shoot him. He healed nicely, however, so Don brought him up to us not long ago. Jeff has kept him in the barn and has been graining him to give him strength for the summer's riding.

The other morning Jeff came in with the full milk pail and a long face, as I was getting breakfast. His first words were, "I have the worst luck of any guy I know." His expression was truly woebegone. I immediately forgot that the sun was shining on a fresh clean world and that I had just heard a meadow lark singing out in the big hay meadow. Anxiously I inquired, "What's happened now?" "It's Booger." Immediately my heart sank. Poor little Booger, his life had been one long series of mishaps, and now, just when he seemed to be getting over his streak of bad luck . . . "I had him in the barn last night and he jumped into the manger and ripped his shoulder open on a big spike," Jeff went on. "I was a fool not to have pulled it out of there long ago. Booger's really ruined this time. Go on out and see him. I turned him into the corral."

Breakfast was forgotten. After a hurried caress for Jeff, I fled through the house and out toward the corral. Halfway to the gate I was halted by Jeff's laughter, from the doorway where he was watching my flight, and a shout of "April Fool" rang in my amazed ears. After a good-natured pommeling, I forgave him, happy in the knowledge that Booger was quite all right.

*Mid-April*

The cattle have been turned out into the big hilly pastures for some time and it has kept Jeff busy riding line on them. The yearling heifers are fidgety, the heel flies are busy at work, and water isn't any too plentiful at the springs; so the cattle work down to the road and try to get through the fence to the river. Don and George are supposed to be up soon to move them back to the main ranch.

Last Sunday Jeff hitched Dick and Jumbo to a little wagon of Houston's (which was, incidentally, minus its springs) and we went to the pasture to scatter salt for the cattle. The trip was rather hazardous, as Dick and Jumbo weigh around sixteen hundred pounds apiece, Dick has the reputation of running away, and we expected the wagon to fall apart at any moment. We jogged along merrily, however, stopping only to explore a couple of old moonshine stills and put some cattle, that had worked through the fence onto the road, back through the gate into the pasture.

We had to go up onto a flat tableland; and when we started almost straight up over niggerhead rocks, through low-hanging pine trees, Dick fidgeting every step of the way, I began to get really jittery. We finally made it to the top and I breathed a deep sigh of relief. We could see for miles—even to the muddy hills along the Yellowstone River, seventy-five miles to the north of us. Southward the mountains loomed, white-capped and misty blue.

After distributing the salt, we started back down. It was even worse than the trip up, but after what seemed like an eternity, we were safely on level ground once more. Jeff turned the horses over to me and I drove home. Jeff pretended he was an Indian buck, seating himself on the floor of the wagon, while the squaw drove the team. If anyone ever saw a squaw attired in pants and cowboy boots, with red hair flaming out from under the brim of a Stetson, I, Lynne Carson Tiernan, was that squaw.

Jeff purchased a two-year-old thoroughbred stallion from Ty the other day. He is a pretty little sorrel with rather odd white markings on his face and a round white spot, about twice the size of a dollar, on his side. He is deep-chested, high-withered, and clean-legged. His name, given him by Ty, is Red Oak. Jeff has been fooling with him and has him gentle enough that he can jump on him bareback and ride him around the corral. Today, just before dinner, Jeff and I were out in the corral, Jeff proudly pointing out his good points, when he jumped and kicked at me. Jeff had him by the halter and jerked him around, so I was untouched save for having my knee barely grazed by his flying hoof.

We sold Goldie to an eastern horse buyer. All spring he has been bucking with Jeff, and he decided I had best not try to ride him any more. Old horses very often get bucking notions after years of apparent docility; when they do, their legs quite frequently go bad and their period of usefulness is at an end. . . .

*April 22*

We were all ready [to return to the home ranch] when it snowed, so we had to stay over two days. We started from Houston's at seven o'clock this morning and reached the Swinging-H at seven o'clock this evening. We started with Dick and Jumbo pulling the load and Doc, Jerry, and Booger tied behind; but before we had gone many miles, Dick and Jumbo broke the doubletrees pulling through the mud; we had an extra, so made the change and put Doc and Jerry on the load too. We had gone only a few yards when Dick popped it again. Luckily we were near a ranch, so borrowed one and traveled on without mishap. We had our dinner at the Brandenburg bridge. Jeff unhitched, fed, and watered the horses; we built a fire and feasted on bacon and eggs, sandwiches, raisin pie, and coffee. From the bridge the road was dry and we made good time. I drove for the last eight or nine miles, feeling very proud of being able to handle a four-horse team. Then I remembered that my father used to freight wool and handle teams of from twelve to sixteen horses, and my head quickly resumed its normal proportions.

About seven miles from home we met Jeff's uncle. He said that our cattle wintered well, with no loss. It was sweet music to our

282

ears. Our herd keeps growing, slowly but surely, and we hope, before too long, to have enough to establish an outfit of our own.

My first winter's sojourn in a cow camp is ended. It was a lot of fun along with the discomfort. I hope we shall spend many more winters in camp, the only reservation I am holding is that the next time our abode will be snugger than the cracker box in which we spent this winter.

*Mid-May*

Last week, mounted on Navajo, little Don's horse, I rode with Jeff and George, moving the bulls to new pasture. It drizzled rain all day, but our long slickers kept us dry. The bulls are naturally restless at this time of year and the rain didn't help matters, but we finally got them moved. We were short three bulls, though, so when we closed the gate on those we had moved we looked for the others, George going south as Jeff and I proceeded west.

As soon as our sorrowful companion was out of sight, Jeff dismounted, "Like to trade horses for a while, Lynne? Navajo's not as easy riding as Rocket."

I'm afraid my mouth fell open—Blue Rocket! I hadn't forgotten his Thanksgiving exhibition. "But," I faltered, "he's never been ridden by a woman. Will it be all right?"

"I wouldn't let you ride him if it wasn't safe, honey; you know that."

Jeff implied an unspoken hurt to think that I wouldn't trust him with my safety. There was no argument I could make against that plea, so I dismounted and Jeff held Rocket as I swung aboard. Jeff was right, nothing happened. Rocket packed me many miles that day, but no one at the ranch shall ever know that I wasn't mounted on Navajo all day. Jeff doesn't want to lose him, as he's by far the best all-around cow horse on the ranch, unequaled either as a rope horse or cutting horse. If Don knew that Rocket was gentle enough to pack a woman, Jeff would be asked to give him up and would be given a green bronc in his place.

*Later*

We had a bit of excitement around here yesterday.

283

Don, with the wagon, and Jeff and George on horseback had gone to the upper meadow to fix fence. About midafternoon, here came the gentle old team down the road, as fast as they could run, with no one in the wagon. Pretty soon Don came along, walking, then Jeff and George on their horses. Rocket was walking as if he'd eaten loco. He stumbled and swayed as if on the verge of falling.

Soon we had the whole story. Jeff was using a hair rope for reins on his bridle; he left Rocket, hobbled, standing with the reins down, while he helped Don and George with the fence. George was riding a little sorrel cyclone called Peanuts. He tied him to a tree. The old team stood quietly without tying, so they were free to go anywhere, had they had such a notion. Blue Rocket closed his eyes, settled on one hind leg, and dozed off. A fresh little breeze swayed the reins, Rocket's eyes popped open— what was that hairy thing in front of his nose? Surely no snake had ever looked like that! Away he went, hobbles and all, past the team and straight over a thirty-foot cut bank. The team, startled, headed for home. George leaped for Peanuts, his one idea to catch the team. In his hurry, he lit, as usual, behind the saddle and was thrown high in the air. While he sat on the ground, feeling cautiously of his bones, Jeff and Don reached the cut bank and gazed morosely on Rocket, lying at the bottom, his head twisted back under his neck.

"By God, Jeff, he's dead!" whispered Don.

Jeff scrambled down the bank, Don close behind. Tenderly, they straightened out his head. Rocket blinked his eyes, gave a snort, and plunged unsteadily to his feet. It was almost unbelievable, yet, there he stood, badly frightened and dazed, but able to travel.

[*Note by Helen Glenn:* During the period from May to December of 1933, Lynne was once again necessarily separated from Jeff. She spent most of this period in Miles City. During this time Jeff traded Booger for a black mare called Doris. Cliff, Jeff's brother, went to work at the Swinging-H. Terry Brown met with difficulty when he branded a "slick" colt and was put on a three-year parole for horse-stealing. In October, the outfit shipped their calves from Rosebud, and Lynne and her sister-in-law joined the boys for the occasion. After the cattle were loaded out, they attended a dance, and were dinner guests at the chuck wagon on the following day.

In early December Jeff contracted scarlatina, but was able to have the Diamond-L in shape for Lynne's home-coming, where she resumes her journal.]

### December 23, 1933

Tonight finds me at home once again, at the Diamond-L on Soda Biscuit Creek. Jeff and Cliff brought me out in the ranch jitney; and although both the brakes and the radiator froze and had to be thawed out before we left Miles City, we reached home without further mishap.

Sam Green and his wife Annie are gone with all of their household belongings; Sam resigned his job; Don has the job of foreman now, permanently. Jeff and Cliff and I staged a triumphal tour of the rather barren-looking rooms tonight, singing "Annie Doesn't Live Here Any More" as loudly as our voices would permit.

Tomorrow I shall unpack my trunk; perhaps I'll be able to give the rooms a more cozy appearance when I hang a few pictures.

### Christmas

Cliff went to the ranch yesterday. Jeff went with him and brought back a fine turkey, so our second Christmas finds us dining on turkey, dressing, cranberries, and all the rest of the trimmings. Terry and Louise sent us an invitation to spend Christmas with them, but fifteen miles is quite a distance to ride horseback to eat Christmas dinner, as it is extremely cold. Besides, Jeff had to get the pump engine in working order so that the cattle could have water; for, as he remarked, "It's just another day to the cattle."

### January 5, 1934

We awoke in the middle of the night to hear rain pattering on the tin roof. Today we are isolated in a sea of ice and water. The creek, frozen over, cannot carry all of the excess water; the cattle are marooned on little islands on either side of the regular creek bed and underneath is a glare of ice. Jeff had to shoe the team this morning so they could get down the hill to the creek to drink.

## Late February

Our winter apparently ended with the unseasonable rain. It has been warm and dry most of the time since.

Cliff came over from the ranch to help Jeff get ice for the cistern. They finally managed to get a small amount from a reservoir a few miles below us. Jeff hauled cottonseed cakes to the cows in a sled while the ice lasted, but now he has an old buggy from the ranch.

Mr. Kent supplied us with calcimine, varnish, and paint; we have completed our renovation of the house and have also cleaned up the yard and outbuildings. We worked longest on the house. We made frames for our pictures out of ash twigs and varnished them. We laid new linoleum in the kitchen; and I hung new drapes in the living room and bedroom. It is very livable and homelike now; but we are not to stay here.

Ever since our marriage we have planned for the day when we might go on a place of our own, with our own stock. Now, it seems, Lady Luck has chosen to smile on us.

Mel Willcox, after making several calls on us, finally came to an agreement with Jeff, in connection with the old home ranch up the creek, which he has been leasing. He is to buy the place, paying cash to Mrs. Tiernan and the two girls, while Jeff and Cliff will take their shares in cattle. With what cattle we already have we should be able to get by. It will mean a great deal of scrimping, as times are very bad, but with a little break we should be able to accumulate a real herd.

Of course, we shall never have the kind of an outfit that the old-timers had. A man used to be able to run his cattle for practically nothing, as the country was unfenced and the grass had not been plowed under by the dry farmers. Now, it is a question of leasing pasture and buying feed for the winter. Even as short a time as twenty-five years ago, the cowman saw all of his cattle only twice a year, during the spring and fall roundups. The roundup covered countless miles of territory and took several weeks to complete. The cowboy's living quarters were his saddle, his bedroll, and the chuck wagon.

Mel and Jeff and I explored the old Diamond-L chuck box one afternoon, which we discovered propped against a corner of the icehouse. In one drawer we found some rusty knives and forks, in a second a broken saucer, in a third a can of mustard and an unmarked can containing something which we judged to be either salt or sugar. Mel took some on the tip of his pocketknife and, tasting it, found it to be sugar. In another drawer, marked "Cowboys," we found a few matches and a stubby pencil. The Diamond-L roundup wagon has not been running since, at least, twenty-five years ago, and we are probably the first who have opened the chuck box in that time.

## April 1

Easter Sunday. Cliff left this afternoon for his new job. He will work for wages, while Jeff and I settle somewhere to look after the stock. Early this morning, Cliff, Jeff, and I headed up the creek for Mel's. I rode Dixie, the horse that filled George's pipe with mud. I found that he really is rather hard to mount, looking at you as though he thought it might be fun to kick your hat off. Cliff held him while I climbed on, my movements somewhat encumbered by Jeff's leather chaps.

We arrived at Mel's about eight o'clock and the boys swung into action. Mel's grandniece and I sat on the corral fence and watched the men brand out the heifers. There are twenty-eight of them, all two-year-olds, nice looking whitefaces. They were rather hard to handle, but the branding went along smoothly and the job was completed by noon. We have, also, a fine three-year-old bull, which we will leave here until the breeding season.

After dinner we started down the creek with the heifers. It was dark by the time Jeff and I finally got them turned into a pasture about a mile west of here which we have had leased during this last year for our horses.

Riding on home in the darkness, we talked of our future. If only it would rain, so that the new grass would have a chance to get started, we could look ahead with even more joy, but we can only hope and pray and strive to somehow retain the supreme optimism which has always been the primary requisite of a dweller in the sage country.

*April 20*

We have secured a place about twenty miles from here, across Tongue River, on the head of Foot Creek, about five miles from where my sister Mary and her husband, Alan, have their ranch.

We have leased a section opening on about twelve sections of unfenced range. Our section has a fine spring on it, and we will have the use of an adjoining farm, which also has a spring and a good well. The buildings are rather dilapidated, but the house will meet our needs for the summer months, after which we will make other arrangements. We plan to leave here the first of May.

Jeff has been breaking Doris, the black for whom he traded Booger. Doris is small and wiry and does a very fancy job of bucking every so often; but Jeff is already roping from her and she is really taking to it quite well. An attempt was made to break her before Jeff got possession of her, and she has the nasty habit of balking. At such moments, if urged too much, she sits down and tries to fall over backward. Thus far, she has had little success in her attempts to buffalo Jeff; but I fear she will never completely give up, for her expression is far from pious. She has a bony nose and a scar over one eye. She reminds me of the witches in the old fairy tales.

Mel's hired man has bequeathed to me a long-legged, homely steed called Darky. Jeff says I look like a mosquito on his back. A ladder would be handy in mounting him, but he is a really good cow horse.

*May*

We are in our new dwelling, a two-room frame shack on the

288

flat above the Foot Creek badlands. After we had moved our household goods, the old-fashioned way, with a borrowed team and wagon, once again I took the role of puncher and helped Jeff move our cattle to their new range.

I have been busy with soap and scrubbing brush since our arrival. The shack has been the home of two bachelors for a number of years, and was in a very sorry state. After much effort, the kitchen cupboards really look clean enough to hold our meager supply of dishes.

*September 15*

This summer has been like a gruesome and never-ending nightmare. Dust, wind, grasshoppers, and starving, choking cattle have imprinted on my mind a picture that can never be banished. Even as early as the latter part of May everyone was in a panic. Although hundreds of people were in Miles City participating in the celebration of the Montana Stockmen's Golden Jubilee, drouth was an actual fact. The gaiety and hilarity of those men and women present was that of doomed people, grasping hysterically for a moment of laughter before disaster should overcome them. The commission companies had already quit buying livestock and in June the government began to buy.

We clung tenaciously to our little herd, hating to sacrifice them for the ridiculously low prices offered by the government. Maximum prices were twenty dollars for cows and ten dollars for calves. Many people got much less than that.

At first we sold only a few of the weaker cattle from Jeff's original herd. The others we watched over carefully, and managed to keep the mud-choked springs dug out enough to keep them watered. Gradually we were forced to sell all but the heifers which Jeff and Cliff got from Mel and two particularly fine cows from the original herd.

Day after endless day we watched the country become more denuded. The wind blew almost constantly. Whenever a bank of clouds appeared in the west we waited for the rain that never came. Only the wind came, and thunder, and the scent of moisture that never fell.

We hopefully planted a garden and dug ditches, irrigating with water pumped by hand from the well; but the seeds never came up. If they had sprouted, the grasshoppers would have devoured the green shoots. They were everywhere, stripping the sagebrush, greasewood, and the few withered blades of grass left from last year. They even settled on the house, striving to find sustenance in the wood. Several times we saw clouds of them flying high in the air. Over everything hung a fog of dust.

In August Cliff quit his job and came hurrying home to see how we were getting along. Jeff had hoped to buy cottonseed cake and pull the cows through the coming winter; but Cliff didn't want to take a gamble on a winter that might be tough, so Jeff agreed to sell.

Now they are gone, all but one heifer which we were unable to find. Here we sit, with no cattle, no job, less than a thousand dollars in cash, a bunch of horses which we hope will live until spring; and I am to have a child in February.

Luckily food costs have been very low and, since we butchered a fat calf in July and I canned it, our expenses have been very small. Our grocery bills have averaged less than fifteen dollars a month.

We shall have to move from our shack soon, however, as it will not be warm enough for the winter months. If our plans do not go awry, we will live just a mile from Mary and Alan this winter, as Pete Schaeffer and his wife plan to go east in search of work and want us to take care of their place while they are gone.

*January 15, 1935*

In October, when Pete and his wife left, we moved into their house and have been quite comfortable here. During November and December, Jeff and Cliff took a job on the North Side, working for a horse outfit. They came back before the holidays and we spent Christmas with Mary and Alan.

Jeff and Cliff butchered our remaining heifer, which we finally located, and Jeff and I made a big batch of mincemeat; since than we have been feasting on mincemeat pies and fresh beef, garnished, of course, by the vegetables which we purchased and stored last fall.

Mary and Alan leave the girls with us whenever they go to town; if I happen to be making bread when they are here, they beg for squaw bread, so into the hot fat go the little pieces of dough, and soon Joan and Gay, Jeff and Cliff are all in the kitchen eating squaw bread as fast as I can get it fried.

Cliff delights in teasing the two youngsters; and there is much noise and excitement, as they insist on playing the piano and drag out Pete's accordion. The "music" causes a great deal of laughter.

Jeff is so horribly worried most of the time that laughter is priceless to me right now. His face is gaunt and lined and to look at him makes my heart ache; but somehow I seem unable to comfort him. He remains aloof from us in his worry, and I am too incoherent to make him understand that I want to help him.

Tomorrow we are going to start canning the rest of the beef, as I plan next Monday to go to town to await the coming of our baby.

Jeff will have to take a job soon; then our little family will be split up until we can once again get a stake. The country is in such a terrible condition right now that it's going to be very hard. But so far, we at least haven't had to go on relief, as the money we received from our stock didn't have to go for mortgages or other debts, as so many people's did.

Jeff's idleness since we sold the cattle has been very wearisome for him. He is never happy except when he is busy. When he starts working again I know he will have a much more optimistic attitude. Jobs are at a premium right now, but Jeff has the offer of a steady job on the North Side and is only waiting until I am safely out of the hospital to take it.

*January 19*

The beef is canned. Jeff and I have had colds and Cliff is developing one. My thoughts are muddled this morning. I have had a headache for two days and nights and it is getting worse every minute. Dave, the old dog, is under the house, as it is terribly cold out. He whines and mourns incessantly. I wish he'd stop it.

My head feels as though it would shatter, like a burned-out electric light bulb, if anyone tapped on it . . . .

# Ranchwoman

## May Vontver

MRS. VONTVER HAS BEEN A TEACHER and a county superintendent of schools. For *Frontier* she wrote a story entitled "The Kiskis" which has been reprinted in more than a dozen anthologies, read several times on radio, and transcribed into Braille. One of her books has been translated into Swedish and published in Stockholm. Her understanding of people and her strong outgoing sympathy account for Mrs. Vontver's appeal to the reader's emotion. In "Ranchwoman" a real ranch person comes clearly and disarmingly before the reader. The sketch appeared in *Frontier*, Vol. X, No. 3, p. 232.

MY FELLOW PASSENGER turned down the seat before me and settled herself with a sigh of relief.

"Nobody takes the local any more," she began. "Only time they do is when the roads are drifted so bad they can't get across the divide in a car. I remember when we used to go to Lewistown with horses. Two days 'twould take a team.

"Yes, we made the trip two, three times a year reg'lar. I took freight out to the ranch myself a few times. The men were harvesting or rounding up cattle or horses or something. Our place is seventeen miles east of Winnett. Sixty and seventeen; seventy-seven miles it was. How much is that for the round trip, now? No, it never did seem so very far. I liked doing it somehow." Her voice drifted off; she was watching the receding landscape. "The little hills," her voice caressed them, "the little hills, they are so pretty."

I, too, looked out. I knew what I would see—bare wind-blown

knolls of singular drabness, dotted with black sage. The coulees between them were filled with snow. A monotonous stretch of gumbo and white, gumbo and white. I said nothing.

"They are just like the hills out on our ranch," she went on. "Our land was not level, either. But it was good pasture."

"How long have you lived in town?" I asked.

"Eleven years it was last month since I moved in. I wanted to stay on out there after Pa died, but Nell she wouldn't hear of it. I told her I wouldn't be alone. I would keep some of the horses and some chickens and a cow. But she thought seventeen miles was too far out if I should run out of groceries or get sick or something. So I got that little house next to hers. We aren't at Teigen already?" She peered out over the bottom lands of one of the oldest ranches in the country. Then she got up, walked to the opposite side of the coach, and looked out once more. After a while she sat down, smiling contentedly.

"I was only just counting the haystacks," she explained. "Must be between thirty and forty. Such big well-made ones old man Teigan always has. Don't you like to see haystacks like that with winter coming on?" She beamed approval.

I did not commit myself. I have never experienced any reaction whatever to hay. In any shape, size, or quantity it leaves me cold —I have had to drive my car dangerously near the edge of the road to avoid collisions with rackloads of it. But to the shriveled little lady with the fairy godmother eyes, hay, hay in early winter, had significance.

The train moved on, slowly taking us past a herd of Mr. Teigen's Herefords.

"Ah, that is the cattle for this country." There was bliss in her inflection. "We had some of them on the ranch. Their faces always looked so clean. Pa, he wasn't as set on the place as I was. He ran for the legislature once, Pa did. He felt pretty bad losing out. I said to him: 'Never mind politics, Pa,' says I. 'You just stay with the whitefaces. They won't go back on you.' And we always did do pretty well with them.

"Is that the *Saturday Evening Post* you have? I sure like that.

Don't know what I'd do with myself if I didn't have something
to read. And the *Post* is so big—all I can read in one week. I
don't need to take no other magazine. Mrs. Johnson, you know
her? Yes, in that shingled shack, she says to me, 'I don't see what
you are so crazy about the *Post* for. It hasn't any recipes in it like
the *Ladies' Home Journal* or the *Woman's Home Companion.*'
And I told her, 'What would I do with recipes, living alone? I
never cook by recipes, anyhow. I just cook what I want.' And
almost every week there is a western story in it. That's what I
like, western stories, with pictures of cowboys and freighting
and riding horses. When my eyes get tired reading I can sit and
look at them pictures."

The train stopped again. We were at Grass Range. With the
eager curiosity of a child my companion slid to the edge of her
seat to take in the sights. Her wrinkled brown hand clawed at
me, missed me, but her face remained glued to the window.
Finally she caught my sleeve and held on.

"Look! See! That team on the loading rack. Did you ever see
such a driving team? Fat! And their harnesses, brand new! Ah, but
that is a fine set. Wonder what they cost. They certainly set off
them horses to perfection."

"Yes?" said I. Never before in my life have I given a second
look to a set of harness.

The team was driven out of sight behind the train. She sat
back and clasped her hands. "Wish I could have had that team
and harness when I had the mail route between Winnett and the
ranch, Meandering Creek Post Office it was then. No, you
couldn't know of it, Mrs. Hilyard, that post office hasn't been run
for a long time. I had the contract eight years and I drove broncs
all the time. Cayuses aren't like them eastern horses that have
been handled and gentled since way back. Western horses, they
just naturally hate a man. They are wild to start with and they
never do get real broke. I drove one team for four years and I
fed them and tended them myself, didn't never let anyone else
do a thing for them, but I never got them over being a little afraid
of me. Keno, now, I always tried specially hard to get him to trust

295